Passing the CPA exam isn't about studying harder...it's about studying smarter.

Kaplan offers a variety of affordable, top-notch options to meet your needs. Whether you choose our internet review course or some of our home-study products, you'll be getting the best CPA review on the market.

CPA WORKBOOK

by the Staff of Kaplan Educational Centers

Simon & Schuster

Kaplan Books
Published by Kaplan Educational Centers and Simon & Schuster
1230 Avenue of the Americas
New York, NY 10020

Material from *Uniform CPA Examination Selected Question and Official Answers*, copyright ©, 1978 through 1997, inclusive, by the American Institute of Certified Public Accountants, Inc., is reprinted/adapted with permission.

The purpose of this publication is to assist individuals in their preparation for the Uniform Certified Public Accountant Examination. It is not intended to be a complete and comprehensive guide to business, legal, investment, and tax matters and should not be used for that purpose. If specific guidance is needed in these areas, the services of a competent professional should be used.

Editor: Joan L. McNamara
Associate Product Director: Lisa Schlesinger, CPA
Product Director: Tamela A. Garrett, CPA
Cover Design: Suzanne Noli
Interior Page Design and Production: gumption design
Production Editor: Maude Spekes
Assistant Managing Editor: Brent Gallenberger
Managing Editor: Kiernan McGuire
Executive Editor: Del Franz

Manufactured in the United States of America
Published simultaneously in Canada

September 1997
10 9 8 7 6 5 4 3

Library of Congress Cataloguing-in-Publication Data
CPA workbook / by the staff of Kaplan Educational Centers.
    p. cm.
  Spine title: CPA 98
  ISBN 0-684-84532-6
  1. Accounting—Examinations, questions, etc. I. Stanley H. Kaplan Educational Centers (New York, N.Y.)
II. Title: CPA 98.
  HF 5635.C875 1997
  657'.076—CD21
                                               97-22920
                                                  CIP

ISBN: 0-684-84532-6

CONTENTS

HOW TO USE THIS BOOK

Kaplan's *CPA Workbook* is designed to provide you with the information, sample tests, and individualized feedback you need to score your best on the Uniform CPA Examination.

A special feature of this book is the computer-assisted feedback that book purchasers are eligible to receive. Simply enter your solutions to the questions on the grids at the back of the book and complete the essays and problems on the response sheets. Kaplan will analyze your exam and send you detailed feedback on how you performed. The feedback will highlight your strengths and weaknesses in each tested subject area. Since this book includes two complete sample CPA exams, you can do one early to get feedback on where to focus your study effort and the other one later to check on your progress.

In addition, you'll find information about the test and how it is administered as well as strategies for doing your best on each part of the exam. However, the bulk of the book is what you need most: practice tests. With each practice test you'll find explanations of all the answers and individualized computer-assisted feedback on how you did.

ABOUT THE CPA EXAM

The first section of this book explains how to register for the test, how the test is administered, and how it is scored. There is also an explanation of the various sections of the exam—Law, Auditing, Accounting and Reporting—Taxation, Managerial, and Governmental and Not-for-profit Oganizations (ARE), and Financial Accounting and Reporting—Busines Enterprises (FARE)—and the different kinds of questions comprising each section of the exam, including multiple-choice and other objective format (OOF) questions.

At the end of this section, you'll find "The Ten Most Frequently Asked CPA Questions and Answers." How to get certified, how long you have to wait for your test results, and why CPA Exams are no longer being released are just some of the questions answered in this section. Of course, this section is by no means exhaustive—feel free to call us today at 1-800-KAP-TEST with any unanswered questions you might have. You can also E-mail us at cpa@kaplan.com, or visit our web site at www.kaplan.com/accounting.

STRATEGIES TO DO YOUR BEST ON THE ESSAYS

The CPA Exam requires essay responses on several sections of the test. In this chapter you'll find strategies you need to write effective, to-the-point essays. Included is a step-by-step guide to the writing process to help you feel more confident when tackling the essay portion of the exam.

STUDY TIPS FOR THE CPA EXAM

Here you'll find a list of study tips that can help you achieve a higher score on the Uniform CPA Examination. We at Kaplan take pride in preparing confident test takers and these tips help to do just that.

TESTS AND SOLUTIONS

Most of this book is devoted to two actual, full-length CPA exams. And for every question, Kaplan has provided a straightforward explanation.

Because these are full-length exams actually given to CPA candidates in previous years, you can see the test elements that you will encounter on the actual exam, including instructions to candidates, time alotted for each section, and the work space allocated to complete problems. Kaplan's *CPA Workbook* helps to simulate the actual test-taking experience.

A scannable grid is included at the back of this book to give you practice filling in an answer sheet. Also at the back of the book, you'll find blank pages for answering the essay questions. After you complete an exam you can mail us your scannable grid and essay questions so that our professional grading staff will process your exam and mail you your results, including individualized feedback on your strengths and weaknesses.

APPENDIX I: STATE BOARDS OF ACCOUNTANCY

Since you'll need to find out the requirements of the state in which you want to be licensed, we've provided a comprehensive list of all the State Accountancy Boards, including addresses and phone and fax numbers.

APPENDIX II: KAPLAN CPA REVIEW PRODUCTS

Kaplan has a number of products designed to help you review for the CPA exam. In case you want additional CPA review materials, we've described the materials Kaplan has developed.

TAKING THE CPA EXAM

ABOUT THE CPA EXAM

CONTENT AND STRUCTURE

The Uniform CPA Examination is divided into the following four sections: (1) Auditing; (2) Business Law & Professional Responsibilities; (3) Accounting & Reporting—Taxation, Managerial, Governmental & Not-for-Profit Accounting (ARE); and (4) Financial Accounting & Reporting—Business Enterprises (FARE).

Since the May 1996 exam, the American Institute of Certified Public Accountants (AICPA), which creates the Uniform CPA Examination, no longer releases a copy of the test after it has been administered. Candidates who sit for the exam no longer receive their answer books by mail, and organizations that prepare candidates for the CPA exam are prevented from publishing answers and explanations for exam questions. As a result, candidates will no longer be able to gain access to the most recent exams, or even see their own exams and answers. The reasons the AICPA has given for its nonrelease policy are: (1) to allow recycling of more questions; (2) to improve the fairness and equality of exam taking; and (3) to prepare for computerization of the exam in the near future—a move that will require a larger pool of questions.

The exam is given every May and November on the first Wednesday and Thursday of the month. It spans fifteen-and-a-half hours of actual test-taking, broken up as follows:

DAY	TIME	TOPIC	HOURS
Wednesday	9:00 A.M.–12:00 P.M.	Business Law & Professional Responsibilites	3.0
Wednesday	1:30 P.M.–6:00 P.M.	Auditing	4.5
Thursday	8:30 A.M.–12:00 P.M.	Accounting & Reporting (ARE)	3.5
Thursday	1:30 P.M.–6:00 P.M.	Financial Accounting & Reporting (FARE)	4.5

Each section of the exam contains multiple-choice questions and other objective format questions (OOF). The other objective format questions may involve matching, true or false, fill-in-the-blank, or numerical-answer questions. Certain sections include essays or problems. Essay and problem questions are designed to test your ability to perceive a problem, analyze the situation, apply judgment, and communicate the results. These questions are usually specific in nature, rather than abstract.

Section	Content	Format
Business Law & Professional Responsibilities	15% Professional and Legal Responsibilities 20% Business Organizations 10% Contracts 10% Debtor-Creditor Relationships 15% Government Regulation 20% Uniform Commercial Code 10% Property	50–60% MC* 20–30% OOF** 20–30% Essays
Auditing	40% Engagement Planning 35% Obtain and Document Information, Form Conclusions 5% Achieve Objectives/Evaluate Information, Document Conclusions 20% Prepare Communications	50–60% MC* 20–30% OOF** 20–30% Essays
Accounting & Reporting (ARE)	20% Federal Taxation—Individuals 20% Federal Taxation—Corporations 10% Federal Taxation—Partnerships, Estates & Trusts, and Exempt Organizations; Preparers Responsibilities 30% Government and Not-for-Profit Organizations 10% Managerial Accounting	50–60% MC 40–50% OOF*
Financial Accounting & Reporting (FARE)	20% Concepts, Standards, & Financial Statements 40% Presentation of Typical Items in Financial Statements 40% Presentation of Specific Types of Transactions & Events	50–60% MC* 20–30% OOF** 20–30% Essays or Problems

* MC = mutiple-choice   ** OOF = other objective format

OTHER THINGS YOU SHOULD KNOW ABOUT THE UNIFORM CPA EXAMINATION

- The exam is closed-book. You are not allowed to use any reference materials.

- You cannot bring your own calculators or electronic devices into the test taking room.

- Calculators are provided for the FARE and ARE sections of the exam.

- You are provided with Examination Question Booklets and Examination Answer Booklets for each section of the exam being taken.

- Be sure to bring plenty of No. 2 pencils and erasers.

Keep in mind that you will need to be familiar with a wide array of material for the exam; however, it does not cover topics to the extent that they may have been covered in a college class. **For this reason, it is important to study from focused test-preparation materials rather than college texts.**

SCORING

CPA examination scores are based on a flat grading scale of one hundred points. In order to pass the exam, you need to get a **75** on each of the four parts. Answers for multiple-choice and other objective questions will be determined to be correct or incorrect—no partial credit will be given. There is no penalty for guessing on the CPA exam, **so always select an answer choice for every question.**

Each set of multiple-choice and OOF questions will be assigned a specific number of points. The number of points earned by the candidate will be based on the *percentage of correct* items in the set multiplied by the point value. For example, if a ten-point matching OOF question calls for fourteen responses and you were to get eleven right, your score would be eleven fourteenths times ten, resulting in eight points.

Essay and problem-type questions are graded by a professional grading staff. Each question is graded by a different group of people who become experts in that particular question. Questions are graded as objectively as possible through the use of grading guides. The grading guides specify essential concepts and/or computations while allowing for alternative approaches. Essays requiring lists usually ask you to include most if not all correct items for a perfect score and are graded on a *percent of all concepts* basis.

Five percent of your overall score will be based on your writing skills. Graders will look for the following six elements in your essay writing:

- Coherent organization
- Conciseness
- Clarity

- Use of standard English

- Responsiveness to the requirements of the question

- Appropriateness for the reader

For more information on writing skills, refer to the section, About Writing Skills.

Once your exam has been initially graded, it will be placed in one of three categories: OBVIOUS PASS, OBVIOUS FAILURE, and MARGINAL PASS. With a score of 75 or above, you will be categorized as an "Obvious Pass." Earning a 69 or below will put you in the category of "Obvious Failure." All remaining exams will be a "Marginal Pass" and subject to additional reviews.

Factors included in the review are: content, neatness, organization, and communication and judgment skills. Those exams that "pass" the review are given a score of 75; those that do not, will receive a 69. (Note: No scores will be given between and including 70 and 74.)

Once all exams have been graded, each individual's exam sections are reviewed for consistency. If a candidate has passed sections of the exam and received a score of 69 on one or more sections, the parts graded 69 will be re-evaluated. If a 75 is still not granted, the Director of Examinations gives the exam section(s) a final review.

In most states, if a candidate passes any two sections of the Uniform CPA Examination, he or she receives conditional credit for the sections passed. You may then pass the remaining sections individually or combined, usually within a three-year period. **Keep in mind if you pass only one section prior to obtaining credit, it will most likely not count, although this varies from state to state.** Also, some states may require a minimum score on all parts not passed in order to get credit for those parts passed. For specific information on the requirements of your state, please contact your State Board of Accountancy (see Appendix I).

TO REGISTER

In today's competitive world, having your CPA certification can make all the difference. You should contact your State Board of Accountancy to determine educational requirements for taking the test, examination fees, deadlines for registration, and application procedures to be followed. Obtain a copy of "Information for Uniform CPA Examination Candidates" from the AICPA. For more information you can also call 1-800-KAP-TEST, or contact Kaplan's CPA team via E-mail at cpa@kaplan.com.

Topic	Day	1997 Test Dates	1998 Test Dates
Law	Wednesday (A.M.)	November 5	May 6, November 4
Audit	Wednesday (P.M.)	November 5	May 6, November 4
ARE	Thursday (A.M.)	November 6	May 7, November 5
FARE	Thursday (P.M.)	November 6	May 7, November 5

TEN MOST FREQUENTLY ASKED CPA QUESTIONS AND ANSWERS

1. **How important is my CPA score?**

The important thing to keep in mind is that you need a score of only 75 (on each section) to pass the CPA exam. Awards and/or honorable mention are given to the top-scoring candidates. However, unless there is a personal reason for scoring in the high 90s (such as a work-related incentive), earning a 95 is exactly the same thing as earning a 75 and could mean that you spent a lot more time studying than you had to.

2. **How do I register for the exam?**

Contact your State Board of Accountancy (see Appendix I) to determine educational requirements for sitting, the examination fees, deadlines for registration, and application procedures to be followed. Obtain a copy of "Information for Uniform CPA Examination Candidates" from the AICPA. You can also call 1-800-CPA-2DAY and ask for the relevant information, or contact Kaplan's CPA team via E-mail at cpa@kaplan.com.

3. **When will I receive my exam results?**

Exam results usually come out three months from the date you take the test.

4. **Do I have to take all four parts at once?**

Not necessarily. Requirements for sitting for the CPA exam vary from state to state. To find out the requirements in your state, call us at 1-800-CPA-2DAY, or contact your State Board of Accountancy.

5. **Am I automatically certified once I pass the CPA exam?**

Probably not. Before becoming a Certified Public Accountant, most states require you have a certain amount of work experience in addition to passing the exam. To find out the requirements in your state, call us at 1-800-KAP-TEST or contact your State Board of Accountancy.

6. How much information do I need to know to pass the CPA exam?

The CPA exam covers a wide array of topics; however, the topics are represented in a lot less detail than that found in college courses. Kaplan CPA review materials condense and simplify the material you need to know for the examination so you don't waste time on unimportant details. Kaplan also provides a percentage breadown of the test by topic for each section of the exam. This information will facilitate your decision about what topics to focus on.

7. What's the pass rate for first-time test takers?

Approximately 10 percent of those candidates sitting for all four parts of the test their first time out pass all four parts.

8. Why do so many candidates fail the exam the first time out?

The CPA exam is very challenging; however, it is an exam that can be passed the first time if you know what to expect and are prepared. Most people who fail do so because they did not study, used materials that were outdated, or failed to manage their time efficiently.

9. Do I have to be a CPA to work in public accounting?

No. In fact, most people starting out in public accounting are recent college or business school graduates and have not passed the CPA exam. However, it is rare for an accountant to obtain a managerial position if he or she has not obtained their CPA certificate.

10. What does it mean that the CPA examinations are no longer being released?

Candidates who sit for the exam will no longer receive their answer books by mail, and CPA review organizations are no longer allowed to publish the answers to the exam. As a result, candidates will not be able to gain access to the most recent exams or even see their own booklets.

STRATEGIES TO DO YOUR BEST ON THE ESSAYS

The essay sections of the exam typically cause candidates more anxiety than any other part. However, essay writing does not have to be a stressful experience if you approach the process in an organized and systematic way. We propose you stick to the following format:

- Plan your strategy

- Check your allotted time

- Analyze the requirements

- Visualize the solution

- Analyze the narrative

- Develop a key-word outline

- Write the essay

- Proofread, edit, and add any missing concepts to your rough draft in arriving at a finalized version

Keep in mind that five percent of your score on the Auditing, Business Law & Professional Responsibilities, and Financial Accounting & Reporting (FARE) sections will be based upon your writing skills. Graders will select either two full essays, two sections of one essay, or one section each of two distinct essays in order to determine your writing skills grade.

FIRST STEPS

Before actually tackling the essays, it is a good strategy to read over all the essay questions first. Then go to the multiple-choice section, and come back to the essays later. The more time you have to think about the essays you need to write, the better your essay will be. Often the multiple-choice questions can help trigger good ideas.

Once you are ready to tackle the essays, **always** start with the easiest one first. Your approach should be to read over the essay questions and jot down the main topics you will need to cover in each one. Then, rank each essay from easiest to hardest according to the subject matter you are most comfortable with, and write the essays in that order.

Each essay question begins with a narrative section and then gives requirements you must fulfill in the essay. Analyzing the narrative and the requirements you are given and organizing and outlining your thoughts are crucial first steps to writing your essay. Before you begin your draft, you should have a clear idea of what conclusions or main points your essay will encompass.

WRITING CRITERIA

Once you have determined what you want to say in your essay, you can start thinking about how to say it. No matter what subject the essay question deals with, it is important to write each essay keeping the following six scoring criteria in mind:

- Coherent organization

- Conciseness

- Clarity

- Use of standard English

- Responsiveness to the requirements of the question

- Appropriateness for the reader

1. Coherent Organization

   Do not write your essays as a stream of consciousness. Your ideas should follow each other logically, and your main idea should always be the first sentence of each paragraph. Also, be sure that each paragraph of your essay contains at least three full sentences.

2. Conciseness

   Ever hear the phrase *Less is more*? Do not use several words when one word will do. Junk phrases are like junk food: They add only fat, no muscle. Many people make the mistake of "overwriting" in an attempt to make their prose seem more scholarly or more formal. It does not work. Their prose ends up seeming inflated and pretentious. Writing junk phrases is a waste of words, a waste of limited time, and a distraction from the point of the essay.

3. Clarity

   Do not waste your time trying to come up with a variety of descriptive phrases. Select words and/or phrases that clearly convey your main ideas and supporting arguments.

4. Use of Standard English

Standard English simply means proper capitalization, proper punctuation, correct spelling, and proper diction (no slang). To avoid careless errors, be sure you spend at least ten minutes proofreading and editing each essay.

5. Answering the Question

Do not forget that every grader will be reading thousands of essays. The grader's job is to make sure you understand the question and, more importantly, know, and can express, the answer. Be sure to specifically address the requirements of each question. Do not make the grader search through multiple lines of prose to find your conclusion. It wastes the person's time and guarantees you a lower grade on your essay.

6. Appropriateness for the Reader

Keep your eye out for essay questions that specify your reader. For instance, a question may ask you to draft a report for a client or for the senior partner in your accounting firm. The same document would be treated differently given the disparity in technical backgrounds of the two audiences. More often than not, the question will not specify a reader; and you should assume he or she is a knowledgeable CPA.

FINAL THOUGHTS

Essay writing is really this easy. It is just a matter of studying, planning out a strategy, and reading the information very carefully. Keep in mind that not every requirement you are given in the test will look the same. Some may ask for conclusions, some may ask you to list items or concepts, and some may ask you to calculate numerical responses for different situations. Remember the fifth criteria for writing essays—"Responsiveness to the requirements of the question." Make sure you read the requirements closely and you are clear about what is being asked of you.

Most important, approach each essay by taking a deep breath. You have studied long enough to know more than enough material to pass the exam. Do not let anxiety stand in the way of your professional goals!

STUDY TIPS FOR THE CPA EXAM

- Always keep a set of flashcards (whether bought or self-made) on hand in order to make use of traveling or commuting time.

- Set up a feasible study schedule early, and plan to stick to it. There is nothing worse than wasting time feeling guilty for not adhering to an impossible schedule.

- When doing problems, read all of the answers, not just those you get right. This will reinforce your understanding as well as ensure that your original mode of thinking was correct.

- As you go through problems, mark the ones you miss. That way, you will be able to review those questions you had trouble with at a later time.

- Do not plan to spend every free moment studying. You need to reward yourself for your hard work once in a while. Make plans to see a movie with a friend, cook dinner, or take a trip to the gym.

- Keep track of your allotted time. Many candidates fall into trouble by spending too long on a particular section of the exam and then not being able to give the proper attention to another area.

- The night before the exam, pull out all of your paperwork and make sure you know where you have to be and at what time. Confirm any lodging and/or travel arrangements you have made, and try to relax. You have studied hard for the test—passing is just a matter of calming down and facing the exam in an objective manner.

- Bring energy food to the exam. A full day of testing can take a lot out of anyone. Raisins, chocolate bars, and nuts are great snacks.

- Make plans to celebrate after your last day of tests. You will have earned it!

TEST ONE

INSTRUCTIONS FOR COMPUTER-ASSISTED FEEDBACK

A special feature of this book is the computer-assisted feedback you can receive. Simply enter your solutions to the questions on the grids at the back of the book and complete the essays and problems on the response sheets, which you will also find at the back of the book. Kaplan will analyze your exam and send you detailed feedback on how you performed. The feedback will highlight your strengths and weaknesses in each subject area of the test. You can do this test early to get feedback on where to focus your study effort and take Test Two later to check on your progress.

1. Be sure that on each answer grid you have entered your name and the test ID. Each of the answer grids you send in should have a different test ID. The test ID can be found can be found on the first page of each the four sections of the test.

2. **Do not fold the answer grids.** Enclose the answer grids and your essay response sheet in an envelope at least 8 1/2 by 11 inches and send to the address below. Affix extra postage for oversized mail. Please include a self-addressed envelope.

KAPLAN
CPA Team
888 Seventh Avenue
New York, NY 10106

TEST 1: QUESTIONS

BUSINESS LAW & PROFESSIONAL RESPONSIBILITIES

Test ID: 4100

INSTRUCTIONS

1. Question Numbers 1, 2, and 3 should be answered on the scannable grid, which is at the back of this book. You should attempt to answer all objective items. There is no penalty for incorrect responses. Since the objective items are computer graded, your comments and calculations associated with them are not considered. Be certain that you have entered your answers on the scannable grid before the examination time is up. The objective portion of your examination will not be graded if you fail to record your answers on the scannable grid.

2. Question Numbers 4 and 5 should be answered on the essay and problem response sheets at the back of this book. If you have not completed answering a question on a page, fill in the appropriate spaces in the wording on the bottom of the page: **"QUESTION NUMBER ___ CONTINUES ON PAGE ___."** If you have completed answering a question, fill in the appropriate space in the wording on the bottom of the page: **"QUESTION NUMBER ___ ENDS ON THIS PAGE."** Always begin the start of an answer to a question on the top of a new page (which may be the back side of a sheet of paper).

3. Although the primary purpose of the examination is to test your knowledge and application of the subject matter, selected essay responses will be graded for writing skills.

The point values for each question, and estimated time allotments based primarily on point value, are as follows:

	Point Value	Estimated Minutes Minimum	Estimated Minutes Maximum
No. 1	60	90	100
No. 2	10	10	15
No. 3	10	10	15
No. 4	10	15	25
No. 5	10	15	25
Totals	**100**	**140**	**180**

Number 1 (Estimated time—90 to 100 minutes)

Select the **best** answer for each of the following items. Use a No. 2 pencil and blacken ovals #1 through #60 on the Multiple-Choice Section of your scannable grid to indicate your answers. **Mark only the one answer for each item. Answer all items.**

1. The profession's ethical standards most likely would be considered to have been violated when a CPA represents that specific consulting services will be performed for a stated fee and it is apparent at the time of the representation that the

A. Actual fee would be substantially higher.
B. Actual fee would be substantially lower than the fees charged by other CPAs for comparable services.
C. CPA would **not** be independent.
D. Fee was a competitive bid.

2. According to the profession's ethical standards, which of the following events may justify a departure from a Statement of Financial Accounting Standards?

	New legislation	Evolution of a new form of business transaction
A.	No	Yes
B.	Yes	No
C.	Yes	Yes
D.	No	No

3. To exercise due professional care an auditor should

A. Critically review the judgment exercised by those assisting in the audit.
B. Examine all available corroborating evidence supporting management's assertions.
C. Design the audit to detect all instances of illegal acts.
D. Attain the proper balance of professional experience and formal education.

4. Must a CPA in public practice be independent in fact and appearance when providing the following services?

	Compilation of personal financial statements	Preparation of a tax return	Compilation of a financial forecast
A.	Yes	No	No
B.	No	Yes	No
C.	No	No	Yes
D.	No	No	No

5. According to the profession's standards, which of the following is **not** required of a CPA performing a consulting engagement?

A. Complying with Statements on Standards for Consulting Services.
B. Obtaining an understanding of the nature, scope, and limitations of the engagement.
C. Supervising staff who are assigned to the engagement.
D. Maintaining independence from the client.

6. According to the profession's standards, which of the following would be considered consulting services?

	Advisory Services	Implementation Services	Product Services
A.	Yes	Yes	Yes
B.	Yes	Yes	No
C.	Yes	No	Yes
D.	No	Yes	Yes

7. According to the profession's standards, which of the following statements is correct regarding the standards a CPA should follow when recommending tax return positions and preparing tax returns?

A. A CPA may recommend a position that the CPA concludes is frivolous as long as the position is adequately disclosed on the return.

B. A CPA may recommend a position in which the CPA has a good faith belief that the position has a realistic possibility of being sustained if challenged.

C. A CPA will usually **not** advise the client of the potential penalty consequences of the recommended tax return position.

D. A CPA may sign a tax return as preparer knowing that the return takes a position that will **not** be sustained if challenged.

8. According to the profession's standards, which of the following actions should be taken by a CPA tax preparer who discovers an error in a client's previously filed tax return?

A. Advise the IRS.
B. Correct the error.
C. Advise the client.
D. End the relationship with the client.

9. In a common law action against an accountant, lack of privity is a viable defense if the plaintiff

A. Is the client's creditor who sues the accountant for negligence.

B. Can prove the presence of gross negligence that amounts to a reckless disregard for the truth.

C. Is the accountant's client.

D. Bases the action upon fraud.

10. Under common law, which of the following statements most accurately reflects the liability of a CPA who fraudulently gives an opinion on an audit of a client's financial statements?

A. The CPA is liable only to third parties in privity of contract with the CPA.

B. The CPA is liable only to known users of the financial statements.

C. The CPA probably is liable to any person who suffered a loss as a result of the fraud.

D. The CPA probably is liable to the client even if the client was aware of the fraud and did **not** rely on the opinion.

11. Under the provisions of Section 10(b) and Rule 10b-5 of the Securities Exchange Act of 1934, which of the following activities must be proven by a stock purchaser in a suit against a CPA?

I. Intentional conduct by the CPA designed to deceive investors.

II. Negligence by the CPA.

A. I only.
B. II only.
C. Both I and II.
D. Neither I nor II.

Items 12 and 13 are based on the following:

Under the liability provisions of Section 11 of the Securities Act of 1933, a CPA may be liable to any purchaser of a security for certifying materially misstated financial statements that are included in the security's registration statement.

12. Under Section 11, a CPA usually will **not** be liable to the purchaser

A. If the purchaser is contributorily negligent.
B. If the CPA can prove due diligence.
C. Unless the purchaser can prove privity with the CPA.
D. Unless the purchaser can prove scienter on the part of the CPA.

13. Under Section 11, which of the following must be proven by a purchaser of the security?

	Reliance on the financial statements	Fraud by the CPA
A.	Yes	Yes
B.	Yes	No
C.	No	Yes
D.	No	No

14. Which of the following statements concerning an accountant's disclosure of confidential client data is generally correct?

A. Disclosure may be made to any state agency without subpoena.
B. Disclosure may be made to any party on consent of the client.
C. Disclosure may be made to comply with an IRS audit request.
D. Disclosure may be made to comply with Generally Accepted Accounting Principles.

15. To which of the following parties may a CPA partnership provide its working papers, without being lawfully subpoenaed or without the client's consent?

A. The IRS.
B. The FASB.
C. Any surviving partner(s) on the death of a partner.
D. A CPA before purchasing a partnership interest in the firm.

16. Which of the following actions requires an agent for a corporation to have a written agency agreement?

A. Purchasing office supplies for the principal's business.
B. Purchasing an interest in undeveloped land for the principal.
C. Hiring an independent general contractor to renovate the principal's office building.
D. Retaining an attorney to collect a business debt owed the principal.

17. Bolt Corp. dismissed Ace as its general sales agent and notified all of Ace's known customers by letter. Young Corp., a retail outlet located outside of Ace's previously assigned sales territory, had never dealt with Ace. Young knew of Ace as a result of various business contacts. After his dismissal, Ace sold Young goods, to be delivered by Bolt, and received from Young a cash deposit for 20% of the purchase price. It was not unusual for an agent in Ace's previous position to receive cash deposits. In an action by Young against Bolt on the sales contract, Young will

A. Lose, because Ace lacked any implied authority to make the contract.
B. Lose, because Ace lacked any express authority to make the contract.
C. Win, because Bolt's notice was inadequate to terminate Ace's apparent authority.
D. Win, because a principal is an insurer of an agent's acts.

18. Easy Corp. is a real estate developer and regularly engages real estate brokers to act on its behalf in acquiring parcels of land. The brokers are authorized to enter into such contracts, but are instructed to do so in their own names without disclosing Easy's identity or relationship to the transaction. If a broker enters into a contract with a seller on Easy's behalf,

A. The broker will have the same actual authority as if Easy's identity had been disclosed.
B. Easy will be bound by the contract because of the broker's apparent authority.
C. Easy will **not** be liable for any negligent acts committed by the broker while acting on Easy's behalf.
D. The broker will **not** be personally bound by the contract because the broker has express authority to act.

19. An agent will usually be liable under a contract made with a third party when the agent is acting on behalf of a(an)

	Disclosed Principal	Undisclosed Principal
A.	Yes	Yes
B.	Yes	No
C.	No	Yes
D.	No	No

20. Unless otherwise provided in a general partnership agreement, which of the following statements is correct when a partner dies?

	The deceased partner's executor would automatically become a partner	The deceased partner's estate would be free from any partnership liabilities	The partnership would be dissolved automatically
A.	Yes	Yes	Yes
B.	Yes	No	No
C.	No	Yes	No
D.	No	No	Yes

21. Which of the following statements is correct concerning liability when a partner in a general partnership commits a tort while engaged in partnership business?

A. The partner committing the tort is the only party liable.
B. The partnership is the only party liable.
C. Each partner is jointly and severally liable.
D. Each partner is liable to pay an equal share of any judgment.

22. The partnership agreement for Owen Associates, a general partnership, provided that profits be paid to the partners in the ratio of their financial contribution to the partnership. Moore contributed $10,000, Noon contributed $30,000, and Kale contributed $50,000. For the year ended December 31, 19X3, Owen had losses of $180,000. What amount of the losses should be allocated to Kale?

    A. $40,000
    B. $60,000
    C. $90,000
    D. $100,000

23. Lark, a partner in DSJ, a general partnership, wishes to withdraw from the partnership and sell Lark's interest to Ward. All of the other partners in DSJ have agreed to admit Ward as a partner and to hold Lark harmless for the past, present, and future liabilities of DSJ. As a result of Lark's withdrawal and Ward's admission to the partnership, Ward

    A. Acquired only the right to receive Ward's share of DSJ profits.
    B. Has the right to participate in DSJ's management.
    C. Is personally liable for partnership liabilities arising before and after being admitted as a partner.
    D. Must contribute cash or property to DSJ to be admitted with the same rights as the other partners.

24. The partners of College Assoc., a general partnership, decided to dissolve the partnership and agreed that none of the partners would continue to use the partnership name. Under the Uniform Partnership Act, which of the following events will occur on dissolution of the partnership?

	Each partner's existing liability would be discharged	Each partner's apparent authority would continue
A.	Yes	Yes
B.	Yes	No
C.	No	Yes
D.	No	No

25. A parent corporation owned more than 90% of each class of the outstanding stock issued by a subsidiary corporation and decided to merge that subsidiary into itself. Under the Revised Model Business Corporation Act, which of the following actions must be taken?

    A. The subsidiary corporation's board of directors must pass a merger resolution.
    B. The subsidiary corporation's dissenting stockholders must be given an appraisal remedy.
    C. The parent corporation's stockholders must approve the merger.
    D. The parent corporation's dissenting stockholders must be given an appraisal remedy.

26. Under the Federal Fair Debt Collection Practices Act, which of the following would a collection service using improper debt collection practices be subject to?

    A. Abolishment of the debt.
    B. Reduction of the debt.
    C. Civil lawsuit for damages for violating the Act.
    D. Criminal prosecution for violating the Act.

27. Which of the following actions between a debtor and its creditors will generally cause the debtor's release from its debts?

	Composition of Creditors	Assignment for the Benefit of Creditors
A.	Yes	Yes
B.	Yes	No
C.	No	Yes
D.	No	No

28. Which of the following prejudgment remedies would be available to a creditor when a debtor owns **no** real property?

	Writ of Attachment	Garnishment
A.	Yes	Yes
B.	Yes	No
C.	No	Yes
D.	No	No

29. Which of the following defenses would a surety be able to assert successfully to limit the surety's liability to a creditor?

A. A discharge in bankruptcy of the principal debtor.
B. A personal defense the principal debtor has against the creditor.
C. The incapacity of the surety.
D. The incapacity of the principal debtor.

30. Which of the following rights does a surety have?

	Right to compel the creditor to collect from the principal debtor	Right to compel the creditor to proceed against the principal debtor's collateral
A.	Yes	Yes
B.	Yes	No
C.	No	Yes
D.	No	No

31. Ingot Corp. lent Flange $50,000. At Ingot's request, Flange entered into an agreement with Quill and West for them to act as compensated cosureties on the loan in the amount of $100,000 each. Ingot released West without Quill's or Flange's consent, and Flange later defaulted on the loan. Which of the following statements is correct?

A. Quill will be liable for 50% of the loan balance.
B. Quill will be liable for the entire loan balance.
C. Ingot's release of West will have **no** effect on Flange's and Quill's liability to Ingot.
D. Flange will be released for 50% of the loan balance.

32. Deft, CPA, is an unsecured creditor of Golf Co. for $16,000. Golf has a total of 10 creditors, all of whom are unsecured. Golf has not paid any of the creditors for three months. Under Chapter 11 of the Federal Bankruptcy Code, which of the following statements is correct?

A. Golf may **not** be petitioned involuntarily into bankruptcy because there are fewer than 12 unsecured creditors.
B. Golf may **not** be petitioned involuntarily into bankruptcy under the provisions of Chapter 11.
C. Three unsecured creditors must join in the involuntary petition in bankruptcy.
D. Deft may file an involuntary petition in bankruptcy against Golf.

33. Which of the following claims will **not** be discharged in bankruptcy?

A. A claim that arises from alimony or child support.
B. A claim that arises out of the debtor's breach of a contract.
C. A claim brought by a secured creditor that remains unsatisfied after the sale of the collateral.
D. A claim brought by a judgment creditor whose judgment resulted from the debtor's negligent operation of a motor vehicle.

34. Under the liquidation provisions of Chapter 7 of the Federal Bankruptcy Code, which of the following statements applies to a person who has voluntarily filed for and received a discharge in bankruptcy?

A. The person will be discharged from all debts.
B. The person can obtain another voluntary discharge in bankruptcy under Chapter 7 after three years have elapsed from the date of the prior filing.
C. The person must surrender for distribution to the creditors amounts received as an inheritance, if the receipt occurs within 180 days after filing the bankruptcy petition.
D. The person is precluded from owning or operating a similar business for two years.

35. For the entire year 19X3, Ral Supermarket, Inc. conducted its business operations without any permanent or full-time employees. Ral employed temporary and part-time workers during each of the 52 weeks in the year. Under the provisions of the Federal Unemployment Tax Act (FUTA), which of the following statements is correct regarding Ral's obligation to file a federal unemployment tax return for 19X3?

A. Ral must file a 19X3 FUTA return only if aggregate wages exceeded $100,000 during 19X3.
B. Ral must file a 19X3 FUTA return because it had at least one employee during at least 20 weeks of 19X3.
C. Ral is obligated to file a 19X3 FUTA return only if at least one worker earned $50 or more in any calendar quarter of 19X3.
D. Ral does **not** have to file a 19X3 FUTA return because it had **no** permanent or full-time employees in 19X3.

36. Which of the following provisions is basic to all workers' compensation systems?

A. The injured employee must prove the employer's negligence.
B. The employer may invoke the traditional defense of contributory negligence.
C. The employer's liability may be ameliorated by a co-employee's negligence under the fellow-servant rule.
D. The injured employee is allowed to recover on strict liability theory.

37. Under the reorganization provisions of Chapter 11 of the Federal Bankruptcy Code, after a reorganization plan is confirmed, and a final decree closing the proceedings entered, which of the following events usually occurs?

A. A reorganized corporate debtor will be liquidated.
B. A reorganized corporate debtor will be discharged from all debts except as otherwise provided in the plan and applicable law.
C. A trustee will continue to operate the debtor's business.
D. A reorganized individual debtor will **not** be allowed to continue in the same business.

38. Under the Federal Age Discrimination in Employment Act, which of the following practices would be prohibited?

	Compulsory retirement of employees below the age of 65	Termination of employees between the ages of 65 and 70 for cause
A.	Yes	Yes
B.	Yes	No
C.	No	Yes
D.	No	No

39. Under the Federal Fair Labor Standards Act, which of the following would be regulated?

	Minimum wage	Overtime	Number of hours in the work week
A.	Yes	Yes	Yes
B.	Yes	No	Yes
C.	Yes	Yes	No
D.	No	Yes	Yes

40. Which of the following statements correctly describes the funding of noncontributory pension plans?

A. All of the funds are provided by the employees.
B. All of the funds are provided by the employer.
C. The employer and employee each provides 50% of the funds.
D. The employer provides 90% of the funds, and each employee contributes 10%.

41. Under the Securities Act of 1933, which of the following statements most accurately reflects how securities registration affects an investor?

A. The investor is provided with information on the stockholders of the offering corporation.
B. The investor is provided with information on the principal purposes for which the offering's proceeds will be used.
C. The investor is guaranteed by the SEC that the facts contained in the registration statement are accurate.
D. The investor is assured by the SEC against loss resulting from purchasing the security.

42. Which of the following securities would be regulated by the provisions of the Securities Act of 1933?

A. Securities issued by not-for-profit, charitable organizations.
B. Securities guaranteed by domestic governmental organizations.
C. Securities issued by savings-and-loan associations.
D. Securities issued by insurance companies.

43. Which of the following requirements must be met by an issuer of securities who wants to make an offering by using shelf registration?

	Original registration statement must be kept updated	The offeror must be a first-time issuer of securities
A.	Yes	Yes
B.	Yes	No
C.	No	Yes
D.	No	No

44. Under the Securities Act of 1933, which of the following statements concerning an offering of securities sold under a transaction exemption is correct?

A. The offering is exempt from the anti-fraud provisions of the 1933 Act.

B. The offering is subject to the registration requirements of the 1933 Act.

C. Resales of the offering are exempt from the provisions of the 1933 Act.

D. Resales of the offering must be made under a registration or a different exemption provision of the 1933 Act.

Items 45 through 47 are based on the following:

Link Corp. is subject to the reporting provisions of the Securities Exchange Act of 1934.

45. Which of the following situations would require Link to be subject to the reporting provisions of the 1934 Act?

	Shares listed on a national securities exchange	More than one class of stock
A.	Yes	Yes
B.	Yes	No
C.	No	Yes
D.	No	No

46. Which of the following documents must Link file with the SEC?

	Quarterly Reports (Form 10-Q)	Proxy Statements
A.	Yes	Yes
B.	Yes	No
C.	No	Yes
D.	No	No

47. Which of the following reports must also be submitted to the SEC?

	Report by any party making a tender offer to purchase Link's stock	Report of proxy solicitations by Link stockholders
A.	Yes	Yes
B.	Yes	No
C.	No	Yes
D.	No	No

48. Which of the following facts will result in an offering of securities being exempt from registration under the Securities Act of 1933?

A. The securities are nonvoting preferred stock.
B. The issuing corporation was closely held prior to the offering.
C. The sale or offer to sell the securities is made by a person other than an issuer, underwriter, or dealer.
D. The securities are AAA-rated debentures that are collateralized by first mortgages on property that has a market value of 200% of the offering price.

49. For an offering to be exempt under Regulation D of the Securities Act of 1933, Rules 504, 505, and 506 each require that

A. The SEC be notified within 10 days of the first sale.
B. The offering be made without general advertising.
C. All accredited investors receive the issuer's financial information.
D. There be a maximum of 35 investors.

50. Under the Sales Article of the UCC, which of the following statements is correct?

A. The obligations of the parties to the contract must be performed in good faith.
B. Merchants and nonmerchants are treated alike.
C. The contract must involve the sale of goods for a price of more than $500.
D. None of the provisions of the UCC may be disclaimed by agreement.

51. Under the Sales Article of the UCC, which of the following statements is correct regarding the warranty of merchantability arising when there has been a sale of goods by a merchant seller?

A. The warranty must be in writing.
B. The warranty arises when the buyer relies on the seller's skill in selecting the goods purchased.
C. The warranty cannot be disclaimed.
D. The warranty arises as a matter of law when the seller ordinarily sells the goods purchased.

52. Which of the following statements concerning an initial intrastate securities offering made by an issuer residing in and doing business in that state is correct?

A. The offering would be exempt from the registration requirements of the Securities Act of 1933.
B. The offering would be subject to the registration requirements of the Securities Exchange Act of 1934.
C. The offering would be regulated by the SEC.
D. The shares of the offering could **not** be resold to investors outside the state for at least one year.

53. High sues the manufacturer, wholesaler, and retailer for bodily injuries caused by a power saw High purchased. Which of the following statements is correct under strict liability theory?

- A. Contributory negligence on High's part will always be a bar to recovery.
- B. The manufacturer will avoid liability if it can show it followed the custom of the industry.
- C. Privity will be a bar to recovery insofar as the wholesaler is concerned if the wholesaler did **not** have a reasonable opportunity to inspect.
- D. High may recover even if he **cannot** show any negligence was involved.

54. Under the Sales Article of the UCC, which of the following events will result in the risk of loss passing from a merchant seller to a buyer?

	Tender of the goods at the seller's place of business	Use of the seller's truck to deliver the goods
A.	Yes	Yes
B.	Yes	No
C.	No	Yes
D.	No	No

55. Under the Sales Article of the UCC, which of the following events will release the buyer from all its obligations under a sales contract?

- A. Destruction of the goods after risk of loss passed to the buyer.
- B. Impracticability of delivery under the terms of the contract.
- C. Anticipatory repudiation by the buyer that is retracted before the seller cancels the contract.
- D. Refusal of the seller to give written assurance of performance when reasonably demanded by the buyer.

56. Rowe Corp. purchased goods from Stair Co. that were shipped C.O.D. Under the Sales Article of the UCC, which of the following rights does Rowe have?

- A. The right to inspect the goods before paying.
- B. The right to possession of the goods before paying.
- C. The right to reject nonconforming goods.
- D. The right to delay payment for a reasonable period of time.

57. Under the Secured Transactions Article of the UCC, which of the following requirements is necessary to have a security interest attach?

	Debtor has rights in the collateral	Proper filing of a security agreement	Value given by the creditor
A.	Yes	Yes	Yes
B.	Yes	Yes	No
C.	Yes	No	Yes
D.	No	Yes	Yes

58. Under the Secured Transactions Article of the UCC, which of the following purchasers will own consumer goods free of a perfected security interest in the goods?

- A. A merchant who purchases the goods for resale.
- B. A merchant who purchases the goods for use in its business.
- C. A consumer who purchases the goods from a consumer purchaser who gave the security interest.
- D. A consumer who purchases the goods in the ordinary course of business.

59. Under the Secured Transactions Article of the UCC, what would be the order of priority for the following security interests in consumer goods?

I. Financing agreement filed on April 1.

II. Possession of the collateral by a creditor on April 10.

III. Financing agreement perfected on April 15.

A. I. II, III.
B. II, I, III.
C. II, III, I.
D. III, II, I.

60. Under the Secured Transactions Article of the UCC, which of the following remedies is available to a secured creditor when a debtor fails to make payment when due?

	Proceed against the collateral	Obtain a general judgment against the debtor
A.	Yes	Yes
B.	Yes	No
C.	No	Yes
D.	No	No

Number 2 (Estimated time—10 to 15 minutes)

Question Number 2 consists of 15 items. Select the **best** answer for each item. Use a No. 2 pencil to blacken ovals #1 through #15 on OOF Section #2 of your scannable grid.

On December 15, Blake Corp. telephoned Reach Consultants, Inc. and offered to hire Reach to design a security system for Blake's research department. The work would require two years to complete. Blake offered to pay a fee of $100,000 but stated that the offer must be accepted in writing, and the acceptance received by Blake no later than December 20.

On December 20, Reach faxed a written acceptance to Blake. Blake's offices were closed on December 20, and Reach's fax was not seen until December 21.

Reach's acceptance contained the following language:

"We accept your $1,000,000 offer. Weaver has been assigned $5,000 of the fee as payment for sums owed Weaver by Reach. Payment of this amount should be made directly to Weaver."

On December 22, Blake sent a signed memo to Reach rejecting Reach's December 20 fax but offering to hire Reach for a $75,000 fee. Reach telephoned Blake on December 23 and orally accepted Blake's December 22 offer.

Required:

a. **Items 61 through 67** relate to whether a contractual relationship exists between Blake and Reach. For each item, determine whether the statement is True (A) or False (B) and blacken ovals #1 through #7 on OOF Section #2 of your scannable grid.

61. Blake's December 15 offer had to be in writing to be a legitimate offer.

62. Reach's December 20 fax was an improper method of acceptance.

63. Reach's December 20 fax was effective when sent.

64. Reach's acceptance was invalid because it was received after December 20.

65. Blake's receipt of Reach's acceptance created a voidable contract.

66. Reach's agreement to a $1,000,000 fee prevented the formation of a contract.

67. Reach's December 20 fax was a counteroffer.

b. Items 68 through 72 relate to the attempted assignment of part of the fee to Weaver. Assume that a valid contract exists between Blake and Reach. For each item, determine whether the statement is True or False. On the scannable grid, blacken (A) if the statement is True or (B) if the statement is False for items #8 through #12 on OOF Section #2.

68. Reach is prohibited from making an assignment of any contract right or duty.

69. Reach may validly assign part of the fee to Weaver.

70. Under the terms of Reach's acceptance, Weaver would be considered a third party creditor beneficiary.

71. In a breach of contract suit by Weaver, against Blake, Weaver would not collect any punitive damages.

72. In a breach of contract suit by Weaver, against Reach, Weaver would be able to collect punitive damages.

c. Items 73 through 75 relate to Blake's December 22 signed memo. For each item, determine whether the statement is True (A) or False (B) and blacken ovals #13 through #15 on OOF Section #2 of your scannable grid.

73. Reach's oral acceptance of Blake's December 22 memo may be enforced by Blake against Reach.

74. Blake's memo is a valid offer even though it contains no date for acceptance.

75. Blake's memo may be enforced against Blake by Reach.

Number 3 (Estimated time—10 to 15 minutes)

Question Number 3 consists of 2 parts. Part A consists of 5 items and Part B consists of 8 items. Select the **best** answer for each item. Use a No. 2 pencil to blacken ovals #1 through #13 on OOF Section #1 of your scannable grid. **Answer all items.**

During an audit of Trent Realty Corp.'s financial statements, Clark, CPA, reviewed the following instruments:

A. Instrument 1.

$300,000	Belle, MD
	September 15, 19X3

For value received, ten years after date, I promise to pay to the order of Dart Finance Co. Three Hundred Thousand and 00/100 dollars with interest at 9% per annum compounded annually until fully paid.

This instrument arises out of the sale of land located in MD.

It is further agreed that:

1. Maker will pay all costs of collection including reasonable attorney fees.

2. Maker may prepay the amount outstanding on any anniversary date of this instrument.

G. Evans
G. Evans

The following transactions relate to Instrument 1.

- On March 15, 19X4, Dart endorsed the instrument in blank and sold it to Morton for $275,000.

- On July 10, 19X4, Evans informed Morton that Dart had fraudulently induced Evans into signing the instrument.

- On August 15, 19X4, Trent, which knew of Evans' claim against Dart, purchased the instrument from Morton for $50,000.

Required:

Items 76 through 80 relate to Instrument 1. For each item, select from List I the correct answer and blacken ovals on OOF Section #1 of your scannable grid, response items #1 through #5. An answer may be selected once, more than once, or not at all.

76. Instrument 1 is a (type of instrument)

77. Instrument 1 is (negotiability)

78. Morton is considered a (type of ownership)

79. Trent is considered a (type of ownership)

80. Trent could recover on the instrument from (liable party/parties)

List I

A. Draft
B. Promissory Note
C. Security Agreement
D. Holder
E. Holder in due course
F. Holder with rights of a holder in due course under the Shelter Provision
G. Negotiable
H. Nonnegotiable
I. Evans, Morton, and Dart
J. Morton and Dart
K. Only Dart

B. Instrument 2.

Front

```
To:Pure Bank
Upton, VT
                                April 5, 19X4
Pay to the order of M. West $1,500.00 One
Thousand Five Hundred and 00/100 dollars
on May 1, 19X4.
                        W. Fields
                        W Fields
```

Back

```
M. West

Pay to C. Larr
T. Keetin

C. Larr
without recourse
```

Required:

Items 81 through 88 relate to Instrument 2. For each item, select from List II the correct answer and blacken ovals on OOF Section #1 of your scannable grid, response items #6 through #13. An answer may be selected once, more than once, or not at all.

81. Instrument 2 is a (type of instrument)

82. Instrument 2 is (negotiability)

83. West's endorsement makes the instrument (type of instrument)

84. Keetin's endorsement makes the instrument (type of instrument)

85. Larr's endorsement makes the instrument (type of instrument)

86. West's endorsement would be considered (type of endorsement)

87. Keetin's endorsement would be considered (type of endorsement)

88. Larr's endorsement would be considered (type of endorsement)

List II

A. Bearer paper
B. Blank
C. Check
D. Draft
E. Negotiable
F. Nonnegotiable
G. Note
H. Order paper
I. Qualified
J. Special

Number 4 (Estimated Time—15 to 25 minutes)

On January 1, 19X3, Stone prepared an *inter vivos* spendthrift trust. Stone wanted to provide financial security for several close relatives during their lives, with the remainder payable to several charities. Stone funded the trust by transferring stocks, bonds, and a commercial building to the trust. Queen Bank was named as Trustee. The trust was to use the calendar year as its accounting period. The trust instrument contained no provision for the allocation of receipts and disbursements to principal and income.

The following transactions involving trust property occurred in 19X3:

- The trust sold stock it owned for $50,000. The cost basis of the stock was $10,000. Forty thousand dollars was allocated to income and $10,000 to principal.

- The trust received a stock dividend of 500 shares of $10 par value common stock selling, at the time, for $50 per share. Twenty thousand dollars was allocated to income and $5,000 to principal.

- The trust received bond interest of $18,000, which was allocated to income. The interest was paid and received semiannually on May 1 and November 1.

- The trust made mortgage amortization payments of $40,000 on the mortgage on the commercial building. The entire amount was allocated to principal.

On December 31, 19X3, all the income beneficiaries and the charities joined in a petition to have the court allow the trust to be terminated and all trust funds distributed.

Required:

a. State the requirements to establish a valid *inter vivos* spendthrift trust and determine whether the Stone trust meets those requirements.

b. State whether the allocations made in the four transactions were correct and, if not, state the proper allocation to be made under the majority rule. Disregard any tax effect of each transactions.

c. State whether the trust will be terminated by the court, and give the reasons for your conclusion.

Number 5 (Estimated time—15 to 25 minutes)

On May 15, 19X3, Strong bought a factory building from Front for $500,000. Strong assumed Front's $300,000 mortgage with Ace Bank, gave a $150,000 mortgage to Lane Finance Co., and paid $50,000 cash.

The Ace mortgage had never been recorded. Lane knew of the Ace mortgage and recorded its mortgage on May 20, 19X3.

Strong bought the factory for investment purposes and, on June 1, 19X3, entered into a written lease with Apex Mfg. for seven years. On December 1, 19X3, Apex subleased the factory to Egan Corp. without Strong's permission. Strong's lease with Apex was silent concerning the right to sublease.

On May 15, 19X3, Strong had obtained a fire insurance policy from Range Insurance Co. The policy had a face value of $400,000. Apex and Egan obtained fire insurance policies from Zone Insurance Co. Each policy contained a standard 80% coinsurance clause. On May 1, 19X4, when the factory had a fair market value of $600,000, a fire caused $180,000 damage.

Strong made no mortgage payments after the fire and, on September 1, 19X4, after the factory had been repaired, the mortgages were foreclosed. The balances due for principal and accrued interest were: Act, $275,000; and Lane, $140,000. At a foreclosure sale, the factory and land were sold. After payment of all expenses, $400,000 of the proceeds remained for distribution.

As a result of the above events, the following actions took place:

- Strong sued Apex for subleasing the factory to Egan without Strong's permission.

- Zone refused to honor the Apex and Egan fire insurance policies claiming neither Apex nor Egan had an insurable interest in the factory.

- Strong sued Range to have Range pay Strong's $180,000 loss. Range refused claiming Strong had insufficient coverage under the coinsurance clause.

- Ace and Lane both demanded full payment of their mortgages from the proceeds of the foreclosure sale.

The preceding took place in a "Notice-Race" jurisdiction.

Required:

Answer the following questions and give the reasons for your conclusions.

a. Would Strong succeed in the suit against Apex for subletting the factory to Egan without Strong's permission?

b. Is Zone correct in claiming that neither Apex nor Egan had an insurable interest in the factory at the time of the fire?

c. What amount will Strong be able to recover from Range?

d. What amount of the foreclosure proceeds will Lane recover?

TEST 1: QUESTIONS

AUDIT

Test ID: 3100

INSTRUCTIONS

1. Question Numbers 1, 2, and 3 should be answered on the scannable grid, which is at the back of this book. You should attempt to answer all objective items. There is no penalty for incorrect responses. Since the objective items are computer graded, your comments and calculations associated with them are not considered. Be certain that you have entered your answers on the scannable grid before the examination time is up. The objective portion of your examination will not be graded if you fail to record your answers on the scannable grid.

2. Question Numbers 4 and 5 should be answered on the essay and problem response sheets at the back of this book. If you have not completed answering a question on a page, fill in the appropriate spaces in the wording on the bottom of the page: **"QUESTION NUMBER ___ CONTINUES ON PAGE ___."** If you have completed answering a question, fill in the appropriate space in the wording on the bottom of the page. **"QUESTION NUMBER ___ ENDS ON THIS PAGE."** Always begin the start of an answer to a question on the top of a new page (which may be the back side of a sheet of paper).

3. Although the primary purpose of the examination is to test your knowledge and application of the subject matter, selected essay responses will be graded for writing skills.

The point values for each question, and estimated time allotments based primarily on point value, are as follows:

	Point Value	Estimated Minutes	
		Minimum	Maximum
No. 1	60	140	150
No. 2	10	15	25
No. 3	10	15	25
No. 4	10	25	35
No. 5	10	25	35
Totals	**100**	**220**	**270**

Number 1 (Estimated time—140 to 150 minutes)

Select the **best** answer for each of the following items. Use a No. 2 pencil and blacken ovals #1 through #90 on the Multiple-Choice Section of your scannable grid to indicate your answers. **Mark only one answer for each item. Answer all items.**

1. Which of the following procedures would an auditor most likely include in the initial planning of a financial statement audit?

A. Obtaining a written representation letter from the client's management.
B. Examining documents to detect illegal acts having a material effect on the financial statements.
C. Considering whether the client's accounting estimates are reasonable in the circumstances.
D. Determining the extent of involvement of the client's internal auditors.

2. Which of the following factors most likely would influence an auditor's determination of the auditability of an entity's financial statements?

A. The complexity of the accounting system.
B. The existence of related party transactions.
C. The adequacy of the accounting records.
D. The operating effectiveness of control procedures.

3. Hill, CPA, has been retained to audit the financial statements of Monday Co. Monday's predecessor auditor was Post, CPA, who has been notified by Monday that Post's services have been terminated. Under these circumstances, which party should initiate the communications between Hill and Post?

A. Hill, the successor auditor.
B. Post, the predecessor auditor.
C. Monday's controller or CFO.
D. The chairman of Monday's board of directors.

4. The senior auditor responsible for coordinating the field work usually schedules a pre-audit conference with the audit team primarily to

A. Give guidance to the staff regarding both technical and personnel aspects of the audit.
B. Discuss staff suggestions concerning the establishment and maintenance of time budgets.
C. Establish the need for using the work of specialists and internal auditors.
D. Provide an opportunity to document staff disagreements regarding technical issues.

5. After field work audit procedures are completed, a partner of the CPA firm who has not been involved in the audit performs a second or wrap-up working paper review. This second review usually focuses on

A. The fair presentation of the financial statements in conformity with GAAP.
B. Irregularities involving the client's management and its employees.
C. The materiality of the adjusting entries proposed by the audit staff.
D. The communication of internal control weaknesses to the client's audit committee.

6. To obtain an understanding of a continuing client's business in planning an audit, an auditor most likely would

A. Perform tests of details of transactions and balances.
B. Review prior-year working papers and the permanent file for the client.
C. Read specialized industry journals.
D. Reevaluate the client's internal control environment.

7. In planning an audit of a new client, an auditor most likely would consider the methods used to process accounting information because such methods

A. Influence the design of the internal control.
B. Affect the auditor's preliminary judgment about materiality levels.
C. Assist in evaluating the planned audit objectives.
D. Determine the auditor's acceptable level of audit risk.

8. Inherent risk and control risk differ from detection risk in that they

A. Arise from the misapplication of auditing procedures.
B. May be assessed in either quantitative or nonquantitative terms.
C. Exist independently of the financial statement audit.
D. Can be changed at the auditor's discretion.

9. The existence of audit risk is recognized by the statement in the auditor's standard report that the

A. Auditor is responsible for expressing an opinion on the financial statements, which are the responsibility of management.
B. Financial statements are presented fairly, in all material respects, in conformity with GAAP.
C. Audit includes examining, on a test basis, evidence supporting the amounts and disclosures in the financial statements.
D. Auditor obtains reasonable assurance about whether the financial statements are free of material misstatement.

10. On the basis of audit evidence gathered and evaluated, an auditor decides to increase the assessed level of control risk from that originally planned. To achieve an overall audit risk level that is substantially the same as the planned audit risk level, the auditor would

A. Decrease substantive testing.
B. Decrease detection risk.
C. Increase inherent risk.
D. Increase materiality levels.

11. Which of the following statements is **not** correct about materiality?

A. The concept of materiality recognizes that some matters are important for fair presentation of financial statements in conformity with GAAP, while other matters are **not** important.
B. An auditor considers materiality for planning purposes in terms of the largest aggregate level of misstatements that could be material to any one of the financial statements.
C. Materiality judgments are made in light of surrounding circumstances and necessarily involve both quantitative and qualitative judgments.
D. An auditor's consideration of materiality is influenced by the auditor's perception of the needs of a reasonable person who will rely on the financial statements.

12. During the annual audit of Ajax Corp., a publicly held company, Jones, CPA, a continuing auditor, determined that illegal political contributions had been made during each of the past seven years, including the year under audit. Jones notified the board of directors about the illegal contributions, but they refused to take any action because the amounts involved were immaterial to the financial statements.

Jones should reconsider the intended degree of reliance to be placed on the

- A. Letter of audit inquiry to the client's attorney.
- B. Prior years' audit programs.
- C. Management representation letter.
- D. Preliminary judgment about materiality levels.

13. Which of the following circumstances most likely would cause an auditor to consider whether material misstatements exist in an entity's financial statements?

- A. Management places little emphasis on meeting earnings projections.
- B. The board of directors makes all major financing decisions.
- C. Reportable conditions previously communicated to management are **not** corrected.
- D. Transactions selected for testing are **not** supported by proper documentation.

14. An entity's income statements were misstated due to the recording of journal entries that involved debits and credits to an unusual combination of expense and revenue accounts. The auditor most likely could have detected this irregularity by

- A. Tracing a sample of journal entries to the general ledger.
- B. Evaluating the effectiveness of the internal control policies and procedures.
- C. Investigating the reconciliations between controlling accounts and subsidiary records.
- D. Performing analytical procedures designed to disclose differences from expectations.

15. Which of the following documentation is **not** required for an audit in accordance with generally accepted auditing standards?

- A. A written audit program setting forth the procedures necessary to accomplish the audit's objectives.
- B. An indication that the accounting records agree or reconcile with the financial statements.
- C. A client engagement letter that summarizes the timing and details of the auditor's planned field work.
- D. The basis for the auditor's conclusions when the assessed level of control risk is below the maximum level.

16. Audit programs should be designed so that

- A. Most of the required procedures can be performed as interim work.
- B. Inherent risk is assessed at a sufficiently low level.
- C. The auditor can make constructive suggestions to management.
- D. The audit evidence gathered supports the auditor's conclusions.

17. The permanent file of an auditor's working papers generally would **not** include

- A. Bond indenture agreements.
- B. Lease agreements.
- C. Working trial balance.
- D. Flowchart of the internal control.

18. Which of the following conditions is necessary for a practitioner to accept an attest engagement to examine and report on an entity's internal control over financial reporting?

- A. The practitioner anticipates relying on the entity's internal control in a financial statement audit.
- B. Management presents its written assertion about the effectiveness of the internal control.
- C. The practitioner is a continuing auditor who previously has audited the entity's financial statements.
- D. Management agrees **not** to present the practitioner's report in a general-use document to stockholders.

19. Which of the following statements is correct concerning an auditor's responsibilities regarding financial statements?

- A. Making suggestions that are adopted about the form and content of an entity's financial statements impairs an auditor's independence.
- B. An auditor may draft an entity's financial statements based on information from management's accounting system.
- C. The fair presentation of audited financial statements in conformity with GAAP is an implicit part of the auditor's responsibilities.
- D. An auditor's responsibilities for audited financial statements are **not** confined to the expression of the auditor's opinion.

20. An accountant has been engaged to review a nonpublic entity's financial statements that contain several departures from GAAP. If the financial statements are **not** revised and modification of the standard review report is **not** adequate to indicate the deficiencies, the accountant should

- A. Withdraw from the engagement and provide **no** further services concerning these financial statements.
- B. Inform management that the engagement can proceed only if distribution of the accountant's report is restricted to internal use.
- C. Determine the effects of the departures from GAAP and issue a special report on the financial statements.
- D. Issue a modified review report provided the entity agrees that the financial statements will **not** be used to obtain credit.

21. Which of the following statements best describes an auditor's responsibility to detect errors and irregularities?

A. An auditor should design an audit to provide reasonable assurance of detecting errors and irregularities that are material to the financial statements.

B. An auditor is responsible to detect material errors, but has **no** responsibility to detect material irregularities that are concealed through employee collusion or management override of the internal control.

C. An auditor has **no** responsibility to detect errors and irregularities unless analytical procedures or tests of transactions identify conditions causing a reasonably prudent auditor to suspect that the financial statements were materially misstated.

D. An auditor has **no** responsibility to detect errors and irregularities because an auditor is **not** an insurer and an audit does **not** constitute a guarantee.

22. Statements on Standards for Accounting and Review Services (SSARS) require an accountant to report when the accountant has

A. Typed client-prepared financial statements, without modification, as an accommodation to the client.

B. Provided a client with a financial statement format that does **not** include dollar amounts, to be used by the client in preparing financial statements.

C. Proposed correcting journal entries to be recorded by the client that change client-prepared financial statements.

D. Generated, through the use of computer software, financial statements prepared in accordance with a comprehensive basis of accounting other than GAAP.

23. An accountant may accept an engagement to apply agreed-upon procedures to prospective financial statements provided that

A. Distribution of the report is restricted to the specified users.

B. The prospective financial statements are also examined.

C. Responsibility for the adequacy of the procedures performed is taken by the accountant.

D. Negative assurance is expressed on the prospective financial statements taken as a whole.

24. The primary purpose of establishing quality control policies and procedures for deciding whether to accept a new client is to

A. Enable the CPA firm to attest to the reliability of the client.

B. Satisfy the CPA firm's duty to the public concerning the acceptance of new clients.

C. Minimize the likelihood of association with clients whose management lacks integrity.

D. Anticipate before performing any field work whether an unqualified opinion can be expressed.

25. When assessing the internal auditor's competence, the independent CPA should obtain information about the

A. Organizational level to which the internal auditors report.

B. Educational background and professional certification of the internal auditors.

C. Policies prohibiting the internal auditors from auditing areas where relatives are employed.

D. Internal auditors' access to records and information that is considered sensitive.

26. Proper segregation of duties reduces the opportunities to allow persons to be in positions to both

  A. Journalize entries and prepare financial statements.
  B. Record cash receipts and cash disbursements.
  C. Establish internal controls and authorize transactions.
  D. Perpetuate and conceal errors and irregularities.

27. Which of the following statements is correct concerning statistical sampling in tests of controls?

  A. As the population size increases, the sample size should increase proportionately.
  B. Deviations from specific internal control procedures at a given rate ordinarily result in misstatements at a lower rate.
  C. There is an inverse relationship between the expected population deviation rate and the sample size.
  D. In determining tolerable rate, an auditor considers detection risk and the sample size.

28. In an audit of financial statements, an auditor's primary consideration regarding an internal control policy or procedure is whether the policy or procedure

  A. Reflects management's philosophy and operating style.
  B. Affects management's financial statement assertions.
  C. Provides adequate safeguards over access to assets.
  D. Enhances management's decision-making processes.

29. Which of the following are considered control environment factors?

	Detection Risk	Personnel Policies and Practices
A.	Yes	Yes
B.	Yes	No
C.	No	Yes
D.	No	No

30. The ultimate purpose of assessing control risk is to contribute to the auditor's evaluation of the risk that

  A. Tests of controls may fail to identify procedures relevant to assertions.
  B. Material misstatements may exist in the financial statements.
  C. Specified controls requiring segregation of duties may be circumvented by collusion.
  D. Entity policies may be overridden by senior management.

31. To obtain evidential matter about control risk, an auditor selects tests from a variety of techniques including

  A. Inquiry.
  B. Analytical procedures.
  C. Calculation.
  D. Confirmation.

32. Which of the following is a step in an auditor's decision to assess control risk at below the maximum?

A. Apply analytical procedures to both financial data and nonfinancial information to detect conditions that may indicate weak controls.

B. Perform tests of details of transactions and account balances to identify potential errors and irregularities.

C. Identify specific internal control policies and procedures that are likely to detect or prevent material misstatements.

D. Document that the additional audit effort to perform tests of controls exceeds the potential reduction in substantive testing.

33. The likelihood of assessing control risk too high is the risk that the sample selected to test controls

A. Does **not** support the auditor's planned assessed level of control risk when the true operating effectiveness of the control justifies such an assessment.

B. Contains misstatements that could be material to the financial statements when aggregated with misstatements in other account balances or transactions classes.

C. Contains proportionately fewer monetary errors or deviations from prescribed internal control policies or procedures than exist in the balance or class as a whole.

D. Does **not** support the tolerable error for some or all of management's assertions.

34. Upon receipt of customers' checks in the mailroom, a responsible employee should prepare a remittance listing that is forwarded to the cashier. A copy of the listing should be sent to the

A. Internal auditor to investigate the listing for unusual transactions.

B. Treasurer to compare the listing with the monthly bank statement.

C. Accounts receivable bookkeeper to update the subsidiary accounts receivable records.

D. Entity's bank to compare the listing with the cashier's deposit slip.

35. Proper authorization of write-offs of uncollectible accounts should be approved in which of the following departments?

A. Accounts receivable.
B. Credit.
C. Accounts payable.
D. Treasurer.

36. Which of the following procedures most likely would **not** be an internal control procedure designed to reduce the risk of errors in the billing process?

A. Comparing control totals for shipping documents with corresponding totals for sales invoices.

B. Using computer programmed controls on the pricing and mathematical accuracy of sales invoices.

C. Matching shipping documents with approved sales orders before invoice preparation.

D. Reconciling the control totals for sales invoices with the accounts receivable subsidiary ledger.

37. Misstatements in a batch computer system caused by incorrect programs or data may **not** be detected immediately because

- A. Errors in some transactions may cause rejection of other transactions in the batch.
- B. The identification of errors in input data typically is **not** part of the program.
- C. There are time delays in processing transactions in a batch system.
- D. The processing of transactions in a batch system is **not** uniform.

38. Which of the following controls is a processing control designed to ensure the reliability and accuracy of data processing?

	Limit Test	Validity Check Test
A.	Yes	Yes
B.	No	No
C.	No	Yes
D.	Yes	No

39. In assessing control risk for purchases, an auditor vouches a sample of entries in the voucher register to the supporting documents. Which assertion would this test of controls most likely support?

- A. Completeness.
- B. Existence or occurrence.
- C. Valuation or allocation.
- D. Rights and obligations.

40. Which of the following internal control procedures is **not** usually performed in the vouchers payable department?

- A. Matching the vendor's invoice with the related receiving report.
- B. Approving vouchers for payment by having an authorized employee sign the vouchers.
- C. Indicating the asset and expense accounts to be debited.
- D. Accounting for unused prenumbered purchase orders and receiving reports.

41. Which of the following questions would an auditor **least** likely include on an internal control questionnaire concerning the initiation and execution of equipment transactions?

- A. Are requests for major repairs approved at a higher level than the department initiating the request?
- B. Are prenumbered purchase orders used for equipment and periodically accounted for?
- C. Are requests for purchases of equipment reviewed for consideration of soliciting competitive bids?
- D. Are procedures in place to monitor and properly restrict access to equipment?

42. The objective of tests of details of transactions performed as tests of controls is to

- A. Monitor the design and use of entity documents such as prenumbered shipping forms.
- B. Determine whether internal control policies and procedures have been placed in operation.
- C. Detect material misstatements in the account balances of the financial statements.
- D. Evaluate whether internal control procedures operated effectively.

43. Which of the following tests of controls most likely would help assure an auditor that goods shipped are properly billed?

    A. Scan the sales journal for sequential and unusual entries.

    B. Examine shipping documents for matching sales invoices.

    C. Compare the accounts receivable ledger to daily sales summaries.

    D. Inspect unused sales invoices for consecutive prenumbering.

44. Reportable conditions are matters that come to an auditor's attention that should be communicated to an entity's audit committee because they represent

    A. Disclosures of information that significantly contradict the auditor's going concern assumption.

    B. Material irregularities or illegal acts perpetrated by high-level management.

    C. Significant deficiencies in the design or operation of the internal control.

    D. Manipulation or falsification of accounting records or documents from which financial statements are prepared.

45. Which of the following statements is correct concerning an auditor's required communication of reportable conditions?

    A. A reportable condition previously communicated during the prior year's audit that remains uncorrected causes a scope limitation.

    B. An auditor should perform tests of controls on reportable conditions before communicating them to the client.

    C. An auditor's report on reportable conditions should include a restriction on the distribution of the report.

    D. An auditor should communicate reportable conditions after tests of controls, but before commencing substantive tests.

46. Snow, CPA, was engaged by Master Co. to examine and report on management's written assertion about the effectiveness of Master's internal control over financial reporting. Snow's report should state that

    A. Because of inherent limitations of any internal control, errors or irregularities may occur and **not** be detected.

    B. Management's assertion is based on criteria established by the American Institute of Certified Public Accountants.

    C. The results of Snow's tests will form the basis for Snow's opinion on the fairness of Master's financial statements in conformity with GAAP.

    D. The purpose of the engagement is to enable Snow to plan an audit and determine the nature, timing, and extent of tests to be performed.

47. Which of the following presumptions is correct about the reliability of evidential matter?

A. Information obtained indirectly from outside sources is the most reliable evidential matter.
B. To be reliable, evidential matter should be convincing rather than persuasive.
C. Reliability of evidential matter refers to the amount of corroborative evidence obtained.
D. An effective internal control provides more assurance about the reliability of evidential matter.

48. Which of the following auditing procedures most likely would provide assurance about a manufacturing entity's inventory valuation?

A. Testing the entity's computation of standard overhead rates.
B. Obtaining confirmation of inventories pledged under loan agreements.
C. Reviewing shipping and receiving cutoff procedures for inventories.
D. Tracing test counts to the entity's inventory listing.

49. In establishing the existence and ownership of a long-term investment in the form of publicly traded stock, an auditor should inspect the securities or

A. Correspond with the investee company to verify the number of shares owned.
B. Inspect the audited financial statements of the investee company.
C. Confirm the number of shares owned that are held by an independent custodian.
D. Determine that the investment is carried at the lower of cost or market.

50. An auditor's purpose in reviewing credit ratings of customers with delinquent accounts receivable most likely is to obtain evidence concerning management's assertions about

A. Valuation or allocation.
B. Presentation and disclosure.
C. Existence or occurrence.
D. Rights and obligations.

51. Determining that proper amounts of depreciation are expensed provides assurance about management's assertions of valuation or allocation and

A. Presentation and disclosure.
B. Completeness.
C. Rights and obligations.
D. Existence or occurrence.

52. In auditing accounts receivable the negative form of confirmation request most likely would be used when

A. Recipients are likely to return positive confirmation requests without verifying the accuracy of the information.
B. The combined assessed level of inherent and control risk relative to accounts receivable is low.
C. A small number of accounts receivable are involved but a relatively large number of errors are expected.
D. The auditor performs a dual purpose test that assesses control risk and obtains substantive evidence.

53. When using confirmations to provide evidence about the completeness assertion for accounts payable, the appropriate population most likely would be

   A. Vendors with whom the entity has previously done business.
   B. Amounts recorded in the accounts payable subsidiary ledger.
   C. Payees of checks drawn in the month after the year end.
   D. Invoices filed in the entity's open invoice file.

54. Which of the following sampling methods would be used to estimate a numerical measurement of a population, such as a dollar value?

   A. Attributes sampling.
   B. Stop-or-go sampling.
   C. Variables sampling.
   D. Random-number sampling.

55. Which of the following courses of action would an auditor most likely follow in planning a sample of cash disbursements if the auditor is aware of several unusually large cash disbursements?

   A. Set the tolerable rate of deviation at a lower level than originally planned.
   B. Stratify the cash disbursements population so that the unusually large disbursements are selected.
   C. Increase the sample size to reduce the effect of the unusually large disbursements.
   D. Continue to draw new samples until all the unusually large disbursements appear in the sample.

56. Which of the following sample planning factors would influence the sample size for a substantive test of details for a specific account?

	Expected Amount of Misstatements	Measure of Tolerable Misstatement
A.	No	No
B.	Yes	Yes
C.	No	Yes
D.	Yes	No

57. In evaluating the reasonableness of an accounting estimate, an auditor most likely would concentrate on key factors and assumptions that are

   A. Consistent with prior periods.
   B. Similar to industry guidelines.
   C. Objective and **not** susceptible to bias.
   D. Deviations from historical patterns.

58. A client maintains perpetual inventory records in both quantities and dollars. If the assessed level of control risk is high, an auditor would probably

   A. Increase the extent of tests of controls of the inventory cycle.
   B. Request the client to schedule the physical inventory count at the end of the year.
   C. Insist that the client perform physical counts of inventory items several times during the year.
   D. Apply gross profit tests to ascertain the reasonableness of the physical counts.

59. In auditing payroll, an auditor most likely would

A. Verify that checks representing unclaimed wages are mailed.
B. Trace individual employee deductions to entity journal entries.
C. Observe entity employees during a payroll distribution.
D. Compare payroll costs with entity standards or budgets.

60. In auditing long-term bonds payable, an auditor most likely would

A. Perform analytical procedures on the bond premium and discount accounts.
B. Examine documentation of assets purchased with bond proceeds for liens.
C. Compare interest expense with the bond payable amount for reasonableness.
D. Confirm the existence of individual bondholders at year end.

61. In performing tests concerning the granting of stock options, an auditor should

A. Confirm the transaction with the Secretary of State in the state of incorporation.
B. Verify the existence of option holders in the entity's payroll records or stock ledgers.
C. Determine that sufficient treasury stock is available to cover any new stock issued.
D. Trace the authorization for the transaction to a vote of the board of directors.

62. An auditor analyzes repairs and maintenance accounts primarily to obtain evidence in support of the audit assertion that all

A. Noncapitalizable expenditures for repairs and maintenance have been recorded in the proper period.
B. Expenditures for property and equipment have been recorded in the proper period.
C. Noncapitalizable expenditures for repairs and maintenance have been properly charged to expense.
D. Expenditures for property and equipment have **not** been charged to expense.

63. Before applying substantive tests to the details of asset accounts at an interim date, an auditor should assess

A. Control risk at below the maximum level.
B. Inherent risk at the maximum level.
C. The difficulty in controlling the incremental audit risk.
D. Materiality for the accounts tested as insignificant.

64. "There are no violations or possible violations of laws or regulations whose effects should be considered for disclosure in the financial statements or as a basis for recording a loss contingency." The foregoing passage most likely is from a (an)

A. Client engagement letter.
B. Report on compliance with laws and regulations.
C. Management representation letter.
D. Attestation report on an internal control.

65. Which of the following statements is correct about the auditor's use of the work of a specialist?

A. The specialist should **not** have an understanding of the auditor's corroborative use of the specialist's findings.
B. The auditor is required to perform substantive procedures to verify the specialist's assumptions and findings.
C. The client should not have an understanding of the nature of the work to be performed by the specialist.
D. The auditor should obtain an understanding of the methods and assumptions used by the specialist.

66. The primary reason an auditor requests letters of inquiry be sent to a client's attorneys is to provide the auditor with

A. The probable outcome of asserted claims and pending or threatened litigation.
B. Corroboration of the information furnished by management about litigation, claims, and assessments.
C. The attorneys' opinions of the client's historical experiences in recent similar litigation.
D. A description and evaluation of litigation, claims, and assessments that existed at the balance sheet date.

67. An auditor issued an audit report that was dual dated for a subsequent event occurring after the completion of field work but before issuance of the auditor's report. The auditor's responsibility for events occurring subsequent to the completion of field work was

A. Limited to include only events occurring up to the date of the last subsequent event referenced.
B. Limited to the specific event referenced.
C. Extended to subsequent events occurring through the date of issuance of the report.
D. Extended to include all events occurring since the completion of field work.

68. In assessing the competence and objectivity of an entity's internal auditor, an independent auditor **least** likely would consider information obtained from

A. Discussions with management personnel.
B. External quality reviews of the internal auditor's activities.
C. Previous experience with the internal auditor.
D. The results of analytical procedures.

69. After determining that a related party transaction has, in fact, occurred, an auditor should

A. Add a separate paragraph to the auditor's standard report to explain the transaction.
B. Perform analytical procedures to verify whether similar transactions occurred, but were **not** recorded.
C. Obtain an understanding of the business purpose of the transaction.
D. Substantiate that the transaction was consummated on terms equivalent to an arm's-length transaction.

70. Which of the following computer-assisted auditing techniques allows fictitious and real transactions to be processed together without client-operating personnel being aware of the testing process?

    A. Integrated test facility.
    B. Input controls matrix.
    C. Parallel simulation.
    D. Data entry monitor.

71. Which of the following conditions or events most likely would cause an auditor to have substantial doubt about an entity's ability to continue as a going concern?

    A. Cash flows from operating activities are negative.
    B. Research and development projects are postponed.
    C. Significant related party transactions are pervasive.
    D. Stock dividends replace annual cash dividends.

72. An auditor ordinarily uses a working trial balance resembling the financial statements without footnotes, but containing columns for

    A. Cash flow increases and decreases.
    B. Audit objectives and assertions.
    C. Reclassifications and adjustments.
    D. Reconciliations and tickmarks.

73. Which of the following factors would **least** likely affect the quantity and content of an auditor's working papers?

    A. The condition of the client's records.
    B. The assessed level of control risk.
    C. The nature of the auditor's report.
    D. The content of the representation letter.

74. Which of the following procedures would an accountant **least** likely perform during an engagement to review the financial statements of a nonpublic entity?

    A. Observing the safeguards over access to and use of assets and records.
    B. Comparing the financial statements with anticipated results in budgets and forecasts.
    C. Inquiring of management about actions taken at the board of directors' meetings.
    D. Studying the relationships of financial statement elements expected to conform to predictable patterns.

75. Which of the following procedures should an accountant perform during an engagement to review the financial statements of a nonpublic entity?

    A. Communicating reportable conditions discovered during the assessment of control risk.
    B. Obtaining a client representation letter from members of management.
    C. Sending bank confirmation letters to the entity's financial institutions.
    D. Examining cash disbursements in the subsequent period for unrecorded liabilities.

76. When an independent CPA is associated with the financial statements of a publicly held entity but has **not** audited or reviewed such statements, the appropriate form of report to be issued must include a (an)

    A. Regulation S-X exemption.
    B. Report on pro forma financial statements.
    C. Unaudited association report.
    D. Disclaimer of opinion.

77. Before reissuing the prior year's auditor's report on the financial statements of a former client, the predecessor auditor should obtain a letter of representations from the

A. Former client's management.
B. Former client's attorney.
C. Former client's board of directors.
D. Successor auditor.

78. An accountant who had begun an audit of the financial statements of a nonpublic entity was asked to change the engagement to a review because of a restriction on the scope of the audit. If there is reasonable justification for the change, the accountant's review report should include reference to the

	Scope limitation that caused the changed engagement	Original engagement that was agreed to
A.	Yes	No
B.	No	Yes
C.	No	No
D.	Yes	Yes

79. Gole, CPA, is engaged to review the 19X4 financial statements of North Co., a nonpublic entity. Previously, Gole audited North's 19X3 financial statements and expressed an unqualified opinion. Gole decides to include a separate paragraph in the 19X4 review report because North plans to present comparative financial statement for 19X4 and 19X3. This separate paragraph should indicate that

A. The 19X4 review report is intended solely for the information of management and the board of directors.
B. The 19X3 auditor's report may **no** longer be relied on.
C. No auditing procedures were performed after the date of the 19X3 auditor's report.
D. There are justifiable reasons for changing the level of service from an audit to a review.

80. Which of the following statements should be included in an accountant's standard report based on the compilation of a nonpublic entity's financial statements?

A. A compilation consists principally of inquiries of company personnel and analytical procedures applied to financial data.
B. A compilation is limited to presenting in the form of financial statements information that is the representation of management.
C. A compilation is **not** designed to detect material modifications that should be made to the financial statements.
D. A compilation is substantially less in scope than an audit in accordance with generally accepted auditing standards.

81. Miller, CPA, is engaged to compile the financial statements of Web Co., a nonpublic entity, in conformity with the income tax basis of accounting. If Web's financial statements do **not** disclose the basis of accounting used, Miller should

A. Disclose the basis of accounting in the accountant's compilation report.
B. Clearly label each page "Distribution Restricted—Material Modification Required."
C. Issue a special report describing the effect of the incomplete presentation.
D. Withdraw from the engagement and provide **no** further services to Web.

82. When an accountant is engaged to compile a nonpublic entity's financial statements that omit substantially all disclosures required by GAAP, the accountant should indicate in the compilation report that the financial statements are

A. Not designed for those who are uninformed about the omitted disclosures.
B. Prepared in conformity with a comprehensive basis of accounting other than GAAP.
C. Not compiled in accordance with Statements on Standards for Accounting and Review Services.
D. Special-purpose financial statements that are **not** comparable to those of prior periods.

83. An accountant's compilation report on a financial forecast should include a statement that

A. The forecast should be read only in conjunction with the audited historical financial statements.
B. The accountant expresses only limited assurance on the forecasted statements and their assumptions.
C. There will usually be differences between the forecasted and actual results.
D. The hypothetical assumptions used in the forecast are reasonable in the circumstances.

84. Which of the following matters is an auditor required to communicate to an entity's audit committee?

A. The basis for assessing control risk below the maximum.
B. The process used by management in formulating sensitive accounting estimates.
C. The auditor's preliminary judgments about materiality levels.
D. The justification for performing substantive procedures at interim dates.

85. Wolf is auditing an entity's compliance with requirements governing a major federal financial assistance program in accordance with *Government Auditing Standards*. Wolf detected noncompliance with requirements that have a material effect on the program. Wolf's report on compliance should express

A. No assurance on the compliance tests.
B. Reasonable assurance on the compliance tests.
C. A qualified or adverse opinion.
D. An adverse or disclaimer of opinion.

86. An auditor concludes that there is a material inconsistency in the other information in an annual report to shareholders containing audited financial statements. If the auditor concludes that the financial statements do **not** require revision, but the client refuses to revise or eliminate the material inconsistency, the auditor may

  A. Revise the auditor's report to include a separate explanatory paragraph describing the material inconsistency.
  B. Issue an "except for" qualified opinion after discussing the matter with the client's board of directors.
  C. Consider the matter closed since the other information is **not** in the audited financial statements.
  D. Disclaim an opinion on the financial statements after explaining the material inconsistency in a separate explanatory paragraph.

87. In the standard report on condensed financial statements that are derived from a public entity's audited financial statements, a CPA should indicate that the

  A. Condensed financial statements are prepared in conformity with another comprehensive basis of accounting.
  B. CPA has audited and expressed an opinion on the complete financial statements.
  C. Condensed financial statements are **not** fairly presented in all material respects.
  D. CPA expresses limited assurance that the financial statements conform with GAAP.

88. Before reporting on the financial statements of a U.S. entity that have been prepared in conformity with another country's accounting principles, an auditor practicing in the U.S. should

  A. Understand the accounting principles generally accepted in the other country.
  B. Be certified by the appropriate auditing or accountancy board of the other country.
  C. Notify management that the auditor is required to disclaim an opinion on the financial statements.
  D. Receive a waiver from the auditor's state board of accountancy to perform the engagement.

89. Subsequent to the issuance of an auditor's report, the auditor became aware of facts existing at the report date that would have affected the report had the auditor then been aware of such facts. After determining that the information is reliable, the auditor should next

  A. Determine whether there are persons relying or likely to rely on the financial statements who would attach importance to the information.
  B. Request that management disclose the newly discovered information by issuing revised financial statements.
  C. Issue revised pro forma financial statements taking into consideration the newly discovered information.
  D. Give public notice that the auditor is **no** longer associated with financial statements.

90. An auditor was engaged to conduct a performance audit of a governmental entity in accordance with *Government Auditing Standards*. These standards do **not** require, as part of this auditor's report

A. A statement of the audit objectives and a description of the audit scope.
B. Indications or instances of illegal acts that could result in criminal prosecution discovered during the audit.
C. The pertinent views of the entity's responsible officials concerning the auditor's findings.
D. A concurrent opinion on the financial statements taken as a whole.

Number 2 (Estimated time—15 to 25 minutes)

Question Number 2 consists of 8 items. Select the **best** answers for each item. Use a No. 2 pencil to blacken the appropriate ovals on your scannable grid to indicate your answers. **Answer all items.**

Required:

Items 91 through 98 present various independent factual situations an auditor might encounter in conducting an audit. List A represents the types of opinions the auditor ordinarily would issue and List B represents the report modification (if any) that would be necessary. For each situation, select one response from List A and one from List B and blacken the corresponding ovals on the OOF Multiple-Response Section of your scannable grid. For List A, use the first response column (#1 through #8). For List B, use the second response column (#1 through #8). Select as the **best** answers for each item, the action the auditor normally would take. The types of opinions in List A and the report modifications in List B may be selected once, more than once, or not at all.

Assume:

- The auditor is independent.

- The auditor previously expressed an unqualified opinion on the prior year's financial statements.

- Only single-year (not comparative) statements are presented for the current year.

- The conditions for an unqualified opinion exist unless contradicted by the facts.

- The conditions stated in the factual situation are material.

- No report modifications are to be made except in response to the factual situation.

91. An auditor hires an actuary to assist in corroborating a client's complex pension calculations concerning accrued pension liabilities that account for 35% of the client's total liabilities. The actuary's findings are reasonably close to the client's calculations and support the financial statements.

92. A client holds a note receivable consisting of principal and accrued interest payable in 19X8. The note's maker recently filed a voluntary bankruptcy petition, but the client failed to reduce the recorded value of the note to its net realizable value, which is approximately 20% of the recorded amount.

93. An auditor is engaged to audit a client's financial statements after the annual physical inventory count. The accounting records are not sufficiently reliable to enable the auditor to became satisfied as to the year-end inventory balances.

94. Big City is required by GASB to present supplementary information outside the basic financial statements concerning the disclosure of pension information. Big City's auditor determines that the supplementary information, which is **not** required to be part of the basic financial statements, is omitted.

95. A client's financial statements do not disclose certain long-term lease obligations. The auditor determines that the omitted disclosures are required by FASB.

96. A principal auditor decides not to take responsibility for the work of another CPA who audited a wholly owned subsidiary of the principal auditor's client. The total assets and revenues of the subsidiary represent 27% and 28%, respectively, of the related consolidated totals.

97. A client changes its method of accounting for the cost of inventories from FIFO to LIFO. The auditor concurs with the change although it has a material effect on the comparability of the financial statements.

98. Due to losses and adverse key financial ratios, an auditor has substantial doubt about a client's ability to continue as a going concern for a reasonable period of time. The client has adequately disclosed its financial difficulties in a note to its financial statements, which do **not** include any adjustments that might result from the outcome of this uncertainty.

List A	List B
Type of Opinions	Report Modifications
A. Either an "except for" qualified opinion or an adverse opinion B. Either a disclaimer of opinion or an "except for" qualified opinion C. Either an adverse opinion o ra disclaimer of opinion D. An "except for" qualified opinion E. An unqualified opinion F. An adverse opinion G. A disclaimer of opinion	A. Describe the circumstances in an explanatory paragraph *without modifying* the three standard paragraphs. B. Describe the circumstances in an explanatory paragraph and modify the opinion paragraph. C. Describe the circumstances in an explanatory paragraph and *modify* the scope and *opinion* paragraphs. D. Describe the circumstances in an explanatory paragraph and *modify* the *introductory, scope,* and *opinion* paragraphs. E. Describe the circumstances within the *scope* paragraph without adding an explanatory paragraph. F. Describe the circumstances within the *opinion* paragraph without adding an explanatory paragraph. G. Describe the circumstances within the *scope* and *opinion* paragraphs without adding an explanatory paragraph. H. Describe the circumstances within the *introductory, scope,* and *opinion* paragraphs without adding an explanatory paragraph. I. Issue the *standard* auditor's report *without modification.*

Number 3 (Estimated time—15 to 25 minutes)

Question Number 3 consists of 6 items. Select the **best** answers for each item. Use a No. 2 pencil to blacken the appropriate ovals on the OOF Section #3 of your scannable grid, response items #1 through #6, to indicate your answers. **Answer all items.**

Required:

Items 99 through 104 represent the items that an auditor ordinarily would find on a client-prepared bank reconciliation. The accompanying **List of Auditing Procedures** represents substantive auditing procedures. For each item, select one procedure, as indicated, that the auditor most likely would perform to gather evidence in support of that item. The procedures on the **List** may be selected once, more than once, or not at all.

Assume:

- The client prepared the bank reconciliation on 10/2/X4.

- The bank reconciliation is mathematically accurate.

- The auditor received a cutoff bank statement dated 10/7/X4 directly from the bank on 10/11/X4.

- The 9/30/X4 deposit in transit, outstanding checks #1281, #1285, #1289, and #1292, and the correction of the error regarding check #1282 appeared on the cutoff bank statement.

- The auditor assessed control risk concerning the financial statement assertions related to cash at the maximum.

General Company
Bank Reconciliation
1st National Bank of U.S. Bank Account
September 30, 19X4

99.	Select 1 Procedure	Balance per bank		$28,375
100.	Select 1 Procedure	Deposits in transit		
		9/29/X4	$4,500	
		9/30/X4	1,525	6,025
				34,400
101.	Select 1 Procedure	Outstanding checks		
		# 988 8/31/X4	2,200	
		#1281 9/26/X4	675	
		#1285 9/27/X4	850	
		#1289 9/29/X4	2,500	
		#1292 9/30/X4	7,225	(13,450)
				20,950
102.	Select 1 Procedure	Customer note collected by bank		(3,000)
103.	Select 1 Procedure	Error: Check #1282, written on 9/26/X4 for $270 was erroneously charged by bank as $720; bank was notified on 10/2/X4		450
104.	Select 1 Procedure	Balance per books		$18,400

List of Auditing Procedures
A.   Trace to cash receipts journal.
B.   Trace to cash disbursements journal.
C.   Compare to 9/30/X4 general ledger.
D.   Confirm directly with bank.
E.   Inspect bank credit memo.

Number 4 (Estimated time—25 to 35 minutes)

Analytical procedures are an important part of the audit process and consist of evaluations of financial information made by the study of plausible relationships among both financial and nonfinancial data. Analytical procedures are used to assist in planning other auditing procedures, as substantive tests in obtaining evidential matter, and as an overall review of the financial information.

Required:

a. Describe the objectives and the characteristics of analytical procedures used in planning an audit.

b. Describe the factors that influence an auditor's decision to select analytical procedures as substantive tests, including the factors that affect their effectiveness and efficiency.

c. Describe an auditor's objectives in applying analytical procedures in the overall review stage of an audit and which analytical procedures generally would be included in the overall review stage.

Number 5 (Estimated time—25 to 35 minutes)

An auditor's working papers include the narrative description below of the cash receipts and billing portions of the internal control of Rural Building Supplies, Inc. Rural is a single-store retailer that sells a variety of tools, garden supplies, lumber, small appliances, and electrical fixtures to the public, although about half of Rural's sales are to construction contractors on account. Rural employs 12 salaried sales associates, a credit manager, three full-time clerical workers, and several part-time cash register clerks and assistant bookkeepers. The full-time clerical workers perform such tasks as cash receipts, billing, and accounting and are adequately bonded. They are referred to in the narrative as "accounts receivable supervisor," "cashier," and "bookkeeper."

Narrative

Retail customers pay for merchandise by cash or credit card at cash registers when merchandise is purchased. A contractor may purchase merchandise on account if approved by the credit manager based only on the manager's familiarity with the contractor's reputation. After credit is approved, the sales associate files a prenumbered charge form with the accounts receivable (A/R) supervisor to set up the receivable.

The A/R supervisor independently verifies the pricing and other details on the charge form by reference to a management-authorized price list, corrects any errors, prepares the invoice, and supervises a part-time employee who mails the invoice to the contractor. The A/R supervisor electronically posts the details of the invoice in the A/R subsidiary ledger; simultaneously, the transaction's details are transmitted to the bookkeeper. The A/R supervisor also prepares a monthly computer-generated A/R subsidiary ledger without a reconciliation with the A/R control account and a monthly report of overdue accounts.

The cash receipts functions are performed by the cashier who also supervises the cash register clerks. The cashier opens the mail, compares each check with the enclosed remittance advice, stamps each check "for deposit only," and lists checks for deposit. The cashier then gives the remittance advices to the bookkeeper for recording. The cashier deposits the checks daily separate from the daily deposit of cash register receipts. The cashier retains the verified deposit slips to assist in reconciling the monthly bank statements, but forwards to the bookkeeper a copy of the daily cash register summary. The cashier does not have access to the journals or ledgers.

The bookkeeper receives the details of transactions from the A/R supervisor and the cashier for journalizing and posting to the general ledger. After recording the remittance advices received from the cashier, the bookkeeper electronically transmits the remittance information to the A/R supervisor for subsidiary ledger updating. The bookkeeper sends monthly statements to contractors with unpaid balances upon receipt of the monthly report of overdue balances from the A/R supervisor. The bookkeeper authorizes the A/R supervisor to write off accounts as uncollectible when six months have passed since the initial overdue notice was sent. At this time, the credit manager is notified by the bookkeeper not to grant additional credit to that contractor.

Required:

Based only on the information in the narrative, describe the internal control weaknesses in Rural's internal control concerning the cash receipts and billing functions. Organize the weaknesses by employee job functions: Credit manager, A/R supervisor, Cashier, and Bookkeeper. Do **not** describe how to correct the weaknesses.

TEST 1: QUESTIONS

ACCOUNTING & REPORTING—
Taxation, Managerial & Governmental and
Not-for-Profit Organizations

Test ID: 1100

INSTRUCTIONS

1. All questions should be answered on the scannable grid, which is at the back of this book. You should attempt to answer all objective items. There is no penalty for incorrect responses. Work space to solve the objective questions is provided. Since the objective items are computer graded, your comments and calculations associated with them will not be considered. Be certain that you have entered your answers on the scannable grid before the examination time is up. At exam time, your examination will not be graded if you fail to record all your answers.

2. At examination time, you will be supplied with an AICPA-approved calculator to help you work through the problems in this section of the CPA exam.

The point values for each question, and estimated time allotments based primarily on point value, are as follows:

	Point Value	Estimated Minutes Minimum	Estimated Minutes Maximum
No. 1	60	120	130
No. 2	5	5	10
No. 3	20	25	40
No. 4	15	20	30
Totals	**100**	**170**	**210**

Number 1 (Estimated time—120 to 130 minutes)

Select the **best** answer for each of the following items. Use a No. 2 pencil to blacken ovals #1 through #60 on the Multiple-Choice Section of your scannable grid to indicate your answers. **Mark only one answer for each item. Answer all items.**

Items 1 through 30 are in the area of Accounting for Governmental and Not-for-Profit Organizations.

1. The governmental fund measurement focus is on the determination of

	Income	Financial Position	Flow of Financial Resources
A.	Yes	Yes	Yes
B.	No	Yes	No
C.	No	Yes	Yes
D.	Yes	No	Yes

2. Which of the following statements is correct regarding comparability of governmental financial reports?

   A. Comparability is **not** relevant in governmental financial reporting.
   B. Similarly designated governments perform the same functions.
   C. Selection of different alternatives in accounting procedures or practices account for the differences between financial reports.
   D. Differences between financial reports should be due to substantive differences in underlying transactions or the governmental structure.

3. The orientation of accounting and reporting for all proprietary funds of governmental units is

   A. Income determination.
   B. Project.
   C. Flow of funds.
   D. Program.

4. On what accounting basis does GASB recommend that governmental fund budgets be prepared?

   A. Cash.
   B. Modified cash.
   C. Accrual.
   D. Modified accrual.

Please use this area for work space.
---

5. If a primary government's general fund has an equity interest in a joint venture, all or a portion of this equity interest should be reported in the

A. General fixed assets account group.
B. Trust fund.
C. Agency fund.
D. Internal service fund.

6. Which of the following statements is correct concerning disclosure of reverse repurchase and fixed coupon reverse repurchase agreements?

A. Related assets and liabilities should be netted.
B. Related interest cost and interest earned should be netted.
C. Credit risk related to the agreements need **not** be disclosed.
D. Underlying securities owned should be reported as "Investments."

7. Fixed assets of a governmental unit, other than those accounted for in proprietary funds or trust funds, should be accounted for in the

A. General fund.
B. Capital projects fund.
C. General long-term debt account group.
D. General fixed assets account group.

8. It is inappropriate to record depreciation expense in a (an)

A. Enterprise fund.
B. Internal service fund.
C. Nonexpendable trust fund.
D. Capital projects fund.

9. When a snowplow purchased by a governmental unit is received, it should be recorded in the general fund as a (an)

A. Encumbrance.
B. Expenditure.
C. Fixed asset.
D. Appropriation.

10. When a capital lease of a governmental unit represents the acquisition of a general fixed asset, the acquisition should be reflected as

A. An expenditure but **not** as an other financing source.
B. An other financing source but **not** as an expenditure.
C. Both an expenditure and an other financing source.
D. Neither an expenditure nor an other financing source.

Please use this area for work space.

11. For which of the following funds do operating transfers affect the results of operations?

	Governmental Funds	Proprietary Funds
A.	No	No
B.	No	Yes
C.	Yes	Yes
D.	Yes	No

12. The debt service fund of a governmental unit is used to account for the accumulation of resources for, and the payment of, principal and interest in connection with a

	Trust Fund	Proprietary Fund
A.	No	No
B.	No	Yes
C.	Yes	Yes
D.	Yes	No

13. The portion of special assessment debt maturing in 5 years, to be repaid from general resources of the government, should be reported in the

A. General fund.
B. General long-term debt account group.
C. Agency fund.
D. Capital projects fund.

14. A major exception to the general rule of expenditure accrual for governmental units relates to unmatured

	Principal of General Long-Term Debt	Interest on General Long-Term Debt
A.	Yes	Yes
B.	Yes	No
C.	No	Yes
D.	No	No

15. Expenditures of a governmental unit for insurance extending over more than one accounting period

A. Must be accounted for as expenditures of the period of acquisition.
B. Must be accounted for as expenditures of the periods subsequent to acquisition.
C. Must be allocated between or among accounting periods.
D. May be allocated between or among accounting periods or may be accounted for as expenditures of the period of acquisition.

Please use this area for work space.

---

16. During the year, a city's electric utility, which is operated as an enterprise fund, rendered billings for electricity supplied to the general fund. Which of the following accounts should be debited by the general fund?

    A. Appropriations.
    B. Expenditures.
    C. Due to electric utility enterprise fund.
    D. Other financing uses-operating transfers out.

17. In which situation(s) should property taxes due to a governmental unit be recorded as deferred revenue?

  I. Property taxes receivable are recognized in advance of the year for which they are levied.

  II. Property taxes receivable are collected in advance of the year in which they are levied.

    A. I only.
    B. Both I and II.
    C. II only.
    D. Neither I nor II.

18. In 19X4, New City issued purchase orders and contracts of $850,000 that were chargeable against 19X4 budgeted appropriations of $1,000,000. The journal entry to record the issuance of the purchase orders and contracts should include a

    A. Credit to vouchers payable of $1,000,000.
    B. Credit to reserve for encumbrances of $850,000.
    C. Debit to expenditures of $1,000,000.
    D. Debit to appropriations of $850,000.

19. Which of the following transactions is an expenditure of a governmental unit's general fund?

    A. Contribution of enterprise fund capital by the general fund.
    B. Transfer from the general fund to a capital projects fund.
    C. Operating subsidy transfer from the general fund to an enterprise fund.
    D. Routine employer contributions from the general fund to a pension trust fund.

Please use this area for work space.

20. Operating transfers received by a governmental-type fund should be reported in the Statement of Revenues, Expenditures, and Changes in Fund Balance as a (an)

A. Addition to contributed capital.
B. Addition to retained earnings.
C. Other financing source.
D. Reimbursement.

21. The following transactions were among those reported by Corfe City's electric utility enterprise fund for 19X3:

Capital contributed by subdividers	$ 900,000
Cash received from customer households	2,700,000
Proceeds from sale of revenue bonds	4,500,000

In the electric utility enterprise fund's statement of cash flows for the year ended December 31, 19X3, what amount should be reported as cash flows from capital and related financing activities?

A. $4,500,000
B. $5,400,000
C. $7,200,000
D. $8,100,000

22. A state government had the following activities:

I.   State-operated lottery $10,000,000
II. State-operated hospital   3,000,000

Which of the above activities should be accounted for in an enterprise fund?

A. Neither I nor II.
B. I only.
C. II only.
D. Both I and II.

23. Deferred compensation plans, for other than proprietary fund employees, adopted under IRC Sec. 457 should be reported in a (an)

A. Governmental fund.
B. Agency fund.
C. Trust fund.
D. Account group.

24. In which of the following funds should the debt service transactions of a special assessment issue for which the government is **not** obligated in any manner be reported?

A. Agency fund.
B. Trust fund.
C. Internal service fund.
D. General fund.

Please use this area for work space.

25. Which type of fund can be either nonexpendable or expendable?

A. Trust fund.
B. Special revenue fund.
C. Enterprise fund.
D. Debt service fund.

26. Cancer Educators, a not-for-profit organization, incurred costs of $10,000 when it combined program functions with fund-raising functions. Which of the following cost allocations might Cancer report in its statement of activities?

	Program Services	Fund Raising	General Services
A.	$0	$0	$10,000
B.	$0	$6,000	$4,000
C.	$6,000	$4,000	$0
D.	$10,000	$0	$0

27. Lea Meditators, a not-for-profit religious organization, elected early adoption of FASB Statement No. 116, *Accounting for Contributions Received and Contributions Made*. A storm broke glass windows in Lea's building. A member of Lea's congregation, a professional glazier, replaced the windows at no charge. In Lea's statement of activities, the breakage and replacement of the windows should

A. Not be reported.
B. Be reported by note disclosure only.
C. Be reported as an increase in both expenses and contributions.
D. Be reported as an increase in both net assets and contributions.

28. Which of the following normally would be included in other operating revenues of a hospital?

	Revenues from Educational Programs	Unrestricted Gifts
A.	No	No
B.	No	Yes
C.	Yes	No
D.	Yes	Yes

Please use this area for work space.

29. In a statement of support, revenue, and expenses and changes in fund balances of the People's Environmental Protection Association, a voluntary community organization, depreciation expense should

A. Not be included.
B. Be included as an element of support.
C. Be included as an element of other changes in fund balances.
D. Be included as an element of expense.

30. FASB Statement No. 117, *Financial Statement of Not-for-Profit Organizations*, focuses on

A. Basic information for the organization as a whole.
B. Standardization of funds nomenclature.
C. Inherent differences of not-for-profit organizations that impact reporting presentations.
D. Distinctions between current fund and noncurrent fund presentations.

*Items 31 through 60 are in the areas of Federal Taxation. The answers should be based on the Internal Revenue Code and Tax Regulations in effect for the tax period specified in the item. If **no** tax period is specified, use the **current** Internal Revenue Code and Tax Regulations.*

31. Banks Corp., a calendar year corporation, reimburses employees for properly substantiated, qualifying business meal expenses. The employees are present at the meals, which are neither lavish nor extravagant, and the reimbursement is not treated as wages subject to withholdings. For 19X4, what percentage of the meal expense may Banks deduct?

A. 0%
B. 50%
C. 80%
D. 100%

32. For the year ended December 31, 19X3, Kelly Corp. had net income per books of $300,000 before the provision for Federal income taxes. Included in the net income were the following items:

Dividend income from an unaffiliated domestic taxable corporation (taxable income limitation does not apply and there is no portfolio indebtedness) $50,000

Bad debt expense (represents the increase in the allowance for doubtful accounts) $80,000

--- Please use this area for work space. ---

Assuming no bad debt was written off, what is Kelly's taxable income for the year ended December 31, 19X3?

A. $250,000
B. $330,000
C. $345,000
D. $380,000

33. For the year ended December 31, 19X6, Taylor Corp. had a net operating loss of $200,000. Taxable income for the earlier years of corporate existence, computed without reference to the net operating loss, was as follows:

Taxable Income

19X1	$ 5,000
19X2	$10,000
19X3	$20,000
19X4	$30,000
19X5	$40,000

If Taylor makes **no** special election to waive the net operating loss carryback, what amount of net operating loss will be available to Taylor for the year ended December 31, 19X7?

A. $200,000
B. $110,000
C. $100,000
D. $95,000

34. On January 2, 19X1, Bates Corp. purchased and placed into service 7-year MACRS tangible property costing $100,000. On December 31, 19X3, Bates sold the property for $102,000, after having taken $47,525 in MACRS depreciation deductions. What amount of the gain should Bates recapture as ordinary income?

A. $0
B. $2,000
C. $47,525
D. $49,525

35. Micro Corp., a calendar year, accrual basis corporation, purchased a 5-year, 8%, $100,000 taxable corporate bond for $108,530, on July 1, 19X3, the date the bond was issued. The bond paid interest semiannually. Micro elected to amortize the bond premium. For Micro's 19X3 tax return, the bond premium amortization for 19X3 should be

I. Computed under the constant yield to maturity method.

II. Treated as an offset to the interest income on the bond.

A. I only.
B. II only.
C. Both I and II.
D. Neither I nor II.

Please use this area for work space.

36. Axis Corp. is an accrual basis calendar year corporation. On December 13, 19X3, the Board of Directors declared a two percent of profits bonus to all employees for services rendered during 19X3 and notified them in writing. None of the employees own stock in Axis. The amount represents reasonable compensation for services rendered and was paid on March 13, 19X4. Axis' bonus expense may

A. Not be deducted on Axis' 19X3 tax return because the per share employee amount **cannot** be determined with reasonable accuracy at the time of the declaration of the bonus.
B. Be deducted on Axis' 19X3 tax return.
C. Be deducted on Axis' 19X4 tax return.
D. Not be deducted on Axis' tax return because payment is a disguised dividend.

37. Tapper Corp., an accrual basis calendar year corporation, was organized on January 2, 19X3. During 19X3, revenue was exclusively from sales proceeds and interest income. The following information pertains to Tapper:

Taxable income before charitable contributions for the year ended December 31, 19X3	$500,000
Tapper's matching contribution to employee-designated, qualified universities made during 19X3	$10,000
Board of directors' authorized contribution to a qualified charity (authorized December 1, 19X3, made February 1, 19X4)	$30,000

What is the maximum allowable deduction that Tapper may take as a charitable contribution on its tax return for the year ended December 31, 19X3?

A. $0
B. $10,000
C. $30,000
D. $40,000

38. Which of the following costs are amortizable organizational expenditures?

A. Professional fees to issue the corporate stock.
B. Printing costs to issue the corporate stock.
C. Legal fees for drafting the corporate charter.
D. Commissions paid by the corporation to an underwriter.

Please use this area for work space.

39. How is the deprecation deduction of nonresidential real property, placed in service in 19X4, determined for regular tax purposes using MACRS?

A. Straight-line method over 40 years.
B. 150% declining-balance method with a switch to the straight-line method over 27.5 years.
C. 150% declining-balance method with a switch to the straight-line method over 39 years.
D. Straight-line method over 39 years.

40. Under the uniform capitalization rules applicable to property acquired for resale, which of the following costs should be capitalized with respect to inventory if **no** exceptions are met?

	Marketing Costs	Off-Site Storage Costs
A.	Yes	Yes
B.	Yes	No
C.	No	No
D.	No	Yes

41. Zinco Corp. was a calendar year S corporation. Zinco's S status terminated on April 1, 19X3, when Case Corp. became a shareholder. During 19X3 (365-day calendar year), Zinco had nonseparately computed income of $310,250. If no election was made by Zinco, what amount of the income, if any, was allocated to the S short year for 19X3?

A. $233,750
B. $155,125
C. $76,500
D. $0

42. Bristol Corp. was formed as a C corporation on January 1, 1980, and elected S corporation status on January 1, 1986. At the time of the election, Bristol had accumulated C corporation earnings and profits, which have not been distributed. Bristol has had the same 25 shareholders throughout its existence. In 19X4 Bristol's S election will terminate if it

A. Increases the number of shareholders to 35.
B. Adds a decedent's estate as a shareholder to the existing shareholders.
C. Takes a charitable contribution deduction.
D. Has passive investment income exceeding 90% of gross receipts in each of the three consecutive years ending December 31, 19X3.

Please use this area for work space.

43. As of January 1, 19X3, Kane owned all the 100 issued shares of Manning Corp., a calendar year S corporation. On the 41st day of 19X3, Kane sold 25 of the Manning shares to Rodgers. For the year ended December 31, 19X3 (a 365-day calendar year), Manning had $73,000 in nonseparately stated income and made no distributions to its shareholders. What amount of nonseparately stated income from Manning should be reported on Kane's 19X3 tax return?

    A. $56,750
    B. $54,750
    C. $16,250
    D. $0

44. On February 10, 19X4, Ace Corp., a calendar year corporation, elected S corporation status and all shareholders consented to the election. There was no change in shareholders in 19X4. Ace met all eligibility requirements for S status during the preelection portion of the year. What is the earliest date on which Ace can be recognized as an S corporation?

    A. February 10, 19X5.
    B. February 10, 19X4.
    C. January 1, 19X5.
    D. January 1, 19X4.

45. Zero Corp. is an investment company authorized to issue only common stock. During the last half of 19X3, Edwards owned 450 of the 1,000 outstanding share of stock in Zero. Another 350 shares of stock outstanding were owned, 10 shares each, by 35 shareholders who are neither related to each other nor to Edwards. Zero could be a personal holding company if the remaining 200 shares of common stock were owned by

    A. An estate of which Edwards is the beneficiary.
    B. Edwards' brother-in-law.
    C. A partnership of which Edwards is **not** a partner.
    D. Edwards' cousin.

Please use this area for work space.
---

46. With regard to consolidated tax returns, which of the following statements is correct?

A. Operating losses of one group member may be used to offset operating profits of the other members included in the consolidated return.

B. Only corporations that issue their audited financial statements on a consolidated basis may file consolidated returns.

C. Of all intercompany dividends paid by the subsidiaries to the parent, 70% are excludable from taxable income on the consolidated return.

D. The common parent must directly own 51% or more of the total voting power of all corporations included in the consolidated return.

47. In the filing of a consolidated tax return for a corporation and its wholly owned subsidiaries, intercompany dividends between the parent and subsidiary corporations are

A. Not taxable.

B. Included in taxable income to the extent of 20%.

C. Included in taxable income to the extent of 80%.

D. Fully taxable.

48. A corporation's penalty for underpaying federal estimated taxes is

A. Not deductible.

B. Fully deductible in the year paid.

C. Fully deductible if reasonable cause can be established for the underpayment.

D. Partially deductible.

49. Which of the following credits is a combination of several tax credits to provide uniform rules for the current and carryback-carryover years?

A. General business credit.

B. Foreign tax credit.

C. Minimum tax credit.

D. Enhanced oil recovery credit.

Please use this area for work space.

50. Blink Corp., an accrual basis calendar year corporation, carried back a net operating loss for the tax year ended December 31, 19X3. Blink's gross revenues have been under $500,000 since inception. Blink expects to have profits for the tax year ending December 31, 19X4. Which method(s) of estimated tax payment can Blink use for its quarterly payments during the 19X4 tax year to avoid underpayment of federal estimated taxes?

    I.   100% of the preceding tax year method.

    II. Annualized income method.

    A. I only.
    B. Both I and II.
    C. II only.
    D. Neither I nor II.

51. Tank Corp., which had earnings and profits of $500,000, made a nonliquidating distribution of property to its shareholders in 19X3 as a dividend in kind. This property, which had an adjusted basis of $20,000 and a fair market value of $30,000 at the date of distribution, did not constitute assets used in the active conduct of Tank's business. How much gain did Tank recognize on this distribution?

    A. $30,000
    B. $20,000
    C. $10,000
    D. $0

52. Adams, Beck, and Carr organized Flexo Corp. with authorized voting common stock of $100,000. Adams received 10% of the capital stock in payment for the organizational services that he rendered for the benefit of the newly formed corporation. Adams did not contribute property to Flexo and was under no obligation to be paid by Beck or Carr. Beck and Carr transferred property in exchange for stock as follows:

	Adjusted Basis	Fair Market Value	Percentage of Flexo Stock Acquired
Beck	5,000	20,000	20%
Carr	60,000	70,000	70%

What amount of gain did Carr recognize from this transaction?

    A. $40,000
    B. $15,000
    C. $10,000
    D. $0

Please use this area for work space.

53. In a type B reorganization, as defined by the Internal Revenue Code, the

I. Stock of the target corporation is acquired solely for the voting stock of either the acquiring corporation or its parent.

II. Acquiring corporation must have control of the target corporation immediately after the acquisition.

A. I only.
B. II only.
C. Both I and II.
D. Neither I nor II.

54. Jackson Corp., a calendar year corporation, mailed its 19X3 tax return to the Internal Revenue Service by certified mail on Friday, March 11, 19X4. The return, postmarked March 11, 19X4, was delivered to the Internal Revenue Service on March 18, 19X4. The statute of limitations on Jackson's corporate tax return begins on

A. December 31, 19X3.
B. March 11, 19X4.
C. March 16, 19X4.
D. March 18, 19X4.

55. A tax return preparer is subject to a penalty for knowingly or recklessly disclosing corporate tax return information, if the disclosure is made

A. To enable a third party to solicit business from the taxpayer.
B. To enable the tax processor to electronically compute the taxpayer's liability.
C. For peer review.
D. Under an administrative order by a state agency that registers tax return preparers.

56. Bell, a cash basis calendar year taxpayer, died on June 1, 19X3. In 19X3, prior to her death, Bell incurred $2,000 in medical expenses. The executor of the estate paid the medical expenses, which were a claim against the estate, on July 1, 19X3. If the executor files the appropriate waiver, the medical expenses are deductible on

A. The estate tax return.
B. Bell's final income tax return.
C. The estate income tax return.
D. The executor's income tax return.

Please use this area for work space.

57. White has a one-third interest in the profits and losses of Rapid Partnership. Rapid's ordinary income for the 19X3 calendar year is $30,000, after a $3,000 deduction for a guaranteed payment made to White for services rendered. None of the $30,000 ordinary income was distributed to the partners. What is the total amount that White must include from Rapid as taxable income in his 19X3 tax return?

    A. $3,000
    B. $10,000
    C. $11,000
    D. $13,000

58. If the executor of a decedent's estate elects the alternate valuation date and none of the property included in the gross estate has been sold or distributed, the estate assets must be valued as of how many months after the decedent's death?

    A. 12
    B. 9
    C. 6
    D. 3

59. An organization that operates for the prevention of cruelty to animals will fail to meet the operational test to qualify as an exempt organization if

	The organization engages in insubstantial nonexempt activities	The organization directly participates in any political campaign
A.	Yes	Yes
B.	Yes	No
C.	No	Yes
D.	No	No

Please use this area for work space.

60. Which one of the following statements is correct with regard to unrelated business income of an exempt organization?

A. An exempt organization that earns any unrelated business income in excess of $100,000 during a particular year will lose its exempt status for that particular year.

B. An exempt organization is not taxed on unrelated business income of less than $1,000.

C. The tax on unrelated business income can be imposed even if the unrelated business activity is intermittent and is carried on once a year.

D. An unrelated trade or business activity that results in a loss is excluded from the definition of unrelated business.

Number 2 (Estimated time—5 to 10 minutes)

Question Number 2 consists of 8 items. Select the **best** answer for each item. Use a No. 2 pencil to blacken the appropriate ovals on the scannable grid. **Answer all items.**

During 19X0, Adams, a general contractor, Brinks, an architect, and Carson, an interior decorator, formed the Dex Home Improvement General Partnership by contributing the assets below.

	Asset	Adjusted Basis	Fair Market	% of Partner Share in Capital, Profits & Losses
Adams	Cash	$40,000	$40,000	50%
Brinks	Land	$12,000	$21,000	20%
Carson	Inventory	$24,000	$24,000	30%

The land was a capital asset to Brinks, subject to a $5,000 mortgage, which was assumed by the partnership.

Please use this area for work space.

For items 61 and 62, determine and select the initial basis of the partner's interest in Dex. Blacken the corresponding ovals on OOF Section #3 of your scannable grid, response items #1 and #2.

61. Brinks' initial basis in Dex is

A. $21,000
B. $12,000
C. $8,000

62. Carson's initial basis in Dex is

A. $25,500
B. $24,000
C. $19,000

During 19X4, the Dex Partnership breaks even but decides to make distributions to each partner.

For items 63 through 68, determine whether the statement is True (A) or False (B). Blacken the corresponding oval on OOF Section #3, response items #3 through #8.

63. A nonliquidating cash distribution may reduce the recipient partner's basis in his partnership interest below zero.

64. A nonliquidating distribution of unappropriated inventory reduces the recipient partner's basis in his partnership interest.

65. In a liquidating distribution of property other than money, where the partnership's basis of the distributed property exceeds the basis of the partner's interest, the partner's basis in the distributed property is limited to his pre-distribution basis in the partnership interest.

66. Gain is recognized by the partner who receives a nonliquidating distribution of property, where the adjusted basis of the property exceeds his basis in the partnership interest before the distribution.

67. In a nonliquidating distribution of inventory, where the partnership has no unrealized receivables or appreciated inventory, the basis of inventory that is distributed to a partner cannot exceed the inventory's adjusted basis to the partnership.

68. The partnership's nonliquidating distribution of encumbered property to a partner who assumes the mortgage does not affect the other partners' basis in their partnership interests.

Please use this area for work space.

Number 3 (Estimated time—25 to 40 minutes)

Question Number 3 consists of 31 items. Select the **best** answer for each item. Use a No. 2 pencil to blacken the appropriate ovals on your scannable grid to indicate your answers. **Answer all items.**

Mrs. Vick, a 40-year-old cash basis taxpayer, earned $45,000 as a teacher and $5,000 as a part-time real estate agent in 19X3. Mr. Vick, who died on July 1, 19X3, had been permanently disabled on his job and collected state disability benefits until his death. For all of 19X3 and 19X4, the Vick's residence was the principal home of both their 11-year-old daughter Joan and Mrs. Vick's unmarried cousin, Fran Phillips, who had no income in either year. During 19X3, Joan received $200 a month in survivor social security benefits that began on August 1, 19X3, and will continue at least until her 18th birthday. In 19X3 and 19X4, Mrs. Vick provided over one-half the support for Joan and Fran, both of whom were U.S. citizens. Mrs. Vick did not remarry. Mr. and Mrs. Vick received the following in 19X3:

Earned income	$50,000
State disability benefits	1,500
Interest on:	
Refund from amended tax return	50
Savings account and certificates of deposit	350
Municipal bonds	100
Gift	3,000
Pension benefits	900
Jury duty pay	200
Gambling winnings	450
Life insurance proceeds	5,000

Additional information:

- Mrs. Vick received the $3,000 cash gift from her uncle.

- Mrs. Vick received the pension distributions from a qualified pension plan, paid for exclusively by her husband's employer. The $5,000 death benefit exclusion did not apply.

- Mrs. Vick had $100 in gambling losses in 19X3.

- Mrs. Vick was the beneficiary of the life insurance policy on her husband's life. She received a lump-sum distribution. The Vicks had paid $500 in premiums.

- Mrs. Vick received Mr. Vick's accrued vacation pay of $500 in 19X4.

— Please use this area for work space. —

For items 69 and 70, *determine and select from the choices below,* **BOTH** *the filing status and the number of exemptions for each item. Blacken the corresponding oval on the Multiple Response Section of your scannable grid. For Filing Status answers, fill in the first column of items #1 and #2 in the Multiple Response Section. For Exemption answers, fill in the second column.*

Filing Status

    A. Single
    B. Married filing joint
    C. Head of household
    D. Qualifying widow with dependent child

Exemptions

    A. 1
    B. 2
    C. 3
    D. 4

69. Determine the filing status and the number of exemptions that Mrs. Vick can claim on the 19X3 federal income tax return, to get the most favorable tax results.

70. Determine the filing status and the number of exemptions that Mrs. Vick can claim on the 19X4 federal income tax return to get the most favorable tax results, if she solely maintains the costs of her home.

For items 71 through 77, *determine the amount, if any, that is taxable and should be included in Adjusted Gross Income (AGI) on the 19X3 federal income tax return filed by Mrs. Vick (round answer to the nearest hundred). To record your answer, write the number in the boxes on the OOF Numeric Response Section of your scannable grid, using response items #9 through #15* **and** *blacken the corresponding oval below each box. Write zeros in any blank boxes preceding your numerical answer, and blacken the zero in the oval below the box.* **You cannot receive credit for your answers if you fail to blacken an oval in each column.**

71. State disability benefits

72. Interest income

73. Pension benefits

74. Gift

75. Life insurance proceeds

76. Jury duty pay

77. Gambling winnings

———————— Please use this area for work space. ————————

During 19X3 the following payments were made or losses were incurred. **For items 78 through 91,** select the appropriate tax treatment and blacken the corresponding oval on OOF Section #1 of your scannable grid using response items #1 through #14. A tax treatment may be selected once, more than once, or not at all.

Payments and Losses

78. Premiums on Mr. Vick's personal life insurance policy.

79. Penalty on Mrs. Vick's early withdrawal of funds from a certificate of deposit.

80. Mrs. Vick's substantial cash donation to the American Red Cross.

81. Payment of estimated state income taxes.

82. Payment of real estate taxes on the Vick home.

83. Loss on the sale of the family car.

84. Cost in excess of the increase in value of residence, for the installation of a stairlift in January 19X3, related directly to the medical care of Mr. Vick.

85. The Vick's health insurance premiums for hospitalization coverage.

86. CPA fees to prepare the 19X2 tax return.

87. Amortization over the life of the loan of points paid to refinance the mortgage at a lower rate on the Vick home.

88. One-half the self-employment tax paid by Mrs. Vick.

89. Mrs. Vick's $100 in gambling losses.

90. Mrs. Vick's union dues.

91. 19X2 federal income tax paid with the Vick's tax return on April 15, 19X3.

Tax Treatment

A. Not deductible.

B. Deductible in Schedule A—Itemized Deductions, subject to threshold of 7.5% of adjusted gross income.

C. Deductible in Schedule A—Itemized Deductions, subject to threshold of 2% of adjusted gross income.

D. Deductible on page 1 of Form 1040 to arrive at adjusted gross income.

E. Deductible in Schedule A—Itemized Deductions.

F. Deductible in Schedule A—Itemized Deductions, subject to threshold of 50% of adjusted gross income.

For items 92 through 99, determine whether the statement is True (A) or False (B) regarding the Vick's 19X3 income tax return. Blacken the corresponding oval on OOF Section #2 of your scannable grid, response items #1 through #8.

92. The funeral expenses paid by Mr. Vick's estate is a 19X3 itemized deduction.

93. Any federal estate tax on the income in respect of decedent, to be distributed to Mrs. Vick, may be taken as a miscellaneous itemized deduction **not** subject to the 2% of adjusted gross income floor.

94. A casualty loss deduction on property used in Mrs. Vick's part-time real estate business is reported as an itemized deduction.

95. The Vick's income tax liability will be reduced by the credit for the elderly or disabled.

96. The CPA preparer is required to furnish a completed copy of the 19X3 income tax return to Mrs. Vick.

97. Since Mr. Vick died during the year, the income limitation for the earned income credit does **not** apply.

98. Mr. Vick's accrued vacation pay, at the time of his death, is to be distributed to Mrs. Vick in 19X4. This income should be included in the 19X3 Federal income tax return.

99. The Vicks paid alternative minimum tax in 19X2. The amount of alternative minimum tax that is attributable to "deferral adjustments and preferences" can be used to offset the alternative minimum tax in the following years.

———— Please use this area for work space. ————

Number 4 (Estimated time—20 to 30 minutes)

Question Number 4 consists of 23 items. Select the **best** answer for each item. Use a No. 2 pencil to blacken the appropriate ovals on your scannable grid. **Answer all items.**

Isle, Inc. commenced operations on January 2, 19X3. Isle's three products (Aran, Bute, Cilly) are produced in different plants located in the same community. The following selected information is taken from Isle's internal 19X3 contribution income statement, based on standard costs.

Isle, Inc.
19X3 CONTRIBUTION INCOME STATEMENT

	Aran	Bute	Cilly	Total
		Products		
Sales (Aran 80,000 units)	$1,200,000	$800,000	$500,000	$2,500,000
Standard Costs:				
Direct Materials	180,000			
Direct Labor (Aran 20,000 hours)	240,000			
Variable Manufacturing Overhead	80,000			
Total Variable Manufacturing Costs	500,000	(Detail omitted)		
Less: Finished Goods Inventory 12/31/X3	100,000			
Variable Cost of Goods Sold	400,000			
Variable Selling and Administrative Costs	120,000			
Total Variable Costs	520,000			
Standard Contribution Margin	680,000	176,000	144,000	1,000,000
Fixed Manufacturing Overhead Costs	440,000	(Detail omitted)		
Fixed Selling and Administrative Costs	140,000			
Total Fixed Costs	580,000			
Standard Operating Income	100,000	35,000	25,000	160,000
Variances—Favorable (F)/Unfavorable (U):				
Direct Materials—Price	2,000 (F)			
Usage	16,000 (U)			
Direct Labor—Rate	12,000 (U)	(Detail omitted)		
Efficiency	24,000 (U)			
Manufacturing Overhead—Total	43,000 (U)			
Selling and Administrative—Total	7,000 (U)			
Operating Income, Net of Variances	$0	$41,000	$36,000	$77,000

Additional Information:

	Aran	Bute	Cilly
• Manufacturing Capacity Utilization	75%	80%	70%
• Average Investment	$1,000,000	$800,000	$400,000
• Demand	Somewhat seasonal and moderately difficult to project more than 3 years	Constant and easy to project more than 3 years	Very seasonal and very difficult to project more than 3 years

- Isle also prepared standard absorption costing statements using full capacity (based on machine hours) to allocate overhead costs.
- Fixed costs are incurred evenly throughout the year.
- There is no ending work-in-process.
- Material price variances are reported when raw materials are taken from inventory.
- Apart from initial build-ups in raw materials, and finished goods inventories, production schedules are based on sales forecasts.

For items 100 through 112, determine whether the statement is Yes (A) or No (B). Blacken the corresponding oval on OOF Section #3 of your scannable grid, response items #9 through #21.

100. Does Isle practice a just-in-time philosophy?

101. Should Isle include standard indirect material costs in standard fixed overhead costs?

102. Should Isle categorize the operation of production equipment as a value-adding activity?

103. If Isle's three products were produced in one plant, would activity-based costing provide more useful total production cost information for Aran, Bute, and Cilly than traditional standard costing?

104. Is the regression analysis technique helpful in determining the variable cost component of Isle's manufacturing overhead costs?

105. In Isle's internal performance reports, should normal spoilage costs be reported in fixed manufacturing overhead costs?

106. The computation of Bute's normal spoilage assumes 10 units in 1,000 contain defective materials and, independently, 15 units in 1,000 contain defective workmanship. Is the probability that is used in computing Bute's normal spoilage less than .025?

107. Isle has contracted to sell units of Aran to a customer in a segregated market during the off-season. Ignore variances and the costs of developing and administering the contract, and assume that standard cost patterns are unchanged except that variable selling and administrative costs are one-half the standard rate. Isle will sell Aran at a price that recoups the variable cost of goods sold at the standard rate, plus variable selling and administrative costs at one-half of the standard rate. Will Isle break even on the contract?

--- Please use this area for work space. ---

108. Were the actual 19X3 direct labor hours used in manufacturing Aran less than the standard hours?

109. Would Aran's 19X3 operating income reported using absorption cost be lower than the amount reported using variable costing?

110. Was the total amount paid for direct materials put into process for the manufacture of Aran more than the standard cost allowed for the work done?

Items 111 and 112 are based on the following:

Isle is considering investing $60,000 in a 10-year property lease that will reduce Aran's annual selling and administration costs by $12,000. Isle's cost of capital is 12%. The present value factor for a 10-year annuity at 12% is 5.65.

111. Is there a positive net present value for the lease investment?

112. Is the internal rate of return for the lease investment lower than the cost of capital?

For items 113 through 117, blacken the corresponding oval on OOF Section #3 of your scannable grid, response items #22 through #26.

113. For which product is evaluation of investments by the payback method likely to be more appropriate?

    A. Aran
    B. Bute
    C. Cilly

114. For which product is the economic order quantity formula likely to be most useful when purchasing raw materials to be used in manufacturing?

115. If Isle sells $10,000 more of Bute and $10,000 less of Cilly, what is the effect on Isle's standard dollar break-even point?

    A. Increase
    B. Decrease
    C. No effect

116. Which product had the greatest actual return on investment?

    A. Aran
    B. Bute
    C. Cilly

—————— Please use this area for work space. ——————

117. Ignore 19X3 reported variances and assume that Isle used expected demand to allocate manufacturing overhead costs. Which product would be most likely to have a substantial percentage of under applied or overapplied fixed manufacturing overhead costs on quarterly statements?

    A. Aran
    B. Bute
    C. Cilly

*For items 118 through 122, to record your answer, write the number in the boxes on the OOF Numeric Response Section of your scannable grid **and** blacken the corresponding oval below each box. Write zeros in any blank boxes preceding your numerical answer, and blacken the zero in the oval below the text. **You cannot receive credit for your answers if you fail to blacken an oval in each column.** For question 118, use response item #1. For questions 119 through 122, use response items #16 through #19 on the OOF Numeric Response Section.*

118. What is Aran's budgeted standard per unit cost for variable selling and administrative costs on sales of 75,000 units?

119. What is Aran's budgeted standard fixed selling and administrative costs on sales of 75,000 units?

120. What is Isle's standard break-even point in sales dollars for the actual sales mix achieved?

121. What amount of Aran's direct material and direct labor variances might be regarded, wholly or partially, as direct labor employees' responsibility?

122. Isle uses the graph below to estimate Aran's total standard manufacturing cost.

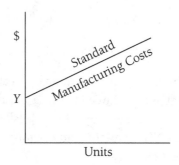

What amount does *Y* represent?

Please use this area for work space.

TEST 1: QUESTIONS

FINANCIAL ACCOUNTING & REPORTING—
Business Enterprises

Test ID: 2100

INSTRUCTIONS

1. Question Numbers 1, 2, and 3 should be answered on the scannable grid, which is at the back of this book. You should attempt to answer all objective items. There is no penalty for incorrect responses. Work space to solve the objective questions is provided. Since the objective items are computer-graded, your comments and calculations associated with them are not considered. Be certain that you have entered your answers on the scannable grid before the examination time is up. The objective portion of your examination will not be graded if you fail to record your answers on the scannable grid. You will not be given additional time to record your answers.

2. Question Numbers 4 and 5 should be answered the essay and problem response sheet at the back of this book. Support **all** answers with properly labeled and legible calculations that can be identified as sources of amounts used to derive your final answer. If you have not completed answering a question on a page, fill in the appropriate spaces in the wording on the bottom of the page. **"QUESTION NUMBER ___ CONTINUES ON PAGE ___ ."** If you have completed answering a question, fill in the appropriate space in the wording on the bottom of the page. **"QUESTION NUMBER ___ ENDS ON THIS PAGE."** Always begin the start of an answer to a question on the top of a new page (which may be the back side of a sheet of paper). Use the entire width of the page to answer requirements of a noncomputational nature. To answer requirements of a computational nature, you may wish to use only a portion of the page.

The point values for each question, and estimated time allotments based primarily on point value, are as follows:

	Point Value	Estimated Minutes Minimum	Estimated Minutes Maximum
No. 1	60	130	140
No. 2	10	15	25
No. 3	10	15	25
No. 4	10	30	40
No. 5	10	30	40
Totals	**100**	**220**	**270**

3. Although the primary purpose of the examination is to test your knowledge and application of the subject matter, selected essay responses will be graded for writing skills.

4. At examination time, you will be provided with an AICPA-approved calculator to help you work through the problems in this section of the CPA exam.

Number 1 (Estimated time—130 to 140 minutes)

Select the **best** answer for each of the following items. Use a No. 2 pencil and blacken ovals #1 through #60 on the Multiple-Choice Section of your scannable grid to indicate your answers. **Mark only one answer for each item. Answer all items.**

1. According to Statements of Financial Accounting Concepts, neutrality is an ingredient of

	Reliability	Relevance
A.	Yes	Yes
B.	Yes	No
C.	No	Yes
D.	No	No

2. In the hierarchy of generally accepted accounting principles, APB Opinions have the same authority as AICPA

A. Statements of Position.
B. Industry Audit and Accounting Guides.
C. Issues Papers.
D. Accounting Research Bulletins.

3. What is the underlying concept that supports the immediate recognition of a contingent loss?

A. Substance over form.
B. Consistency.
C. Matching.
D. Conservatism.

4. A company that wishes to disclose information about the effect of changing prices in accordance with Statement of Financial accounting Standards No. 89, *Financial Accounting and Changing Prices*, should report this information in

A. The body of the financial statements.
B. The notes to the financial statements.
C. Supplementary information to the financial statements.
D. Management's report to shareholders.

5. In analyzing a company's financial statements, which financial statement would a potential investor primarily use to assess the company's liquidity and financial flexibility?

A. Balance sheet.
B. Income statement.
C. Statement of retained earnings.
D. Statement of cash flows.

Please use this area for work space.

6. Thorn Co. applies Statement of Financial Accounting Standards No. 109, *Accounting for Income Taxes*. At the end of 19X3, the tax effects of temporary differences were as follows:

	Deferred tax assets (liabilities)	Related asset classification
Accelerated tax depreciation	($75,000)	Noncurrent asset
Additional costs in inventory for tax purposes	25,000	Current asset
	$50,000	

A valuation allowance was not considered necessary. Thorn anticipates that $10,000 of the deferred tax liability will reverse in 19X4. In Thorn's December 31, 19X3, balance sheet, what amount should Thorn report as noncurrent deferred tax liability?

A. $40,000
B. $50,000
C. $65,000
D. $75,000

7. Which of the following should not be disclosed in an enterprise's statement of cash flows prepared using the indirect method?

A. Interest paid, net of amounts capitalized.
B. Income taxes paid.
C. Cash flow per share.
D. Dividends paid on preferred stock.

Items 8 and 9 are based on the following:

The following trial balance of Trey Co. at December 31, 19X3, has been adjusted except for income tax expense.

	Dr.	Cr.
Cash	$ 550,000	
Accounts receivable, net	1,650,000	
Prepaid taxes	300,000	
Accounts payable		$ 120,000
Common stock		500,000
Additional paid-in capital		680,000
Retained earnings		630,000
Foreign currency translation adjustment	430,000	
Revenues		3,600,000
Expenses	2,600,000	
	$5,530,000	$5,530,000

———————— Please use this area for work space. ————————

Additional information:

- During 19X3, estimated tax payments of $300,000 were charged to prepaid taxes. Trey has not yet recorded income tax expense. There were no differences between financial statement and income tax income, and Trey's tax rate is 30%.

- Included in accounts receivable is $500,000 due from a customer. Special terms granted to this customer require payment in equal semi-annual installments of $125,000 every April 1 and October 1.

8. In Trey's December 31, 19X3 balance sheet, what amount should be reported as total current assets?

   A. $1,950,000
   B. $2,200,000
   C. $2,250,000
   D. $2,500,000

9. In Trey's December 31, 19X3 balance sheet, what amount should be reported as total retained earnings?

   A. $1,029,000
   B. $1,200,000
   C. $1,330,000
   D. $1,630,000

10. Kale Co. has adopted Statement of Financial Accounting Standards No. 115, *Accounting for Certain Investments in Debt and Equity Securities.* Kale purchased bonds at a discount on the open market as an investment and intends to hold these bonds to maturity. Kale should account for these bonds at

   A. Cost.
   B. Amortized cost.
   C. Fair value.
   D. Lower of cost or market.

11. Mare Co.'s December 31, 19X3 balance sheet reported the following current assets:

Cash	$70,000
Accounts Receivable	120,000
Inventories	60,000
Total	$250,000

An analysis of the accounts disclosed that accounts receivable consisted of the following:

Trade accounts	$ 96,000
Allowance for uncollectible accounts	(2,000)
Selling price of Mare's unsold goods out on consignment, at 130% of cost, **not** included in Mare's ending inventory	26,000
Total	$120,000

Please use this area for work space.

At December 31, 19X3, the total of Mare's current assets is

A. $224,000
B. $230,000
C. $244,000
D. $270,000

12. When the allowance method of recognizing uncollectible accounts is used, the entry to record the write-off of a specific account

A. Decreases both accounts receivable and the allowance for uncollectible accounts.
B. Decreases accounts receivable and increases the allowance for uncollectible accounts.
C. Increases the allowance for uncollectible accounts and decreases net income.
D. Decreases both accounts receivable and net income.

13. Herc Co.'s inventory at December 31, 19X3, was $1,500,000 based on a physical count priced at cost, and before any necessary adjustment for the following:

• Merchandise costing $90,000, shipped FOB shipping point from a vendor on December 30, 19X3, was received and recorded on January 5, 19X4.

• Goods in the shipping area were excluded from inventory although shipment was not made until January 3, 19X4. The goods, billed to the customer FOB shipping point on December 30, 19X3, had a cost of $120,000.

What amount should Herc report as inventory in its December 31, 19X3, balance sheet?

A. $1,500,000
B. $1,590,000
C. $1,620,000
D. $1,710,000

14. Which of the following statements are correct when a company applying the lower of cost or market method reports its inventory at replacement cost?

I. The original cost is less than replacement cost.

II. The net realizable value is greater than replacement cost.

A. I only.
B. II only.
C. Both I and II.
D. Neither I nor II.

———————————————— Please use this area for work space. ————————————————

15. Moss Corp. owns 20% of Dubro Corp.'s preferred stock and 80% of its common stock. Dubro's stock outstanding at December 31, 19X3, is as follows:

10% cumulative preferred stock	$100,000
Common stock	700,000

Dubro reported net income of $60,000 for the year ended December 31, 19X3. What amount should Moss record as equity in earnings of Dubro for the year ended December 31, 19X3?

A. $42,000
B. $48,000
C. $48,400
D. $50,000

16. On January 2, 19X3, Well Co. purchased 10% of Rea, Inc.'s outstanding common shares for $400,000. Well is the largest single shareholder in Rea, and Well's officers are a majority on Rea's board of directors. Rea reported net income of $500,000 for 19X3, and paid dividends of $150,000. In its December 31, 19X3, balance sheet, what amount should Well report as investment in Rea?

A. $450,000
B. $435,000
C. $400,000
D. $385,000

17. On January 2, 19X3, Paye Co. purchased Shef Co. at a cost that resulted in recognition of goodwill of $200,000 having an expected benefit period of 10 years. During the first quarter of 19X3, Paye spent an additional $80,000 on expenditures designed to maintain goodwill. Due to these expenditures, at December 31, 19X3, Paye estimated that the benefit period of goodwill was 40 years. In its December 31, 19X3, balance sheet, what amount should Paye report as goodwill?

A. $180,000
B. $195,000
C. $252,000
D. $273,000

18. In its 19X3 financial statements, Cris Co. reported interest expense of $85,000 in its income statement and cash paid for interest of $68,000 in its cash flow statement. There was no prepaid interest or interest capitalization either at the beginning or end of 19X3. Accrued interest at December 31, 19X2, was $15,000. What amount should Cris report as accrued interest payable in its December 31, 19X3, balance sheet?

A. $2,000
B. $15,000
C. $17,000
D. $32,000

Please use this area for work space.

19. On July 1, 19X3, Ran County issued realty tax assessments for its fiscal year ended June 30, 19X4. On September 1, 19X3, Day Co. purchased a warehouse in Ran County. The purchase price was reduced by a credit for accrued realty taxes. Day did not record the entire year's real estate tax obligation, but instead records tax expenses at the end of each month by adjusting prepaid real estate taxes or real estate taxes payable, as appropriate. On November 1, 19X3, Day paid the first of two equal installments of $12,000 for realty taxes. What amount of this payment should Day record as a debit to real estate taxes payable?

  A. $4,000
  B. $8,000
  C. $10,000
  D. $12,000

20. At the inception of a capital lease, the guaranteed residual value should be

  A. Included as part of minimum lease payments at present value.
  B. Included as part of minimum lease payments at future value.
  C. Included as part of minimum lease payments only to the extent that guaranteed residual value is expected to exceed estimated residual value.
  D. Excluded from minimum lease payments.

21. For $50 a month, Rawl Co. visits its customers' premises and performs insect control services. If customers experience problems between regularly scheduled visits, Rawl makes service calls at no additional charge. Instead of paying monthly, customers may pay an annual fee of $540 in advance. For a customer who pays the annual fee in advance, Rawl should recognize the related revenue

  A. When the cash is collected.
  B. At the end of the fiscal year.
  C. At the end of the contract year after all of the services have been performed.
  D. Evenly over the contract year as the services are performed.

***Items 22 and 23** are based on the following:*

House Publishers offered a contest in which the winner would receive $1,000,000, payable over 20 years. On December 31, 19X3, House announced the winner of the contest and signed a note payable to the winner for $1,000,000, payable in $50,000 installments every January 2. Also on December 31, 19X3, House purchased an annuity for $418,250 to provide the $950,000 prize monies remaining after the first $50,000 installment, which was paid on January 2, 19X4.

Please use this area for work space.

22. In its December 31, 19X3, balance sheet, what amount should House report as note payable-contest winner, net of current portion?

A. $368,250
B. $418,250
C. $900,000
D. $950,000

23. In its 19X3 income statement, what should House report as contest prize expense?

A. $0
B. $418,250
C. $468,250
D. $1,000,000

24. On January 2, 19X4, West Co. issued 9% bonds in the amount of $500,000, which mature on January 2, 2004. The bonds were issued for $469,500 to yield 10%. Interest is payable annually on December 31. West uses the interest method of amortizing bond discount. In its June 30, 19X4, balance sheet, what amount should West report as bonds payable?

A. $469,500
B. $470,475
C. $471,025
D. $500,000

25. Black Co. requires advance payments with special orders for machinery constructed to customer specifications. These advances are nonrefundable. Information for 19X3 is as follows:

Customer advances—	
balance 12/31/X2	$118,000
Advances received with order in 19X3	184,000
Advances applied to orders shipped in 19X3	164,000
Advances applicable to order canceled in 19X3	50,000

In Black's December 31, 19X3, balance sheet, what amount should be reported as a current liability for advances from customer?

A. $0
B. $88,000
C. $138,000
D. $148,000

26. Management can estimate the amount of loss that will occur if a foreign government expropriates some company assets. If expropriation is reasonably possible, a loss contingency should be

A. Disclosed but **not** accrued as a liability.
B. Disclosed and accrued as a liability.
C. Accrued as a liability but not disclosed.
D. Neither accrued as a liability nor disclosed.

Please use this area for work space.

27. Vadis Co. sells appliances that include a three-year warranty. Service calls under the warranty are performed by an independent mechanic under a contract with Vadis. Based on experience, warranty costs are estimated at $30 for each machine sold. When should Vadis recognize these warranty costs?

A. Evenly over the life of the warranty.
B. When the service calls are performed.
C. When payments are made to the mechanic.
D. When the machines are sold.

28. East Co. issued 1,000 shares of its $5 par common stock to Howe as compensation for 1,000 hours of legal services performed. Howe usually bills $160 per hour for legal services. On the date of issuance, the stock was trading on a public exchange at $140 per share. By what amount should the additional paid-in capital account increase as a result of this transaction?

A. $135,000
B. $140,000
C. $155,000
D. $160,000

29. During 19X2, Brad Co. issued 5,000 shares of $100 par convertible preferred stock for $110 per share. One share of preferred stock can be converted into three shares of Brad's $25 par common stock at the option of the preferred shareholder. On December 31, 19X3, when the market value of the common stock was $40 per share, all of the preferred stock was converted. What amount should Brad credit to Common Stock and to Additional Paid-in Capital—Common Stock as a result of the conversion?

	Common Stock	Additional Paid-In Capital
A.	$375,000	$175,000
B.	$375,000	$225,000
C.	$500,000	$50,000
D.	$600,000	$0

30. When a company declares a cash dividend, retained earnings is decreased by the amount of the dividend on the date of

A. Declaration.
B. Record.
C. Payment.
D. Declaration or record, whichever is earlier.

31. Long Co. had 100,000 shares of common stock issued and outstanding at January 1, 19X3. During 19X3, Long took the following actions:

March 15—Declared a 2-for-1 stock split, when the fair value of the stock was $80 per share.

December 15—Declared a $.50 per share cash dividend.

In Long's statement of stockholders' equity for 19X3, what amount should Long report as dividends?

    A. $50,000
    B. $100,000
    C. $850,000
    D. $950,000

32. If a corporation sells some of its treasury stock at a price that exceeds its cost, this excess should be

    A. Reported as a gain in the income statement.
    B. Treated as a reduction in the carrying amount of remaining treasury stock.
    C. Credited to additional paid-in capital.
    D. Credited to retained earnings.

33. On January 2, 19X3, Farm Co. granted an employee an option to purchase 1,000 shares of Farm's common stock at $40 per share. The option became exercisable on December 31, 19X3, after the employee had completed one year of service, and was exercised on that date. The market prices of Farm's stock were as follows:

January 2, 19X3	$50
December 31, 19X3	65

What amount should Farm recognize as compensation expense for 19X3?

    A. $0
    B. $10,000
    C. $15,000
    D. $25,000

Please use this area for work space.

---

34. The following data relates to Nola Co.'s defined benefit pension plan as of December 31, 19X3:

Unfunded accumulated benefit
  obligation $140,000
Unrecognized prior service cost   45,000
Accrued pension cost   80,000

What amount should Nola report as excess of additional pension liability over unrecognized prior service cost in its statement of stockholders' equity?

  A. $15,000
  B. $35,000
  C. $95,000
  D. $175,000

35. When Mill retired from the partnership of Mill, Yale, and Lear, the final settlement of Mill's interest exceeded Mill's capital balance. Under the bonus method, the excess

  A. Was recorded as goodwill.
  B. Was recorded as an expense.
  C. Reduced the capital balances of Yale and Lear.
  D. Had **no** effect on the capital balances of Yale and Lear.

36. On January 2, 19X3, Smith purchased the net assets of Jones' Cleaning, a sole proprietorship, for $350,000, and commenced operations of Spiffy Cleaning, a sole proprietorship. The assets had a carrying amount of $375,000 and a market value of $360,000. In Spiffy's cash-basis financial statements for the year ended December 31, 19X3, Spiffy reported revenues in excess of expenses of $60,000. Smith's drawings during 19X3 were $20,000. In Spiffy's financial statements, what amount should be reported as Capital-Smith?

  A. $390,000
  B. $400,000
  C. $410,000
  D. $415,000

37. The primary purpose of a quasi-reorganization is to give a corporation the opportunity to

  A. Obtain relief from its creditors.
  B. Revalue understated assets to their fair values.
  C. Eliminate a deficit in retained earnings.
  D. Distribute the stock of a newly created subsidiary to its stockholders in exchange for part of their stock in the corporation.

Please use this area for work space.

38. Leaf Co. purchased from Oak Co. a $20,000, 8%, 5-year note that required five equal annual year-end payments of $5,009. The note was discounted to yield a 9% rate to Leaf. At the date of purchase, Leaf recorded the note at its present value of $19,485. What should be the total interest revenue earned by Leaf over the life of this note?

A. $5,045
B. $5,560
C. $8,000
D. $9,000

39. Stock dividends on common stock should be recorded at their fair market value by the investor when the related investment is accounted for under which of the following methods?

	Cost	Equity
A.	Yes	Yes
B.	Yes	No
C.	No	Yes
D.	No	No

40. Wren Corp.'s trademark was licensed to Mont Co. for royalties of 15% of sales of the trademarked items. Royalties are payable semi-annually on March 15 for sales in July through December of the prior year, and on September 15 for sales in January through June of the same year. Wren received the following royalties from Mont:

	March 15	September 15
19X2	$10,000	$15,000
19X3	12,000	17,000

Mont estimated that sales of the trademarked items would total $60,000 for July through December 19X3.

In Wren's 19X3 income statement, the royalty revenue should be

A. $26,000
B. $29,000
C. $38,000
D. $41,000

41. As an inducement to enter a lease, Graf Co., a lessor, granted Zep, Inc., a lessee, twelve months of free rent under a five year operating lease. The lease was effective on January 1, 19X3, and provides for monthly rental payments to begin January 1, 19X4. Zep made the first rental payment on December 30, 19X3. In its 19X3 income statement, Graf should report rental revenue in an amount equal to

A. Zero.
B. Cash received during 19X3.
C. One-fourth of the total cash to be received over the life of the lease.
D. One-fifth of the total cash to be received over the life of the lease.

Please use this area for work space.

---

42. On July 31, 19X3, Dome Co. issued $1,000,000 of 10%, 15-year bonds at par and used a portion of the proceeds to call its 600 outstanding 11%, $1,000 face value bonds, due on July 31, 2003, at 102. On that date, unamortized bond premium relating to the 11% bonds was $65,000. In its 19X3 income statement, what amount should Dome report as gain or loss, before income taxes, from retirement of bonds?

    A. $53,000 gain.
    B. $0
    C. $(65,000) loss.
    D. $(77,000) loss.

43. Bren Co.'s beginning inventory at January 1, 19X3, was understated by $26,000, and its ending inventory was overstated by $52,000. As a result, Bren's cost of goods sold for 19X3 was

    A. Understated by $26,000.
    B. Overstated by $26,000.
    C. Understated by $78,000.
    D. Overstated by $78,000.

44. During 19X3, Orr Co. incurred the following costs:

Research and development services performed by Key Corp. for Orr	$150,000
Design, construction, and testing of preproduction prototypes and models	200,000
Testing in search for new products or process alternatives	175,000

In its 19X3 income statement, what should Orr report as research and development expense?

    A. $150,000
    B. $200,000
    C. $350,000
    D. $525,000

—————— Please use this area for work space. ——————

45. Inge Co. determined that the net value of its accounts receivable at December 31, 19X3, based on an aging of the receivables, was $325,000. Additional information is as follows:

Allowance for uncollectible accounts—1/1/X3	$ 30,000
Uncollectible accounts written off during 19X3	18,000
Uncollectible accounts recovered during 19X3	2,000
Accounts receivable at 12/31/X3	350,000

For 19X3, what would be Inge's uncollectible accounts expense?

A. $5,000
B. $11,000
C. $15,000
D. $21,000

46. An increase in the cash surrender value of a life insurance policy owned by a company would be recorded by

A. Decreasing annual insurance expense.
B. Increasing investment income.
C. Recording a memorandum entry only.
D. Decreasing a deferred charge.

47. Clark Co.'s advertising expense account had a balance of $146,000 at December 31, 19X3, before any necessary year-end adjustment relating to the following:

- Included in the $146,000 is the $15,000 cost of printing catalogs for a sales promotional campaign in January 19X4.

- Radio advertisements broadcast during December 19X3 were billed to Clark on January 2, 19X4. Clark paid the $9,000 invoice on January 11, 19X4.

What amount should Clark report as advertising expense in its income statement for the year ended December 3, 19X3?

A. $122,000
B. $131,000
C. $140,000
D. $155,000

Please use this area for work space.

48. Able Co. provides an incentive compensation plan under which its president receives a bonus equal to 10% of the corporation's income before income tax but after deduction of the bonus. If the tax rate is 40% and net income after bonus and income tax was $360,000, what was the amount of the bonus?

    A. $36,000
    B. $60,000
    C. $66,000
    D. $90,000

Items 49 and 50 are based on the following:

Kent, Inc.'s reconciliation between financial statement and taxable income for 19X3 follows:

Pretax financial income	$150,000
Permanent difference	(12,000)
	138,000
Temporary difference—depreciation	(9,000)
Taxable income	$129,000

Additional information:

	At	
	12/31/X2	12/31/X3
Cumulative temporary differences (future taxable amounts)	$11,000	$20,000

The enacted tax rate was 34% for 19X2, and 40% for 19X3 and years thereafter.

49. In its December 31, 19X3 balance sheet, what amount should Kent report as deferred income tax liability?

    A. $3,600
    B. $6,800
    C. $7,340
    D. $8,000

50. In its 19X3 income statement, what amount should Kent report as current portion of income tax expense?

    A. $51,600
    B. $55,200
    C. $55,860
    D. $60,000

——————— Please use this area for work space. ———————

51. In its 19X3 income statement, Cere Co. reported income before income taxes of $300,000. Cere estimated that, because of permanent differences, taxable income for 19X3 would be $280,000. During 19X3 Cere made estimated tax payments of $50,000, which were debited to income tax expense. Cere is subject to a 30% tax rate. What amount should Cere report as income tax expense?

A. $34,000
B. $50,000
C. $84,000
D. $90,000

52. On October 1, 19X3, Wand, Inc. committed itself to a formal plan to sell its Kam division's assets. On that date, Wand estimated that the loss from the disposal of assets in February 19X4 would be $25,000. Wand also estimated that Kam would incur operating losses of $100,000 for the period of October 1, 19X3, through December 31, 19X3, and $50,000 for the period January 1, 19X4 through February 28, 19X4. These estimates were materially correct. Disregarding income taxes, what should Wan report as loss from discontinued operations in its comparative 19X3 and 19X4 income statements?

	19X3	19X4
A.	$175,000	$0
B.	$125,000	$50,000
C.	$100,000	$75,000
D.	$0	$175,000

Please use this area for work space.

53. A transaction that is unusual in nature and infrequent in occurrence should be reported separately as a component of income

A. After cumulative effect of accounting changes and before discontinued operations of a segment of business.
B. After cumulative effect of accounting changes and after discontinued operations of a segment of a business.
C. Before cumulative effect of accounting changes and before discontinued operations of a segment of a business.
D. Before cumulative effect of accounting changes and after discontinued operations of a segment of a business.

54. How should the effect of a change in accounting estimate be accounted for?

A. By restating amounts reported in financial statements of prior periods.
B. By reporting pro forma amounts for prior periods.
C. As a prior period adjustment to beginning retained earnings.
D. In the period of change and future periods if the change affects both.

55. Foy Corp. failed to accrue warranty costs of $50,000 in its December 31, 19X2, financial statements. In addition, a change from straight-line to accelerated depreciation made at the beginning of 19X3 resulted in a cumulative effect of $30,000 on Foy's retained earnings. Both the $50,000 and the $30,000 are net of related income taxes. What amount should Foy report as prior period adjustments in 19X3?

A. $0
B. $30,000
C. $50,000
D. $80,000

56. Sun, Inc. is a wholly-owned subsidiary of Patton, Inc. On June 1, 19X3, Patton declared and paid a $1 per share cash dividend to stockholders of record on May 15, 19X3. On May 1, 19X3, Sun bought 10,000 shares of Patton's common stock for $700,000 on the open market, when the book value per share was $30. What amount of gain should Patton report from this transaction in its consolidated income statement for the year ended December 31, 19X3?

A. $0
B. $390,000
C. $400,000
D. $410,000

Please use this area for work space.
---

57. During 19X3, Park Corp. recorded sales of inventory costing $500,000 to Small Co., its wholly owned subsidiary, on the same terms as sales made to third parties. At December 31, 19X3, Small held one-fifth of these goods in its inventory. The following information pertains to Park and Small's sales for 19X3.

	Park	Small
Sales	$2,000,000	$1,400,000
Cost of sales	800,000	700,000
	$1,200,000	$700,000

In its 19X3 consolidated income statement, what amount should Park report as cost of sales?

- A. $1,000,000
- B. $1,100,000
- C. $1,260,000
- D. $1,500,000

58. The following information pertains to Eagle Co.'s 19X3 sales:

Cash sales

Gross	$80,000
Returns and allowances	4,000

Credit sales

Gross	120,000
Discounts	6,000

On January 1, 19X3, customers owed Eagle $40,000. On December 31, 19X3, customers owed Eagle $30,000. Eagle uses the direct write-off method for bad debts. No bad debts were recorded in 19X3. Under the cash basis of accounting, what amount of net revenue should Eagle report for 19X3?

- A. $76,000
- B. $170,000
- C. $190,000
- D. $200,000

59. Which of the following information should be disclosed in the summary of significant accounting policies?

- A. Refinancing of debt subsequent to the balance sheet date.
- B. Guarantees of indebtedness of others.
- C. Criteria for determining which investments are treated as cash equivalents.
- D. Adequacy of pension plan assets relative to vested benefits.

Please use this area for work space.

60. In financial reporting for segments of a business enterprise, the operating profit or loss of a manufacturing segment includes a portion of

	General Corporate Expenses	Indirect Operating Expenses
A.	Yes	Yes
B.	Yes	No
C.	No	Yes
D.	No	No

Number 2 (Estimated time—15 to 25 minutes)

Question Number 2 consists of 14 items. Select the best answer for each item. Use a No. 2 pencil to blacken OOF Section #2 of your scannable grid. **Answer all items.**

Items 61 through 66 represent expenditures for goods held for resale and equipment.

Required:

For items 61 through 66, determine for each item whether the expenditure should be Capitalized (A) or Expensed as a Period Cost (B) and blacken the corresponding oval on response items #1 through #6 on OOF Section #2.

61. Freight charges paid for goods held for resale.

62. In-transit insurance on goods held for resale purchased F.O.B. shipping point.

63. Interest on note payable for goods held for resale.

64. Installation of equipment.

65. Testing of newly purchased equipment.

66. Cost of current year service contract on equipment.

Items 67 through 70 are based on the following 19X3 transactions:

- Link Co. purchased an office building and the land on which it is located by paying $800,000 cash and assuming an existing mortgage of $200,000. The property is assessed at $960,000 for realty tax purposes, of which 60% is allocated to the building.

- Link leased construction equipment under a 7-year capital lease requiring annual year-end payments of $100,000. Link's incremental borrowing rate is 9%, while the lessor's implicit rate, which is not known to Link, is 8%. Present value factors for an ordinary

---

Please use this area for work space.

annuity for seven periods are 5.21 at 8% and 5.03 at 9%. Fair value of the equipment is $515,000.

- Link paid $50,000 and gave a plot of undeveloped land with a carrying amount of $320,000 and a fair value of $450,000 to Club Co. in exchange for a plot of undeveloped land with a fair value of $500,000. The land was carried on Club's books at $350,000.

Required:

For items 67 through 70, calculate the amount to be recorded for each item. To record your answer, write the number in the boxes on the OOF Numeric Response Section of your scannable grid, using response items #9 through #12. Blacken the corresponding oval below each box. Write zeros in any blank boxes preceding your numerical answer, and blacken the zero in the oval below the box. You cannot receive credit for your answers if you fail to blacken an oval in each column.

67. Building.

68. Leased equipment.

69. Land received from Club on Link's books.

70. Land received from Link on Club's books.

Please use this area for work space.

Items 71 through 74 are based on the following information:

On January 2, 19X2, Half, Inc. purchased a manufacturing machine for $864,000. The machine has a 8-year estimated life and a $144,000 estimated salvage value. Half expects to manufacture 1,800,000 units over the life of the machine. During 19X3, Half manufactured 300,000 units.

Required:

Items 71 through 74 represent various depreciation methods. For each item, calculate depreciation expense for 19X3 (the second year of ownership) for the machine described above under the method listed. To record your answer, write the number in the boxes on the OOF Numeric Response Section of your scannable grid, using response items #13 through #16. Blacken the corresponding oval below each box. Write zeros in any blank boxes preceding your numerical answer, and blacken the zero in the oval below the box. You cannot receive credit for your answers if you fail to blacken an oval in each column.

71. Straight-line.

72. Double-declining balance.

73. Sum-of-the-years'-digits.

74. Units of production.

Numbers 3 and 4 (Estimated time—45 to 65 minutes)

Question Numbers 3 and 4 are based on the following information. **Question Number 3** consists of items 75 through 80. **Question Number 4** is a computational question.

The following condensed trial balance of Probe Co., a publicly held company, has been adjusted except for income tax expense.

Please use this area for work space.

Probe Co.
CONDENSED TRIAL BALANCE

	12/31/X3 Balances Dr. (Cr.)	12/31/X2 Balances Dr. (Cr.)	Net change Dr. (Cr.)
Cash	$ 473,000	$ 817,000	$ (344,000)
Accounts receivable, net	670,000	610,000	60,000
Property, plant, and equipment	1,070,000	995,000	75,000
Accumulated depreciation	(345,000)	(280,000)	(65,000)
Dividends payable	(25,000)	(10,000)	(15,000)
Income taxes payable	35,000	(150,000)	185,000
Deferred income tax liability	(42,000)	(42,000)	—
Bonds payable	(500,000)	(1,000,000)	500,000
Unamortized premium on bonds	(71,000)	(150,000)	79,000
Common stock	(350,000)	(150,000)	(200,000)
Additional paid-in capital	(430,000)	(375,000)	(55,000)
Retained earnings	(185,000)	(265,000)	80,000
Sales	(2,420,000)		
Cost of sales	1,863,000		
Selling and administrative expense	220,000		
Interest income	(14,000)		
Interest expense	46,000		
Depreciation	88,000		
Loss on sale of equipment	7,000		
Gain on extinguishment of bonds	(90,000)		
	$ 0	$ 0	$ 300,000

Additional information:

- During 19X3 equipment with an original cost of $50,000 was sold for cash, and equipment costing $125,000 was purchased.

- On January 1, 19X3, bonds with a par value of $500,000 and related premium of $75,000 were redeemed. The $1,000 face value, 10% par bonds had been issued on January 1, 1984, to yield 8%. Interest is payable annually every December 31 through 2003.

- Probe's tax payments during 19X3 were debited to Income Taxes Payable. Probe elected early adoption of Statement of Financial Accounting Standards No. 109, Accounting for Income Taxes, for the year ended December 31, 19X2, and recorded a deferred income tax liability of $42,000 based on temporary differences of $120,000 and an enacted tax rate of 35%. Probe's 19X3 financial statement income before income taxes was greater than its 19X3 taxable income, due entirely to temporary differences by $60,000. Probe's cumulative net taxable temporary differences at December 31, 19X3 were $180,000. Probe's enacted tax rate for the current and future years is 30%.

- 60,000 shares of common stock, $2.50 par, were outstanding on December 31, 19X2. Probe issued an additional 80,000 shares on April 1, 19X3.

- There were no changes to retained earnings other than dividends declared.

Number 3 (Estimated time—15 to 25 minutes)

Question Number 3 consists of 6 items. Select the best answer for each item. Use a No. 2 pencil to blacken the appropriate ovals on the OOF Numeric Response Section of your scannable grid, response items #19 through #24. **Answer all items.**

Required:

For each transaction in **items 75 through 80,** the following **two** responses are required:

- Determine the amount to be reported in Probe's 19X3 statement of cash flows prepared using the indirect method. To record your answer, write the number in the boxes on the scannable grid **and** blacken the corresponding oval below the box. Write zeros in any blank boxes preceding your numerical answer, and blacken the zero in the oval below the box. **You cannot receive credit for your answers if you fail to blacken an oval in each column.**

- Select from the list below where the specific item should be separately reported on the statement of cash flows prepared using the indirect method and blacken the corresponding oval on the Scannable Grid.

  A. Operating.
  B. Investing.
  C. Financing.
  D. Supplementary information.
  E. Not reported on Probe's statement of cash flows.

75. Cash paid for income taxes.

76. Cash paid for interest.

77. Redemption of bonds payable.

78. Issuance of common stock.

79. Cash dividends paid.

80. Proceeds from sale of equipment.

Please use this area for work space.

Number 4 (Estimated time—30 to 40 minutes)

Question Number 4 is a computational question.

Required:

Prepare Probe Co.'s multiple-step income statement for the year ended December 31, 19X3, with earnings per share information and supporting computations for current and deferred income tax expense.

Number 5 (Estimated time—30 to 40 minutes)

Wyatt, CPA, is meeting with Brown, the controller of Emco, a wholesaler, to discuss the accounting issues regarding two unrelated items:

- Emco is considering offering its customers the right to return its products for a full refund within one year of purchase. Emco expects its sales to increase as a result, but is unable to estimate the amount of future returns.

- Brown is aware that Statement of Financial Accounting Standards (FAS) No. 106, *Employers Accounting for Postretirement Benefits Other Than Pensions*, is effective for years beginning after December 15, 19X2. Brown is uncertain about the benefits and beneficiaries covered by this Statement. Brown believes that, regardless of FAS 106, no estimate of postretirement obligation can be reasonable because it would be based on too many assumptions. For this reason, Brown wishes to continue to account for the postretirement benefits that Emco pays to its retirees on the pay-as-you-go (cash) basis.

Brown has asked Wyatt to write a brief memo to Brown that Brown can use to explain these issues to Emco's president.

Required:

Write a brief advisory memo from Wyatt to Brown to:

a. Explain the general principle of revenue recognition, the method of revenue recognition when right to return exists, and the impact of offering a right to return on Emco's ability to recognize revenue, if any.

b. State the principal benefit covered by FAS 106 and give an example of other benefits covered by FAS 106. Explain the reasoning given in FAS 106 for requiring accruals based on estimates. Indicate the primary recipients of postretirement benefits other than pensions.

Please use this area for work space.

1. A Stating a particular fee for specific consulting services would violate the profession's ethical standards if it was apparent to the CPA consultant that the actual fee would be much higher. Independence is not required when performing consulting services.

2. C A departure from a Statement of Financial Accounting Standards may be justified by unusual circumstances including new legislation or the development of a new form of business transaction. The CPA must describe the approximate effects of the departure and justify why the departure is appropriate in the circumstances.

3. A An auditor will exercise due professional care by carefully reviewing the levels of judgment used by all individuals assisting in the audit. Auditors need not examine all available evidence or design audits to discover all illegal acts. Balancing professional experience with formal education relates to the competence of the auditor, not to due professional care.

4. D Independence in fact and appearance is required when performing audit, attest, or review services. Independence is not required when performing compilations or tax returns.

5. D Independence in fact or appearance is not required of a CPA when performing a consulting engagement. A CPA is required to comply with Statements on Standards for Consulting Engagements, obtain an understanding of the nature, scope, and limitations of the engagement, and supervise staff assigned to the engagement.

6. A Consulting services could include advisory services, implementation services, and product services.

7. B A CPA in tax practice should ensure that tax advice reflects professional competence. This would include recommending a position that the CPA believes has a reasonable possibility of being sustained if challenged. A CPA may not recommend a frivolous position, even if disclosed, and may not sign a return knowing a position that cannot be sustained has been taken. A CPA should advise a client of potential penalties that may result from taking a certain position.

8. C When a CPA tax preparer discovers an error in a client's previously filed tax return, the CPA should advise the client of the discovery. The CPA may not notify the IRS without client permission.

9. A Lack of privity would be a viable defense in a common law action if a third party sues based on negligence. Lack of privity would not be a viable defense for negligence if the third party had been known and forseen as the intended beneficiary of the accountant's work. Suits based on gross negligence or fraud do not require privity. The accountant's client would have privity, and thus lack of privity would be an ineffective defense if the plaintiff is the client.

10. C The CPA will generally be liable to all those who rely on the accountant's audit of financial statements if there has been a material misstatement or omission, the accountant committed scienter, the accountant intended reliance on the financial statements, reliance occurred, and a loss resulted for the plaintiff.

11. A Provisions of section 10(b) and Rule 10b-5 of the Act of 1934 require that scienter and reliance must be shown by the plaintiff in a suit against a CPA. Scienter is intentional misconduct and includes reckless conduct. Negligence need not be proven by the plaintiff in suits brought under the provisions of section 10(b) and Rule 10b-5.

12. B Under section 11 of the 1933 Act, a CPA will usually avoid liability to a securities purchaser if the CPA can prove due diligence. Due diligence means the CPA followed the standards of the auditing profession. The CPA could also likely avoid liability by showing the plaintiff's loss was caused by other things or if the plaintiff knew of the material misstatement or omission.

13. D Under section 11 of the 1933 Act, neither plaintiff reliance on the financial statements nor fraud by the CPA are required to be proven by the purchaser of securities.

14. B Accountants may respond to a valid subpoena for confidential client data but may not disclose such information to a state agency without subpoena. Accountants may disclose client information to any party if the client consents to the disclosure.

15. C Within a partnership, working papers may be reviewed by any surviving partner or partners upon the death of a partner. This is consistent with the responsibilities of partners within a general partnership.

16. B Written agency agreements are required when the agency agreement cannot be completed within one year or when the subject of the agency agreement is subject to the statute of frauds. As a result, an agent's purchase of land on behalf of a principal would require a written agency agreement.

17. C While the principal provided actual notice by sending letters to the agent's known customers, no public announcements were made. As a result, Young received no actual or constructive notice of the termination of the agency agreement. Young will win against the principal due to Ace's apparent authority since they had no notice of the agent's dismissal.

18. A The authority of an agent is unaffected by whether the principal is disclosed or undisclosed. The principal cannot be bound by apparent authority unless the third party knows that there is an agency relationship. Principals are liable for their agents' negligent acts while acting on the principal's behalf. When the principal is undisclosed, the agent will be personally bound because a good faith third party would assume that the agent was the principal.

19. C Agents are usually not liable to a third party when the principal is disclosed. When the principal is undisclosed, however, the agent usually will be liable because the third party would assume that the agent was the principal.

20. D   Unless otherwise provided in the partnership agreement, the executor of a deceased partner's estate will not become a partner but will include the partnership interest in the estate. The estate will not be free of partnership liabilities existing at the partner's death. A partnership is automatically dissolved whenever a partner dies.

21. C   When a partner commits a tort while pursuing partnership business all of the partners are jointly and severally liable. In these cases, the third party can sue one or any combination of the partners.

22. D   Unless agreed otherwise, losses are shared in the same proportion as profits. Kale will be allocated 5/9 of the partnership's $180,000 loss, or $100,000.

23. B   Ward has become a partner because Ward sought to buy Lark's partnership interest and because all of the other partners have agreed to admit Ward to the partnership. Partners in a general partnership are entitled to participate in the partnership's management. New partners are not personally responsible for liabilities arising prior to their admission but are personally responsible for liabilities after their admission.

24. C   An agreement among the partners will not change or discharge any partner's liability. Each partner will continue to have apparent authority and could bind the dissolved partnership unless proper notice is given.

25. B   When a parent firm owns more than 90% of the shares of each class of stock of a subsidiary, the parent firm may accomplish a "short form" merger by mere resolution by its board of directors. Neither the group of stockholders nor the subsidiary's board of directors need approve the merger. The right of appraisal exists only for the minority shareholders of the subsidiary.

26. C   The Fair Debt Collection Act generally prohibits those who collect debts for others from making contact with third parties regarding the debtor's liabilities. Debtors may bring civil suits against collection agencies who violate the provisions of this act.

27. B   A debtor will be released from debts when the debtor and the creditors enter into a composition of creditors. This occurs when the debtor and creditors agree among themselves that the creditors will accept partial payment in full settlement of the entire debt. An assignment for the benefit of creditors occurs when a debtor makes a voluntary transfer of nonexempt property to an assignee who liquidates the assets and settles the debtor's liabilities on a pro rata basis. The debtor is not released from unsatisfied liabilities at the conclusion of an assignment for the benefit of creditors.

28. A   A writ of attachment is a prejudgment remedy which prevents the debtor from disposing of assets. Another prejudgment remedy available to a creditor is garnishment, which requires third parties to continue holding assets owned by the debtor or prevents third parties from paying amounts owed directly to the debtor.

29. C   The incapacity of the surety would excuse the surety from liability to the creditor. The debtor's discharge in bankruptcy has no impact on the surety's obligation to the creditor. Personal defenses of the debtor or incapacity of the principal debtor would also have no impact on the surety's obligation to the creditor.

30. D A surety enters in to a contract with the credititor related to amounts owed by the debtor. The surety does not have rights to compel the creditor to proceed against the prinipcal debtor or the collateral. The creditor could, however, pursue either of the actions voluntarily. In addition, once the surety has made payment to the creditor, the surety may pursue the principal debtor and is entitled to the debtor's collateral.

31. A When a creditor releases a cosurety from an obligation all the cosureties are released to the extent that they have lost the right of contribution from the released cosurety. West and Quill were cosureties with equal liabilities to the creditor. Release of West and Quill from 50% of the loan balance, which is that amount that West would be required to contribute.

32. D In general, 3 or more unsecured creditors owed an aggregate of $10,000 or more by a debtor who is behind in making payments may successfully file an involuntary petition in bankruptcy. If there are fewer than 12 unsecured creditors owed an aggregate of $10,000 or more by a debtor, one or two of these creditors can successfully file the involuntary petition in bankruptcy.

33. A Certain claims are not discharged in bankruptcy at the conclusion of the proceedings. Undischarged claims include alimony or child support obligations. Debts arising from negligence are discharged unless the debtor's behavior had been willful.

34. C Under Chapter 7 of the Federal Bankruptcy Code, a debtor must surrender to the trustee all property receivable or received within 180 days of the filing of a voluntary petition if the property results from inheritances, life insurance settlements, and divorce settlements. All debts are not discharged, and another discharge in bankruptcy is not available within 6 years of a previous discharge.

35. B An employer has an obligation to file a FUTA tax return if, in the current year, it had at least one employee, whether full or part-time, in at least 20 weeks, or paid $1,500 or more in wages in any calendar quarter.

36. D One basic component in all workers' compensation systems is that negligence by the employer, employee, or co-employees do not prevent recovery by the injured employee. This is consistent with recovery under strict liability theory.

37. B Under the reorganization provisions of Chapter 11, a reorganized corporate debtor will receive a discharge of debts, except as provided in the plan and available law. The debtor has avoided liquidation through reorganization and the debtor's business affairs would be turned over to a trustee only in the unlikely event that a trustee had been appointed. The debtor may remain in the same business.

38. B The Federal Age Discrimination in Employment Act prohibits discrimination in any employment practice based on age. The act benefits individuals who have attained age 40 without any upper age limit. Termination of employees for cause is not prohibited by this act.

39. A The Federal Fair Labor Standards Act regulates minimum hourly wages and payment of overtime at 150% for hours in excess of forty per week. Some jobs are exempted from these provisions, such as professionals, managers, and outside sales persons. By regulating overtime for hours in excess of 40 per week, the act regulates the number of hours in the work week.

40. B Noncontributory pension plans are paid for entirely by the employer.

41. B The SEC does not guarantee the accuracy of information contained in a registration statement, but reviews the information for completeness. The SEC gives no assurance against investor losses. The investor does receive information about the primary uses to which the proceeds will be applied.

42. D The Securities Act of 1933 provides for exemptions from registration for securities issued by charitable organizations, regulated industries such as savings and loan associations, and state or local governmental organizations. Securities issued by insurance companies are not exempt. Insurance policies or contracts, however, would be exempt.

43. B An on-going registration is called a shelf registration and requires appropriate updating of the original registration statement in order to remain effective. There is no requirement that shelf-registrations are available only to first-time issuers.

44. D All securities are subject to the anti-fraud provisions of the 1933 Act regardless of whether they are exempt from registration. If securities were exempt when issued, either a resale must be registered or a different exemption under the 1933 Act must be identified.

45. B The 1934 Act requires continuous reporting by firms whose shares are listed on a national securities exchange. The number of classes of stock has no relevance to the reporting requirements under the 1934 Act.

46. A A company subject to the reporting requirements of the 1934 Act must file periodic reports, such as the 10K, 10Q, and 8K, and must file proxy statements with the SEC.

47. A When a company is subject to the reporting requirements of the 1934 Act, appropriate reports must be submitted to the SEC by parties making a tender offer to buy shares and by stockholders making a proxy solicitation.

48. C An exemption from registering securities under the 1933 Act is available for sales of securities by persons other than an issuer, underwriter, or dealer.

49. B An offering will be exempt under Rules 505 and 506 if it is made without general advertising. Notice to the SEC must be within 15 days of the first sale. Accredited investors are not required to receive any specific financial information, and there is no upper limit on the total number of investors, including accredited and nonaccredited investors.

50. A The parties to a sale of goods contract must perform in good faith. Merchants and non-merchants are not treated alike under the UCC. The UCC applies to all sales of goods without regard to the dollar value of the contract, but certain provisions of the UCC, such as implied warranties, can be disclaimed by agreement.

51. D The warranty of merchantability arises as a matter of law when a merchant selling goods has failed to exclude the warranty. The warranty of merchantability can be disclaimed by oral or conspicuous written language that specifically mentions merchantability.

52. A An intrastate securities offering would be exempt from registration under the 1933 and 1934 Acts. Resales of these securities cannot occur within 9 months from the final sale.

53. D Recoveries under strict liability theory do not require negligence be shown. Contributory negligence by the plaintiff is not a bar to recovery, though it might impact the settlement amount. The manufacturer cannot escape liability by showing it followed the custom of the industry. Privity is irrelevant in cases of product liability, including strict liability.

54. D Use of the seller's truck suggests the contract is a destination contract and the risk of loss would remain with the seller until successful delivery occurred. Tender of the goods to the buyer at the seller's place of business would not shift risk of loss to the buyer when the seller is a merchant.

55. D When either buyer or seller has reasonable doubts about the other party's willingness or ability to perform its obligations under a contract for the sale of goods, the doubting party may ask for reasonable assurance that performance will be forthcoming as contracted. Destruction of the goods after risk of loss had passed to buyer would not release the buyer. Had the buyer expressed an anticipatory repudiation and retracted the repudiation prior to a seller's cancellation of a contract, the contract would continue in force.

56. C When goods are shipped on a C.O.D. basis, the buyer cannot take possession of the goods or inspect the goods until payment is made. After paying for the goods the buyer has the right to reject nonconforming goods.

57. C Attachment is accomplished when 3 requirements have been accomplished. The debtor must have rights in the collateral, a security interest must be signed by the debtor or possession of the collateral must be given to the creditor, and the creditor must have given value to the debtor. The sequence in which these requirements are fulfilled is irrelevant.

58. D Consumer goods are items to be used personally by the buyer. When a consumer buys goods from a merchant in the ordinary course of business, the goods are taken free of a perfected security interest. The consumer's knowledge of a creditor's perfection by filing is irrelevant. If a merchant bought the goods, they would not be consumer goods in the merchant's hands. A consumer who buys goods from another consumer purchaser who had given a security interest to a creditor would not take the goods free of the creditor's perfected security interest if the second consumer has knowledge of the creditor's perfected security interest.

59. A In general, a security interest in consumer goods has its priority established on the basis of when the security interest is perfected. A security interest can be perfected by filing a financing statement with the appropriate governmental office or by taking possession of the collateral. Since all 3 security interest are perfected in this case, they would be given priority in the order they were perfected, April 1, followed by April 10, followed by April 15.

60. A A secured creditor may proceed against collateral when the debtor fails to make a scheduled payment. The secured creditor may also seek to obtain an agreement by the debtor granting the creditor authority to enter a judgment against the debtor.

61. B Blake's oral offer of December 15 was a legitimate offer. Offers need not be written to be legitimate.

62. B Reach's December 20 fax was a proper method of accepting because the offer did not indicate that a fax would be unacceptable and, given the offer's terms, it was imperative that the written acceptance be received by December 20. Use of a fax was a reasonable method by which to communicate a timely acceptance.

63. B Since Blake indicated acceptance must be received by December 20, the acceptance will not be effective when sent.

64. B Reach's acceptance was effectively received on December 20 since it was delivered to Blake's office on that date. Since Blake's office was closed on December 20, the fax to the office would be considered reasonable delivery.

65. B Reach's acceptance was actually a counteroffer. As a result, no contract was formed.

66. A or B Reach's agreement to $1,000,000 prevented the formation of the first ($100,000) contract but not the subsequent ($75,000) one. Hence the ambiguity of the question makes either answer acceptable depending on the context.

67. A Reach's December 20 fax was a counteroffer. In order to be valid as an acceptance, it would need to duplicate the terms of the offer without modification.

68. B Reach is not prohibited from assigning any contract right. The contract did not forbid assignment of rights. In general, rights and obligations may be assigned.

69. A Reach may assign all or part of Reach's rights under the contract.

70. A A creditor beneficiary exists when an assignment of rights is made to a third party who is owed a legal duty by the assignor. Reach owes money to Weaver, and Reach has assigned part of Blake's performance to Weaver.

71. A In a breach of contract suit by Weaver against Blake, Weaver would not collect any punitive damages. Punitive damages are not recoverable in breach of contract suits unless the defendant's actions were of a malicious and willful nature. Compensatory damages, however, might be collectible.

72. B In a breach of contract suit by Weaver against Reach, Weaver would not collect any punitive damages. Punitive damages are not recoverable in breach of contract suits unless the defendant's actions were of a malicious and willful nature. Compensatory damage might, however, be collectible.

73. **B** Reach's oral acceptance of Blake's December 22 memo did form a valid contract. Under the statute of frauds, however, personal service contracts that cannot be completed within one year or less will be only enforceable against one who signed the writing.

74. **A** An offer need not contain a deadline for acceptance.

75. **A** Reach can enforce the contract formed by Reach's oral acceptance against Blake. An oral acceptance forms a valid contract that can be enforced against Blake because there is written evidence demonstrating Blake's intent to form a contract.

76 **B** The instrument is a promissory note. It contains a promise to pay and is a two-party instrument.

77. **G** The instrument is negotiable because the six requirements are met. The sum due at the maturity date can be calculated, the instrument is payable to order, it contains an unconditional promise to pay, and is payable only in money. In addition, the instrument is signed by the party who will pay. Prepayment dates do not cause the instrument to be non-negotiable.

78. **E** Morton is a holder in due course. The instrument became bearer paper when Dart endorsed it in blank. The negotiable bearer instrument has been properly transferred to Morton by delivery. Morton has no notice of defenses by the note's maker, and Morton has given value for the note.

79. **F** Since Trent obtained the instrument from a holder in due course, Trent will obtain comparable status despite the knowledge of a personal defense against the instrument.

80. **I** Trent could recover on the note from Evans, Morton, and Dart. Recovery from Evans is justified because Evans has only a personal defense while Trent has the rights of a holder in due course. Recovery from Morton is justified based on warranty theory of liability which provides that a transferer of a negotiable instrument who receives consideration is liable to the immediate transferee if the warranties are broken, as in this case. Recovery from Dart is based on signature theory, which provides that all who sign a negotiable instrument are potentially liable to a current holder. Recovery from Dart is also based on warranty theory, which provides that all transferers of a negotiable instrument who receive consideration have made certain warranties to all subsequent holders if transfer occurred by endorsement. The warranties are not all valid in this case, and Dart is liable to Trent under the warranty theory of liability.

81. **D** This is a three party instrument and is a draft.

82. **E** The draft is negotiable. All the requirements for negotiability have been satisfied.

83. **A** West's endorsement in blank causes the negotiable draft to become bearer paper.

84. **H** Keetin's special endorsement names C. Larr as the new payee, making the draft order paper again.

85. A Larr's endorsement in blank causes the negotiable draft to be bearer paper again. The phrase *without recourse* has no impact on the draft's status as bearer paper.

86. B West's endorsement is an endorsement in blank since it does not name a new payee.

87. J Keetin's endorsement is a special endorsement since it names a new payee.

88. I Larr's endorsement is a qualified endorsement because of the phrase "without recourse."

4.

a. The requirements to establish any trust include the need for a beneficiary, a reasonable purpose, assets, a trustee, and a specified life. These requirements have been met. The beneficiaries are "several close relatives." The reasonable purpose is "financial security" for the beneficiaries. Assets have been placed in the trust. A trustee has been named. The trust term is the lifetimes of the beneficiaries.

b. All four allocations were incorrect. The $50,000 sale price of stock should have been entirely allocated to principal. The stock dividend should have been entirely allocated to principal. The interest received should have been allocated to principal if it was accrued prior to the trust creation on January 1, 19X3. Three thousand dollars of the interest had been accrued and should have been allocated to principal with the remainder allocated to income in 19X3. The mortgage amortization payments should have the interest portion allocated to income and the remainder allocated to principal.

c. The court will not terminate the trust at the beneficiaries' request if the trust's purposes have not been accomplished.

5.

a. Strong will not succeed in a suit against Apex for subletting the factory to Egan, unless explicitly prohibited by the lease terms subleases and assignments are acceptable.

b. Zone is not correct in the claim that neither Apex nor Egan had an insurable interest in the factory at the time of the loss. Lessees and sublessees do have insurable interests in the property.

c. Strong will be able to recover $150,000 from Range. The ratio of the policy's face value over the required amount of insurance is $400,000/480,000. This ratio is multiplied by the $180,000 in damages to the property to yield a recovery of $150,000.

d. Lane will recover only $125,000. The $400,000 available for the mortgagees will be used first to satisfy in full Ace's unrecorded claim of $275,000 before any payment to Lane. Ace's unrecorded claim is superior to Lane's claim in this situation because of the "Notice-Race" statute and Lane's knowledge that Ace's mortgage existed prior to Lane's mortgage.

TEST 1: SOLUTIONS
AUDIT

1. **D** Audit planning involves developing an overall strategy for the expected conduct and scope of the audit. One important factor is the extent to which the work of internal auditors is considered, and one of the procedures that should be performed by an external auditor is determining the extent of involvement of the client's internal auditors. Obtaining a representation letter, examining documents to detect illegal acts, and considering the reasonableness of client's estimates are all procedures performed as part of the audit, but are not part of the planning.

2. **C** Without adequate accounting records, the auditor would be unable to gather sufficient, competent evidential matter upon which to base an opinion. While the complexity of the client's accounting system, existence of related party transactions, and operating effectiveness of the client's internal control affect the evidence gathered by the auditor, these factors would ordinarily not preclude a financial statement audit from being conducted.

3. **A** Communication between the predecessor and successor auditor should be initiated by Hill, the successor auditor. While the client must authorize any communications between the predecessor and successor auditor, client personnel would not initiate this communication.

4. **A** The pre-audit conference between the senior auditor and audit team focuses on providing staff with guidance about the technical and personnel aspects of the audit. While issues relating to time budgets and the need for specialists and internal auditors may be discussed during the pre-audit conference, these are not the primary purposes of the conference. Any disagreements with technical issues would arise during the audit examination, which occurs after the pre-audit conference.

5. **A** The second, or wrap-up, review of working paper is performed after the completion of field work and focuses on the overall presentation of the financial statements and the ability of the audit procedures to support the auditor's opinion.

6. **B** Prior-year working papers and information contained in the permanent file would provide the auditor with an understanding of a continuing client's business. While industry journals would also provide this information, this source would be more appropriate in the audit of a new, not continuing, audit client. Evaluating the client's internal control and performing tests of details would be done after obtaining an understanding of the client's business.

7. **A** The methods used by the entity to process accounting information influence the design of the client's internal control. While both audit risk and materiality are considered in the planning stages of the audit, these judgments are made by auditors independent of the methods used to process accounting information. The audit objectives remain the same in all audits, regardless of the methods used by clients to process accounting information.

8. C Inherent risk and control risk relate to the susceptibility of an account balance to misstatement and the effectiveness of the client's internal control, respectively. These risks exist independently of the auditor's procedures, cannot be changed at the auditor's discretion, and are unaffected by the misapplication of auditing procedures. The misapplication of auditing procedures affects the level of detection risk. All three types of risk can be assessed by the auditor in either quantitative or nonquantitative terms.

9. D Audit risk is the risk that a material misstatement will occur in an account balance, not be prevented or detected by the client's internal control, and not be detected by the auditor's substantive testing procedures. The result of audit risk is that financial statements could contain a material misstatement. Due to audit risk the auditor can provide reasonable assurance, but not absolute assurance, that the financial statements are free of material misstatements.

10. B If the auditor's assessment of control risk is increased, the auditor feels that the client's internal control is less effective in preventing or detecting misstatements than originally anticipated. This would indicate that the auditor is willing to accept a lower level of detection risk and would need to perform more effective substantive testing procedures. The levels of inherent risk and materiality are assessed independently of the client's internal control.

11. B Because of interrelationships among the financial statements, the auditor considers materiality in terms of the **smallest** level of misstatements that could be material to any one of the financial statements. Materiality judgments are related to the presentation of the financial statements according to GAAP and the needs of reasonable people who rely on the financial statements. In addition, any judgments of materiality should consider both quantitative and qualitative factors.

12. C When illegal acts have been identified by the auditor, the implications of these illegal acts on the reliability of any representations received from management should be considered. This would be of particular concern in situations where the board of directors did not take action with respect to identified illegal acts.

13. D The lack of proper documentation to support transactions indicates the possible existence of material misstatements. Material misstatements would ordinarily be more likely when management places **high** emphasis on meeting earnings projections and when major decisions are dominated by a **single person** within the organization. While reportable conditions represent deficiencies in the internal control, they are not considered to have the potential to result in material financial statement misstatements.

14. D Analytical procedures allow the auditor to identify differences from expectations, such as the existence of unusual relationships within the financial statements. When unusual relationships exist, the auditor would investigate the cause and likely discover the recording of journal entries involving unusual combinations of expense and revenue accounts.

15. C While encouraged, engagement letters are not required in audits conducted according to generally accepted auditing standards. Preparing written audit programs, agreeing the client's accounting records with the financial statements, and identifying the basis for assessing control risk at less than the maximum are all required forms of documentation in an audit conducted in accordance with generally accepted auditing standards.

16. D The purpose of an audit program is to summarize the procedures considered necessary to accomplish the objectives of the audit. Audit programs ensure that the evidence gathered by the auditor supports conclusions on the fairness of the financial statements. Audit procedures can be performed at either the interim period or at year-end, whichever is deemed more appropriate. Inherent risk may be assessed at either high or low levels, depending on the susceptibility of an account balance to misstatement. Making constructive suggestions to management to improve its internal control is normally done in an audit, but this is not as important as gathering evidence on the fairness of the financial statements.

17. C The permanent file of an auditor's working papers includes information that is expected to be useful in both current and future audits. Examples include bond indenture agreements, lease agreements, and flowcharts of the internal control. In contrast, the working trial balance would only be of interest in the current year's audit.

18. B In an attest engagement, a practitioner issues a conclusion about another party's written assertion. In order to perform an attest engagement on an entity's internal control over financial reporting, management must present its written assertion about the effectiveness of its internal control. This assertion can be provided to shareholders in a general-use document, such as the annual report. Attest engagements on an entity's internal control over financial reporting can be performed regardless of the intended reliance to be placed on the internal control in an audit and whether or not the auditor has performed an audit of the client's financial statements.

19. B Auditors may draft an entity's financial statements and make suggestions about the form and content of the entity's financial statements. The statements are the responsibility of the client's management, however, not the auditor. The auditor's responsibility is limited to expressing an opinion on the fairness of the financial statements based on the audit.

20. A When departures from GAAP are noted in a review engagement, the accountant should disclose these departures in a separate paragraph of the review report. When departures from GAAP cannot be adequately disclosed in the review report and the client refuses to revise the financial statements, the accountant should withdraw from the review engagement and not provide any further services with respect to the financial statements. A special report or a report with limited distribution would not be appropriate in this circumstance.

21. A The auditor's responsibility in an audit conducted according to generally accepted auditing standards is to provide reasonable assurance of detecting errors and irregularities having a material effect on the client's financial statements.

22. D When an accountant submits unaudited financial statements to clients or to others, the financial statements must be accompanied by an appropriate compilation or review report. An accountant submits financial statements when the accountant has generated them, either manually or through the use of computer software. An accountant is not submitting financial statements by typing client-prepared financial statements, providing a client with a financial statement format, or proposing correcting journal entries.

23. A In an engagement to perform agreed-upon procedures to prospective financial statements, the users of the prospective financial statements assist in determining the scope of the engagement. The distribution of any report resulting from this type of engagement should be limited to the specified users who participated in determining the scope of the engagement. This type of report does not provide negative assurance, but provides a summary of the accountant's procedures and findings.

24. C The primary purpose of establishing quality control policies and procedures for deciding whether to accept a new client is to minimize the likelihood of association with clients whose management lacks integrity. Auditors do not attest to the reliability of their clients nor do they have an obligation to the public with respect to the acceptance of new clients. The type of opinion on the financial statements is not considered until after the field work has been performed.

25. B When considering how the work of internal auditors affects the external audit examination, the external auditors should consider the competence, objectivity, and work performance of the internal auditors. An internal auditor's competence would be evidenced by their educational background and certification. The organizational level to which internal auditors report, policies preventing internal auditors from auditing areas where relatives are employed, and access to sensitive records and information are related to the objectivity of the internal audit function.

26. D Proper segregation of duties divides the responsibilities of authorizing a transaction, having custody of any related assets, recording the transaction, and reconciling the related accounts. This prevents individuals from committing errors or irregularities and concealing them. Journalizing entries and preparing financial statements, recording cash receipts and cash disbursements, and establishing internal control policies and authorizing transactions are not incompatible duties as they do not permit an employee to commit and conceal an error or irregularity.

27. B While deviations from control procedures increase the risk of material misstatement in the financial statements, these deviations do not necessarily result in material misstatements of the same magnitude. In general, deviations from internal control procedures at a given rate would ordinarily be expected to result in misstatements at a lower rate. Because of the large size of most internal control populations, the population size has almost no effect on sample size. A direct, not an inverse, relationship exists between the expected population deviation rate and the sample size. The tolerable rate is determined based on the auditor's anticipated reliance on the internal control and does not consider either the detection risk or the sample size.

28. B The primary purpose of the auditor's understanding of the internal control is to determine the nature, timing, and extent of substantive tests. The auditor is therefore interested in determining whether internal control policies and procedures affect management's financial statement assertions.

29. C The control environment is the element of the internal control that reflects management's attitude about the importance of the internal control. One example of a control environment factor is the existence of personnel policies and procedures. Detection risk reflects the nature, timing, and extent of the auditor's substantive tests and is not a part of the client's control environment or the internal control.

30. B The primary purpose of the auditor's understanding of the internal control and assessment of control risk is to determine the nature, timing, and extent of substantive tests. This is done to limit audit risk to a reasonably low level, reducing the possibility that material misstatements exist in the financial statements. Tests of controls are performed after the assessment of control risk. Collusion and management override are inherent limitations of any internal control.

31. A In performing tests of controls, the auditor may inquire of client personnel, observe client employees, inspect documentary evidence, or re-perform the procedure to determine the operating effectiveness of control policies and procedures. Analytical procedures, confirmation, and calculation are examples of methods used by the auditor when performing substantive tests.

32. C When control risk is assessed at less than the maximum, the auditor will identify specific control policies and procedures that are likely to prevent or detect material misstatements. Analytical procedures and tests of details of transactions and account balances are substantive tests that will be performed after the auditor's final assessment of control risk. If the effort necessary to perform tests of controls exceeds the expected reduction in substantive testing, the auditor will normally assess control risk at the maximum level.

33. A When an auditor assesses control risk too high, it indicates that the internal control can be relied upon to a greater degree than the auditor has decided to rely upon it. This will occur if the sample selected in a test of controls includes a higher proportionate number of errors than those included in the population. As a result, the test will not support the auditor's planned assessment of control risk even though a sample that is more reflective of the population would support such an assessment.

34. C Remittance listings represent a record of cash received from the organization's customers for sales made on account. This document contains the customer's account number along with the amount of cash received from the customer. One copy of the remittance listing should be used by the accounts receivable bookkeeper to update the subsidiary accounts receivable records.

35. D For effective segregation of duties, the write-off of uncollectible accounts receivable should be authorized by an individual who has no other responsibilities with respect to accounts receivable. Since the accounts receivable department records accounts receivable transactions and the credit department authorizes sales to customers on account, neither of these departments should approve write-offs. The treasurer would normally approve write-offs.

36. D Comparing control totals for shipping documents and invoices will assist in determining that all goods shipped have been billed. Using computer controls to verify the mathematical accuracy of sales invoices will assist in detecting errors on billings. Matching shipping documents with approved sales orders will assist in determining that all goods shipped were based on authorized sales. All of these procedures enable a company to detect errors in the billing process. Reconciling control totals for sales invoices with the accounts receivable subsidiary ledger, enables the company to determine that all invoices have been recorded, but this does not relate to errors in the billing process.

37. C An important characteristic of a batch processing system is that a delay normally exists between the creation of a transaction and its processing. As a result, any misstatements resulting from incorrect programs or data may not be detected immediately. The rejection of transactions because of errors in other transactions would not affect the timeliness of error detection. Input controls are commonly used in both batch and interactive systems. In addition, like interactive systems, the processing of all transactions is uniform.

38. A Limit tests are controls where information is compared against some upper or lower amount for reasonableness. A validity check is an example of a computer hardware control where an item is compared to a list of all possible valid structures to determine if input data were properly coded. Both of these tests are commonly used to ensure the reliability of data processing.

39. B By tracing entries in the voucher register to the supporting documents, the auditor can verify that the entries recorded are all supported by actual transactions, testing the assertion of existence or occurrence. To test completeness, the auditor would select from the supporting documents and trace a sample to the voucher register, determining that all transactions have been recorded.

40. D In examining invoices received from vendors, the vouchers payable department will match the invoice with the receiving report and approve the invoice for payment. Once the invoice has been examined, the account distribution could also be provided on the voucher itself to assist in record keeping. In contrast, unused prenumbered purchase orders and receiving reports would be accounted for in purchasing and receiving, the departments that issue these documents.

41. D Restricting access to equipment relates to safeguarding of assets, but does not concern the initiation and execution of equipment transactions. The approval of major repairs, use of prenumbered purchase orders, and solicitation of competitive bids are all related to the initiation of equipment transactions.

42. D The purpose of tests of controls is to verify the operating effectiveness of the organization's internal control policies and procedures that have been placed in operation. Substantive tests are used to detect material misstatements in account balances.

43. B To verify that goods shipped are properly billed, the auditor would locate evidence of shipment, usually a shipping document, and trace it to a sales invoice. Scanning the sales journals and comparing accounts receivable ledgers to sales summaries will provide evidence only about sales that were billed, but would not provide evidence indicating that shipments may not have been billed. By inspecting unused sales invoices, the auditor can determine that there are no missing invoices which might indicate unrecorded, but not unbilled, sales.

44. C Reportable conditions are significant deficiencies in the design or operation of the client's internal control, which could affect the organization's ability to record, process, summarize, and report financial data. Reportable conditions do not necessarily represent irregularities, intentional distortions of the financial statements, or illegal acts committed by client personnel. In addition, reportable conditions do not necessarily suggest potential going-concern uncertainties.

45. C The auditor's communication of reportable conditions should state that the communication is intended solely for the use and information of the audit committee, management, and others within the organization. Scope limitations are the result of the inability to perform substantive testing procedures. Reportable conditions may be detected by auditors without performing tests of controls and may be communicated by the auditor at any time during the examination.

46. A An accountant's report regarding management's written assertion about the effectiveness of its internal control would mention the inherent limitations of the internal control. Management's assertion can be based on any reasonable criteria for effective internal control established by a recognized body, not only the AICPA. Snow's tests in an engagement to examine management's written assertion about the effectiveness of its internal control will not relate to the nature, timing, and extent of substantive tests nor enable Snow to form an opinion on the entity's financial statements.

47. D The more effective an internal control, the more reliable the accounting data and financial statements prepared under that internal control. Information obtained directly by the auditor or obtained directly from outside parties is more reliable than information obtained indirectly from outside parties. To be reliable, evidence is normally persuasive rather than convincing. Sufficiency, not reliability, relates to the amount of corroborative evidence obtained.

48. A The computation of standard overhead rates is directly related to the valuation of a manufacturing entity's inventory. Obtaining confirmation of inventories pledged under loan agreements primarily relates to the presentation and disclosure of inventories. Reviewing shipping and receiving cutoff procedures and tracing test counts to the entity's inventory listing are related to the completeness assertion.

49. C The existence and ownership of a long-term investment would be determined by inspecting the securities or confirming the shares held by an independent custodian. Inspecting the audited financial statements of the investee company and determining if the investment is accounted for at the lower of cost or market both relate to the valuation of the investment. It is not ordinarily feasible for the auditor to confirm ownership of shares with the investee company.

50. A Reviewing credit ratings of customers with delinquent accounts will provide the auditor with information about the ultimate collectibility of those accounts. This is most closely related to the valuation or allocation assertion, since accounts receivable are presented at net realizable value.

51. A The auditor's primary motivation for determining that proper amounts of depreciation are expensed is to verify the valuation or allocation assertion. In addition, the auditor makes certain that the depreciation is properly presented and that the appropriate disclosures are made, obtaining assurance about management's assertion of presentation and disclosure.

52. B Negative accounts receivable confirmations are a less reliable form of evidence than positive confirmations. This form should be used when the combined assessed level of inherent risk and control risk is low. Positive confirmations are more appropriate for higher assessed levels of inherent risk and control risk and for situations when a large number of errors are expected. Confirmations do not provide any evidence regarding the operating effectiveness of internal control policies and procedures and, therefore, would not be employed as a dual-purpose test.

53. A By confirming with vendors with whom the entity has previously done business, the auditor can determine that there are no unrecorded transactions that should be included in accounts payable. This assists the auditor in determining that the amount reported as accounts payable is complete. Confirming amounts in the accounts payable subsidiary ledger or represented by invoices filed in the open invoice file would provide evidence of the existence or occurrence and valuation and allocation assertions. While examining checks drawn in the month after year-end may allow the auditor to identify unrecorded accounts payable, some items may be paid subsequent to this and it would not ordinarily

serve as the most appropriate population for confirmation.

54. C Variables sampling would be used to estimate a numerical measurement of a population, such as a dollar value. Attributes sampling and stop-or-go sampling are normally used to estimate a rate of occurrence or deviation in a population. Random number sampling is a method used to select sample items and can be employed under either variables or attribute sampling.

55. B One of the advantages of stratifying a sample is that different sampling methods can be employed with different strata. In cases in which unusually large cash disbursements exist, the auditor could establish the strata in such a manner that all items in one strata are selected for examination. A lower tolerable deviation rate would affect the auditor's sample size for tests of controls, not substantive tests. Increasing the sample size would result in a larger number of items being selected, but the large disbursements are not necessarily more likely to be selected. Drawing additional samples to select the desired items violates the basic assumptions of statistical sampling.

56. B In determining the sample size for a substantive test of details, the auditor would consider both the expected amount of misstatements and a measure of tolerable misstatement. The amount of expected misstatements has a direct effect on sample size and the amount of tolerable misstatement an inverse effect on sample size.

57. D When evaluating the reasonableness of an accounting estimate, the auditor should concentrate on any factors or assumptions that deviate from historical patterns. Deviations from historical patterns may represent situations where management is attempting to influence the financial statements through changing estimates. Any factors or assumptions that are consistent with prior periods, similar to industry guidelines, or objective and not susceptible to bias do not indicate potential concerns to the auditor.

58. B A high level of control risk would indicate that the auditor will not rely on the internal control in relation to inventory. As a result, there would be no need to increase the tests of controls of the inventory cycle. The auditor would desire to verify the inventory amounts presented on the financial statements, which could best be accomplished if a physical count is performed at the balance sheet date. Only if control risk is low, could the auditor inspect inventory counts throughout the year. While gross profit tests can be applied by the auditor, physical counts of inventory should still be observed.

59. D The auditor will compare payroll costs with entity standards or budgets to determine if payroll is reasonable. A significant difference from expected results will alert the auditor to a potential problem. The auditor may observe a payroll distribution to be certain that the employees exist, but this can be accomplished by other procedures. Unclaimed checks should be maintained by the entity in a secure place, not mailed to employees. Individual employee deductions would be reflected in the payroll journal, not general journal entries.

60. C A common procedure performed for long-term bonds payable is verifying the reasonableness of the interest expense account. The auditor would normally recalculate the bond premium and discount accounts and not verify these through performing analytical procedures. Examining documentation of liens on assets would be performed in the audit of the related asset accounts, not long-term bonds payable. The auditor ordinarily confirms the existence of bonds with the trustee, not the individual bondholders.

61. D When examining the granting of stock options, the auditor's primary concern is that this transaction has been properly authorized. Granting stock options is normally authorized by the company's board of directors.

62. D By analyzing the repairs and maintenance account, the auditor is examining all items charged to expense by the company during the period, allowing the auditor to identify any expenditures for property and equipment that have been improperly charged to expense. To determine that all noncapitalizable expenditures are recorded in the proper period, the auditor would need to analyze items recorded in the current period, as well as the previous and subsequent periods. To determine whether noncapitalizable expenditures have been properly charged to expense, the auditor should investigate items recorded in the property and equipment account during the period.

63. C The auditor's primary concern with respect to performing interim tests is controlling the incremental audit risk between the interim date and the balance sheet date. Neither inherent risk nor materiality affect the auditor's ability to perform interim tests. While interim tests are normally more appropriate when control risk is assessed at less than the maximum level, auditors can perform interim tests when control risk is assessed at the maximum level as long as the audit conclusions can be extended to the balance-sheet date.

64. C At the conclusion of the audit, the auditor obtains written representations from the client's management. Among the topics that are ordinarily discussed in those representations is the existence of any violations of laws and regulations that may result in the recognition of a loss contingency.

65. D When using a specialist, the auditor is required to obtain an understanding of the methods and assumptions used by the specialist. The auditor is not required to corroborate the specialist's findings through performing substantive tests. Both the client and the specialist should have an understanding of the nature of the specialist's work and the auditor's use of the specialist's findings.

66. B A letter of inquiry from the client's attorney provides the auditor with corroboration of the information furnished by management about litigation, claims, and assessments, which is the auditor's primary source of information about such items. While the potential outcome of claims and pending litigation may be discussed in the letter of inquiry, this is not the primary reason the auditor obtains the letter from the attorney. The letter would not ordinarily provide the attorney's opinions of the client's historical experience with respect to litigation, claims, and assessments.

67. B The auditor's purpose for dual-dating a report is to limit responsibility for events occurring after the last day of field work. When a report is dual-dated, the auditor's responsibility for these events is limited to the specific event

that serves as the basis for the dual-dating. The auditor's responsibility for all other subsequent events is the date of the audit report, which is the last day of field work.

68. D The competence and objectivity of an entity's internal auditor can be assessed through discussions with management personnel, external quality reviews of the internal auditor's activities, and prior experience with the internal auditor. Analytical procedures are a form of substantive test and would not provide the external auditor with information about the competence and objectivity of the internal audit function.

69. C The auditor should obtain an understanding of the business purpose of any related party transactions to determine that the economic substance of the transactions are disclosed. Related party transactions would not cause a modification of the auditor's report unless these transactions were not properly disclosed or recorded. Analytical procedures would ordinarily not be effective in identifying unrecorded, related party transactions, as these types of transactions are generally nonrecurring. The auditor has no obligation to substantiate that any related party transactions were consummated at arm's length.

70. A An integrated test facility combines fictitious transactions and real transactions to examine the client's processing of transactions. A parallel simulation also examines the processing of transactions, but does not involve client personnel since a program created by the auditor is used. An input controls matrix and data entry monitor are input controls, not computer-assisted audit techniques.

71. A Among the factors that may cause an auditor to have substantial doubt about an entity's ability to continue in existence are negative cash flows from operating activities. The existence of related party transactions, postponement of research and development projects, and use of stock, as opposed to cash, dividends may be indicative of going-concern problems but are not individually significant enough to cause the auditor to have substantial doubt.

72. C The auditor's working trial balance will contain columns for any reclassifications and adjustments noted during the audit examination. Information about cash flows is not normally contained on a working trial balance. The audit objectives and assertions form the basis for the audit program and do not appear in the working trial balance. Reconciliations and tickmarks would appear on the actual working papers supporting the amounts contained in the working trial balance.

73. D The representation letter is ordinarily obtained by the auditor at the conclusion of the audit examination. It would not influence the quantity and content of the auditor's working papers. The condition of the client's records, assessed level of control risk, and nature of the auditor's report all affect the evidence gathered by the auditor and, therefore, would influence the working papers.

74. A In a review engagement of a nonpublic entity's financial statements, the auditor performs inquiry and analytical procedures. Comparing the financial statements with anticipated results and studying the relationship among financial statement elements are types of analytical procedures. No understanding of the entity's internal control is contemplated during this type of engagement.

75. B The auditor should obtain representations from management during a review engagement. Other than inquiries and analytical procedures, the auditor does not perform substantive tests during a review. Sending bank confirmations and examining subsequent cash disbursements would not be appropriate. Since the auditor does not obtain an understanding of the client's internal control during a review, reportable conditions would not be identified based on the auditor's assessment of control risk.

76. D A disclaimer of opinion is appropriate when the auditor is associated with the financial statements of a publicly held company, but has not audited or reviewed the statements.

77. D Prior to reissuing a report on the financial statements of a former client, a predecessor auditor should consider whether the opinion on those financial statements is still appropriate. In doing so, the predecessor auditor will obtain a letter of representations from the successor auditor to determine whether any matters in the current audit affect the predecessor's previous opinion on the financial statements.

78. C When the accountant feels that there is reasonable justification for a change in the scope of an engagement from an audit to a review, the review report should not refer to the scope limitation that caused the change or the original engagement that was to be performed.

79. C When the current period financial statements of a nonpublic entity have been reviewed and those of the prior period have been audited, the accountant can either reissue the prior period report or include a paragraph in the current report describing the responsibility assumed for the prior period financial statements. This paragraph should indicate that no auditing procedures were performed after the date of the previous report.

80. B   In a compilation, the accountant presents the representations of management in the form of financial statements. While a compilation is not designed to detect material misstatements and is less in scope than an audit, statements to that effect are not included in a compilation report. Inquiries of company personnel and analytical procedures are performed in a review engagement, not a compilation.

81. A   Accountants may compile financial statements for a client using a comprehensive basis of accounting other than GAAP. The accountant will include a paragraph in the compilation report disclosing the basis of accounting and indicating that it is not GAAP. A special report would be appropriate only when the financial statements prepared using a comprehensive basis of accounting other than GAAP have been audited.

82. A   Financial statements that omit substantially all disclosures required by GAAP may still be compiled, but the accountant should indicate that the financial statements are not designed for individuals who are not informed about these matters. Compiled financial statements that omit substantially all disclosures required by GAAP are not considered to be special purpose financial statements.

83. C   An accountant's compilation report on a financial forecast should indicate that differences between the forecasted and actual results will usually occur. Forecasts can be read and used apart from the historical financial statements. In addition, the accountant does not provide any assurance on the forecasted financial statements or the assumptions used to prepare these statements in a compilation engagement.

84. B   During an audit, certain matters should be communicated to the client's audit committee. The matters to be communicated include the process used by management in formulating sensitive accounting judgments. The basis for assessing control risk at below maximum, the auditor's preliminary judgments about materiality, and justification for performing substantive tests at interim dates are not communicated to the audit committee.

85. C   Under *Government Auditing Standards,* auditors are required to examine the governmental entity's compliance with the requirements of federal financial assistance programs. When instances of noncompliance are detected that have a material effect on the program, the report on compliance should express a qualified or adverse opinion.

86. A   When a material inconsistency exists between other information presented in an annual report to shareholders and the audited financial statements, the auditor should determine whether the financial statements, the other information, or both require revision. If the financial statements do not require revision, but the client refuses to revise the other information, the report should be modified to describe the material inconsistency in the other information. The auditor's opinion on the financial statements, however, is not affected by inconsistencies in the other information.

87. B When reporting on condensed financial statements derived from a public entity's audited financial statements, the CPA will indicate that the complete financial statements were audited and an opinion on them was expressed. In addition, the CPA's report will indicate whether the condensed financial statements are fairly stated in relation to the audited financial statements from which they have been derived.

88. A When auditing the financial statements of a U.S. entity prepared in conformity with accounting principles generally accepted in another country, the auditor should obtain an understanding of the accounting principles generally accepted in that country. The auditor may issue an opinion on the financial statements, as long as both U.S. GAAS and the general and fieldwork standards of the other country can be observed. The auditor is not required to be certified for practice in the other country, nor does the auditor need to receive a waiver to perform an engagement on financial statements prepared in conformity with accounting principles of another country.

89. A When facts existing at the report date become known after issuance of the auditor's report, the auditor should first determine whether persons relying or likely to rely on the financial statements would find the newly discovered facts important. If so, the auditor would then suggest that the client's management disclose the newly discovered information to individuals relying on or likely to rely on the financial statements.

90. D A performance audit under *Government Auditing Standards* requires a statement of the audit objectives and description of the audit scope, indications of any illegal acts that could result in criminal persecution, and the views of the entity's officials concerning the auditor's findings. A concurrent opinion on the financial statements taken as a whole is not required in a performance audit.

91. E, I When the auditor uses a specialist and the specialist's findings corroborate information presented in the client's financial statements, a standard unqualified opinion would be issued.

92. A, B The failure to reduce the value of a note receivable to its net realizable value is an example of a departure from generally accepted accounting principles. Either a qualified or adverse opinion would be issued, with the effects of the departure from GAAP disclosed in a paragraph preceding the opinion paragraph.

93. B, C The inability to observe year-end inventory balances may preclude the auditor from issuing an opinion on the entity's financial statements or require the issuance of an "except for" qualified opinion, depending upon the materiality of the inventory. The scope limitation would be discussed in an explanatory paragraph preceding the opinion paragraph and the scope and opinion paragraphs would be modified.

94. E, A When supplementary information required by the FASB or GASB is omitted, the auditor would identify the omission of this information in an explanatory paragraph. Omission of this information, however, does not require modification of the auditor's opinion on the financial statements.

95. A, B The failure to disclose long-term lease obligations is an example of a departure from generally accepted accounting principles. Either a qualified or adverse opinion, would be issued, with the effects of the departure from GAAP disclosed in a paragraph preceding the opinion paragraph.

96. E, H When a division of responsibility is indicated in the auditor's report, the circumstances are described in the introductory, scope, and opinion paragraphs. The auditor still issues an unqualified opinion and an explanatory paragraph would not be added to the auditor's report.

97. E, A When a change in accounting principle occurs, and the auditor agrees with the change, an unqualified opinion is appropriate. The change in accounting principle is mentioned in an explanatory paragraph following the opinion paragraph.

98. E, A As long as the circumstances have been adequately disclosed in the client's financial statements, an auditor is not precluded from issuing an unqualified opinion when substantial doubt exists about an entity's ability to continue in existence. The auditor's doubts about continued existence should be disclosed in an explanatory paragraph following the opinion paragraph.

99. D The auditor can verify the "balance per bank" by confirming this balance directly with the bank or comparing it to the balance on the cutoff bank statement.

100. A The deposits in transit should be traced to the cash receipts journal, with any unusual delays noted. The auditor would then trace deposits in transit on the bank reconciliation to deposits in transit returned with the cutoff bank statement to determine that all deposits listed on the reconciliation are legitimate (existence or occurrence). By tracing deposits in transit returned with the cutoff bank statement to those listed on the bank reconciliation, the auditor can verify that all deposits in transit are listed on the reconciliation (completeness). Finally, for any deposits in transit not returned with the cutoff bank statement, the auditor should examine supporting documents.

101. B The outstanding checks should be traced to the cash disbursements journal, with any unusual delays noted. The auditor would then trace outstanding checks on the bank reconciliation to outstanding checks returned with the cutoff bank statement to determine that all checks listed on the reconciliation are legitimate (existence or occurrence). By tracing outstanding checks returned with the cutoff bank statement to those listed on the bank reconciliation, the auditor can verify that all outstanding checks are listed on the reconciliation (completeness). Finally, for any outstanding checks not returned with the cutoff bank statement, the auditor should examine supporting documents.

102. E For notes collected by the bank, the auditor should investigate bank credit memos.

103. E Because the bank deducted an excessive amount for check #1282, they would increase (credit) the account, as evidenced by a credit memorandum. In addition, the auditor would trace the reconciling item from the client's bank reconciliation to information received with the cutoff bank statement.

104. C The balance per books should be compared to the general ledger balance.

4.

a. The purpose of applying analytical procedures (APs) in the planning stages of the audit is to assist the auditor in planning the nature, timing, and extent of substantive tests. APs used in the planning stages of the audit should focus on enhancing the auditor's understanding of the client's business and the transactions and events occurring since the last audit date and identifying areas that may represent specific risks relevant to the audit.

b. In deciding whether to use APs as substantive tests of details to achieve an audit objective, the auditor considers the level of assurance to be obtained and whether APs can provide that level of assurance. Factors that affect the effectiveness and efficiency of APs include the nature of the assertion examined, the plausibility and predictability of the relationship, the availability and reliability of data used to develop the expectation used in performing APs, and the precision of that expectation.

c. The auditor's objective of using APs in the overall review stage of the audit is to allow the auditor to assess the conclusions reached and evaluate the client's overall financial statement presentation. The overall review would include considering the adequacy of evidence gathered in response to unusual or unexpected balances identified by APs in the planning stages or during the course of the audit. In addition, the auditor should investigate any unusual or unexpected balances identified by APs that were not noted in earlier stages of the audit.

5.

Credit Manager

1. No formal process is used to authorize credit to customers.

2. Multiple copies of the charge form, which authorizes sales to a customer on account, should be prepared.

Accounts Receivable Supervisor

1. The charge form should be submitted to the billing department for invoice preparation.

2. The accounts receivable supervisor should not have responsibility for both recording sales on account and invoice preparation.

3. Multiple copies of the invoice should be prepared.

4. No reconciliation of the subsidiary accounts receivable and control accounts receivable is performed.

Cashier

1. Cash should be received in the mail by someone other than the cashier.

2. A separate remittance listing should be prepared upon receipt of the cash.

3. The cashier should not have access to the cash receipts and have responsibility for reconciling the bank accounts.

Bookkeeper

1. The bookkeeper should not be responsible for sending monthly statements to customers.

2. It does not appear that any formal procedures exist for handling discrepancies between statements and customer records.

3. The bookkeeper should not have responsibility for record keeping and authorizing write-offs to customer accounts.

4. Additional efforts to collect customer accounts should be made.

1. C Measurement focus refers to what is being measured by the information in the financial statements. For the governmental funds, the measurement focus is on the sources and uses or flow of financial resources. It is also on the balance of these resources, indicated by financial position.

2. D Governmental financial reports have the same qualitative characteristics as for-profit enterprise financial reports, including comparability. Differences should be due to substantive differences in underlying transactions or the governmental structure. Similarly designated governments may not perform the same functions. For example, some city governments have school districts as part of the government entity, while others have school districts that are independent government units. Selection of different alternatives in accounting procedures or practices may account for **some** of the differences, but not the more substantive differences.

3. A Proprietary funds are accounted for similarly to businesses operated for profit. As a result, the orientation or measurement focus is income determination.

4. D GASB recommends that governmental fund budgets be prepared on the modified accrual basis of accounting. That is the basis of accounting required of funds that must record the budget, including the general fund, special revenue fund, and debt service fund.

5. A A government should report its equity interest in a joint venture investment as an asset in the general fixed assets account group to the extent that the equity interest exceeds the amount reported in the governmental funds. The general fixed asset account group is where assets acquired by the general fund that must be accounted for are reported.

6. D In a reverse repurchase agreement, a financial institution or broker transfers cash to a governmental entity. The entity transfers securities to the broker and promises to repay the cash plus interest in exchange for the same securities. The governmental entity should disclose the carrying value and market value of the underlying securities under a caption such as "Investments held by broker under reverse repurchase agreements." Neither related assets and liabilities, nor related interest cost and interest earned should be netted. These should all be reported as separate items. Credit risk related to the agreements should also be disclosed.

7. D Fixed assets of a governmental unit, except those accounted for in proprietary funds or trust funds, should be accounted for in the general fixed-assets account group.

8. D Depreciation expense is not recorded in a governmental fund such as a capital projects fund, in an agency fund, or in an expendable trust fund. These funds use the modified accrual basis of accounting and record expenditures, not expenses. Depreciation expense is recorded in the funds that use full accrual accounting, including the enterprise fund, the internal service fund, the nonexpendable trust fund, and the pension trust fund.

9. B When a fixed asset, such as a snowplow, purchased by a governmental unit is received, it should be recorded in the general fund as an expenditure. The fixed asset itself would be recorded in the general fixed assets account group. The encumbrance would be recorded in the general fund when the asset is ordered. The appropriation is recorded at the beginning of the year for the budgeted expenditures.

10. C When a capital lease of a governmental unit represents the acquisition of a general fixed asset, the purchase should be reflected in a governmental fund as a debit to expenditures and a credit to other financing sources. The amount would be the present value of the future lease payments or the fair value of the leased asset, whichever is less.

11. C Operating transfers are reported in the operating statements of governmental funds and proprietary funds. They affect the results of operations of both types of funds.

12. A The debt service fund is used to account for the accumulation of resources for the payment of principal and interest in connection with general long-term debt. Proprietary funds and trust funds that have long-term debt, such as a nonexpendable trust fund and a pension trust fund, have specific debt that would be accounted for and serviced through the funds themselves, not the debt service fund.

13. B Special assessment long-term debt to be repaid from general resources of the government is considered general long-term debt. It should be reported in the general long-term debt account group.

14. A Unmatured principal and interest expenditures on general long-term debt are **not** accrued at year-end. This is the major exception to the general rule of accruing all expenditures when the fund liability is incurred. The reason for the exception is that the debt service fund usually obtains its resources as transfers from other funds when the principal or interest must be paid. The amounts are not expenditures and current liabilities at year-end since they will not require expenditure of existing fund assets but rather future fund assets that will be transferred to the debt service fund.

15. D A government may use either the consumption basis or the purchases basis to account for inventories and prepayments such as prepaid insurance. Under the consumption basis, expenditures are allocated between periods as only the amount used is reported as an expenditure. Under the purchases basis, the amount purchased during the period is reported as an expenditure.

16. B When an enterprise fund bills a general fund for goods or services supplied or rendered, the general fund debits expenditures and credits vouchers payable or due to other funds. The enterprise fund credits revenues and debits due from other funds.

17. B Property taxes receivable can be recognized only with a debit to a receivable account, while collections are recognized with a debit to cash. If either of these occur in advance of the year for which they are levied, the credit cannot be to revenues. The credit will instead be recorded in a deferred revenue account.

18. B The journal entry to record the issuance of the purchase orders and contracts would be:

Encumbrances	850,000	
Reserve for Encumbrances		850,000

19. D Routine employer contributions from the general fund to a pension trust fund would be an expenditure of the general fund. Contribution of enterprise fund capital would be an equity transfer out. Transfers to a capital projects fund and operating subsidy transfers are operating transfers out, which are other financing uses.

20. C Operating transfers received by a governmental fund are other financing sources in the Statement of Revenues, Expenditures, and Changes in Fund Balance.

21. B The proceeds from the sale of revenue bonds of $4,500,000 and the capital contributed by subdividers of $900,000 should both be reported as cash flows from capital and related financing activities, for a total of $5,400,000. Cash received from customer households would be a cash flow from operating activities.

22. D Both state lotteries and state hospitals are activities that should be accounted for in an enterprise fund.

23. B IRC Sec. 457 authorizes state and local governments to establish eligible deferred compensation plans for their employees if the plans meet certain requirements. GASB standards require that the plan assets and liabilities be reported in an agency fund, provided that the plan is not for proprietary fund employees.

24. A When a governmental unit has no obligation in relation to the debt service transactions of a special assessment issue, the governmental unit acts as an agent by collecting the special assessments and making the principal and interest payments. These transactions would be accounted for in an agency fund.

25. A Trust funds can be either expendable or nonexpendable. Special revenue funds and debt service funds are expendable since they are governmental funds. An enterprise fund is nonexpendable since it is a proprietary fund.

26. C When program services costs are combined with fund-raising costs, the total should be allocated between the program services and the fund-raising categories of expenses. No portion should be allocated to general services, eliminating answers A and B. Since D allocates all of the cost to program services, the only logical answer is C.

27. C Contributed services are recorded as both expenses and revenues, in the form of contributions, if (1) they create or enhance nonfinancial assets; or (2) require special skills, are provided by those possessing such skills, and would normally be purchased if not obtained by donation. The replacement of the windows by the professional glazier at no charge, qualifies under the second criterion for recognition as both an expense and a contribution. This entry has no effect on net assets.

28. C Revenues from education programs are reported as other operating revenue for a hospital. Unrestricted gifts are non-operating revenues or gains.

29. D In a voluntary community organization, depreciation expense should be included as an element of expense in the unrestricted net asset section of the activities statement.

30. A Not-for-profit organizations are required to report certain basic information that focuses on the organization as a whole. The basic information would include a statement of financial position, a statement of activities, a statement of cash flows, and accompanying notes. The intent is to eliminate the differences in reporting among colleges, hospitals, voluntary health and welfare organizations, and other not-for-profit organizations, rather than creating or highlighting differences or distinctions.

31. B A corporation, like a sole proprietorship, may deduct 50% of qualifying business meals. There is no problem with the employees being present at the meals.

32. C The dividends received deduction on dividend income from an unaffiliated corporation is 70% of the dividend income, or $35,000. Bad debt expense may only be deducted for tax purposes using the direct write-off method, not the allowance method. As a result, financial statement income will be reduced by the dividends received deduction and increased by the bad debt expense. Taxable income will be $300,000 − $35,000 + $80,000 or $345,000.

33. B A net operating loss (NOL) may be carried back 3 years, then forward 15 years. In this case, the 19X6 $200,000 NOL would be first carried back to 19X3, then 19X4, then 19X5, for a total carryback of $20,000 + $30,000 + $40,000 or $90,000. This leaves $110,000 ($200,000 − $90,000) to be carried forward to 19X7.

34. C Depreciation recapture on tangible personal property used in a business involves reporting the gain on the sale of such property as ordinary income to the extent of the depreciation taken, but limited to the realized gain. The property has an adjusted basis of $100,000 −$47,525 or $52,475. The realized gain is $102,000 − $52,475 or $49,525. Of the $49,525 realized gain, $47,525 would be recaptured as ordinary income, while the remaining $2,000 would be Sec. 1231 gain.

35. C The amount of bond premium that can be amortized for a tax year is calculated under the constant yield to maturity method, also referred to as the interest method for financial reporting purposes. The amortization amount is treated as an offset to the interest income on the bond. Bond owners can elect to amortize the premium and reduce their basis or not amortize the premium and instead treat the premium as part of the bond basis.

36. B An accrual basis employer may deduct bonuses paid to nonshareholder employees in the year of accrual if the bonuses are subsequently paid within 2 1/2 months after the close of the tax year. The exact amount does not have to be determined at the time of declaration of the bonus.

37. D An accrual basis corporation can deduct the amount of charitable contributions actually made during the year plus any amounts authorized during the year by the board of directors if actually paid to the charity by the 15th day of the third month after the close of the tax year. In this case, the contributions total $10,000 + $30,000 or $40,000. This total is less than the limitation of 10% of taxable income, before taking the contribution deduction. The allowable deduction is $40,000.

38. C Qualifying organizational expenditures are costs incurred to form the corporation. They include legal fees for drafting the corporate charter, state incorporation fees, expenses of temporary directors, and organizational meeting costs. They do **not** include professional fees to issue the corporate stock, printing costs to issue the corporate stock, or underwriter's commissions to sell the stock.

39. D For regular tax purposes using MACRS, nonresidential real property is depreciated using the straight-line method over 39 years. The straight-line method over 40 years is used under the alternative depreciation system (ADS) for all real property.

40. D Under the uniform capitalization rules applicable to inventories, off-site storage costs should be capitalized as part of the inventory cost. Marketing costs are expensed.

41. C Zinco's status as a calendar-year S corporation terminated an April 1, 19X3. It was an S corporation **through** March 31 for a total of 90 days. Under the per-day allocation method, the amount of income allocated to the S short year would be $310,250 × 90/365 or $76,500.

42 D S election termination occurs when, for 3 consecutive tax years, the corporation has both accumulated C corporation earnings and profits and passive investment income greater than 25% of gross receipts. An S corporation can have as many as 35 shareholders, can have a decedent's estate as a shareholder, and can flow through charitable contributions to its shareholders for deduction by them.

43. A For the first 40 days of 19X3, Kane owned 100% of Manning Corp for a pro-rata income of $73,000 × 100% × 40/365 or $8,000. For the remainder of the year, Kane owned 75% for a pro-rata income of $73,000 × 75% × 325/365 or $48,750. The total is $8,000 + $48,750 or $56,750.

44. D   An S corporation election must be made within the first 2 1/2 months of the beginning of the corporation's tax year to be effective from the first day of that tax year. The election for Ace Corp., a calendar year corporation, was made on February 10, 19X4. This is within 2 1/2 months of the beginning of the corporation's tax year. The earliest date on which Ace can be recognized as an S corporation is January 1, 19X4.

45. A   To be a personal holding company, at any time during the last half of the taxable year more than 50 percent of the value of the corporation's outstanding stock must be owned, directly or indirectly, by 5 or fewer individuals. Indirect ownership would include those shares owned by an estate where the shareholder is the beneficiary. Indirect ownership would also include those shares owned by family members such as brothers, sisters, a spouse, ancestors, and lineal descendants. In-laws and cousins are not considered family members for the indirect ownership rules. A partnership in which the shareholder is not a partner would also not qualify under the indirect ownership rules.

46. A   Operating losses of one consolidating entity may offset operating profits of another. There is no requirement about issuing audited financial statements in order to file a consolidated tax return. The intercompany dividends are 100% excludable in a consolidated return and the common parent must directly own 80% or more of one of the subsidiaries in order to be able to file a consolidated return.

47. A   In consolidated returns, intercompany dividends between the parent and wholly owned subsidiaries are not taxable. They are 100% eliminated in the consolidation.

48. A   No deduction is allowed for a federal tax penalty, including a corporation's penalty for underpaying federal estimated taxes.

49. A   The general business credit is a combination of several tax credits to provide uniform rules for the current and carryback or carryover years. Some of the credits under the general business credit are the targeted jobs credit, the alcohol fuel credit, and the low-income housing credit.

50. C   Blink Corp. can use 100% of the preceding tax year method **only** if it had a positive tax liability in the preceding year and it consisted of 12 months. In the preceding year Blink had a net operating loss, so it **cannot** use 100% of the preceding tax year method. Blink **can** use the annualized income method for its quarterly payments.

51. C   A corporation recognizes gain on nonliquidating distributions of appreciated property. The gain is calculated as if the property had been sold for its fair market value of $30,000. The amount by which that exceeds the basis of $20,000 is a taxable gain, $10,000 in this case.

52. D   Carr and Beck contributed property solely in exchange for stock and immediately after the exchange they had control in the form of 80% of the ownership of the corporation. Neither will recognize gain or loss on the exchange. Adams, who contributed services, will recognize a $10,000 gain equal to the value received, 10% × $100,000, in exchange for his services.

53. C In a type B, or stock-for-stock reorganization, stock of the target corporation is acquired solely for the voting stock of either the acquiring corporation or its parent. In addition, the acquiring corporation must have control of the target corporation immediately after the exchange. Control requires ownership of 80% or more.

54. C The normal statute of limitations is 3 years from the later of the normal due date, March 15, 19X4, or the filing date, March 11, 19X4. The statute in this case would begin on March 16, 19X4, the day after the normal due date of the return, and end March 15, 19X7, 3 years later.

55. A A tax return preparer may not disclose or use tax return information without the taxpayer's consent except pursuant to a court or administrative order, in connection with the preparation of the tax return, or to be evaluated for quality or peer review. The preparer may not disclose tax return information to enable a third party to solicit business from the taxpayer.

56. B If medical expenses are paid out of an estate they are deductible on the decedent's final income tax return. In order for this to be the case, they must be paid within one year of the date of death and the estate must waive the right to claim the expense as a deduction.

57. D White must include in his taxable income the $3,000 guaranteed payment made to White for services rendered plus 1/3 × $30,000 or $10,000 for a total of $13,000. Guaranteed payments are deductible to arrive at ordinary income.

58. C The alternate valuation date is 6 months after the decedent's death.

59. C A not-for-profit organization such as one for the prevention of cruelty to animals would fail to achieve tax exempt status if it does not meet the operation test by directly participating in any political campaign. Insubstantial nonexempt activities, while they may result in taxable unrelated business income, do not violate the operational test.

60. B An exempt organization is not taxed an unrelated business income (UBI) of less than $1,000. Having UBI in excess of $100,000 does not necessarily jeopardize the organization's tax exempt status. To be UBI, the trade or business must be regularly, not intermittently, carried on. An unrelated business activity that results in a loss is still an unrelated business by definition.

61. C Brink's initial basis in Dex is calculated as follows:

Brink's basis in the land contributed	$12,000
Less: Brink's liability assumed by partnership	(5,000)
	7,000
Add: Brink's share of the liability (20% × $5,000)	1,000
	$ 8,000

62. A Carson's initial basis in Dex is calculated as follows:

Carson's basis in the inventory	$24,000
Add: Carson's share of the liability (30% × $5,000)	1,500
	$25,500

63. B A partner's basis cannot be reduced below zero. The partner will recognize gain to the extent a cash distribution exceeds his basis in the partnership in order to avoid a negative basis.

64. A A nonliquidating distribution of unappreciated inventory reduces the recipient partner's basis in the partnership.

65. A In a liquidating distribution of property other than money, where the partnership's basis in the property exceeds the partner's basis in the partnership, the partner will recognize no gain or loss, but would carry the basis in the partnership to the property. The partner's basis in the distributed property would be limited to his predistribution basis in the partnership.

66. B In a nonliquidating distribution, gain is not recognized on property distribution. In this case, the property's basis to the partner would be limited to his predistribution basis in the partnership.

67. A In a nonliquidating distribution of inventory, where the partnership has no appreciated inventory, the partner's basis in the inventory distributed will be the same as the partnership's basis in the inventory. The amount, however, will be lower if it exceeds the partner's basis in the partnership.

68. B The partnership's nonliquidating distribution of encumbered property to a partner who assumes the liability does affect the other partners' bases. It will decrease partnership liabilities thereby decreasing each partner's basis by his share of that decrease.

69. B, D

Since Mrs. Vick's husband died during 19X3, she can file married filing jointly in 19X3, the year of death of her spouse.

She will receive one exemption for herself and her spouse in 19X3, a third exemption for her dependent daughter, and a fourth exemption for her dependent unmarried cousin who lived with her in 19X3. The support, income, citizenship, and relationship or member of household tests are all met for both the daughter and cousin to be claimed as dependents.

70. D, C

In 19X4 Mrs. Vick is a surviving spouse since she provides over half the cost of maintaining a home in which a dependent son or daughter lives for the entire year and her husband died last year. The surviving spouse filing status can be used for 2 years after the year of death of one's spouse.

She will receive one exemption for herself and 2 dependency exemptions for her daughter and her unmarried cousin who lived with her in 19X4. All of the 5 dependency tests are met for these two individuals.

71. $0 State disability benefits, including workers' compensation, is excludable from income.

72. $400 Interest on tax refunds of $50 and interest on savings accounts and CDs of $350 are taxable, for a total of $400. Interest on municipal bonds is tax-exempt.

73. $900 Pension benefits paid for exclusively by Mrs. Vick's husband's employer are fully taxable.

74. $0 Gifts are excludable from income.

75. $0 Life insurance proceeds are excludable from income.

76. $200 Jury duty pay is taxable as other income.

77. $450 Gambling winnings are taxable as other income.

78. A Premiums on life insurance are not deductible since the proceeds are not taxable.

79. D A penalty on the early withdrawal of funds from a CD is deductible to arrive at adjusted gross income (AGI).

80. F Cash contributions are deductible as an itemized deduction on Schedule A, but are limited to 50% of AGI.

81. E A payment for estimated state income taxes is fully deductible as an itemized deduction on Schedule A.

82. E A payment for real estate taxes on a personal residence is fully deductible as an itemized deduction on Schedule A.

83. A A loss on the sale of personal use assets, like the family car, is not deductible.

84. B To the extent that it exceeds any increase in the value of the residence, the cost of installation of a stairlift in 19X3, related directly to the medical care of Mr. Vick is deductible as a medical expense on Schedule A. It is subject to the 7.5% of AGI floor.

85. B Health insurance premiums are deductible as a medical expense on Schedule A, subject to the 7.5% of AGI floor.

86. C Tax preparation fees are deductible on Schedule A, but are subject to the 2% of AGI floor.

87. E Points paid to refinance the personal home mortgage at a lower rate are amortized over the life of the loan. The amortization is fully deductible as interest expense on Schedule A.

88. D One-half of the self-employment tax paid by Mrs. Vick is deductible to arrive at AGI.

89. E Gambling losses are deductible on Schedule A to the extent of gambling winnings. Since the $100 in gambling losses are less than the $450 in gambling winnings, the losses are fully deductible.

90. C Union dues are unreimbursed employee business expenses and are deductible on Schedule A, subject to the 2% of AGI floor.

91. A Federal income taxes paid are not deductible.

92. B Funeral expenses are not deductible on the income tax return.

93. A Any federal income tax on the income in respect of a decedent (IRD) must be claimed as a miscellaneous deduction and is not subject to the 2% of AGI floor. It is claimed in the same tax year that the income is included in gross income.

94. B A casualty loss deduction on property used in a business is reported as a business deduction to arrive at AGI, not as an itemized deduction.

95. B The Vicks' cannot claim the credit for the elderly or disabled because their AGI is $20,000 or more. In addition, Mr. Vick received nontaxable disability benefits in 19X3, another reason the credit cannot be taken.

96. A One of the preparer's responsibilities is to furnish a completed copy of the tax return to the taxpayer.

97. B The income limitation on the earned income credit applies, even in the year in which one of the spouses dies.

98. B Income in respect of a decedent (IRD) is included in the income of the person to whom the estate properly distributes the right to receive it in the tax year in which it is received. The vacation pay will be included in 19X4.

99. B The minimum tax credit, which is the amount of AMT attributable to "deferral adjustments and preferences," can be used to offset the regular tax liability in the following years. It is not offset against the AMT.

100. B The just-in-time inventory philosophy is characterized by maintaining low levels of inventory and producing inventory for customers based primarily "on demand." Although Isle has no work-in-process inventories, the facts indicate that Isle's production schedules are based on sales forecasts, which is not consistent with the just-in-time philosophy.

101. B Indirect material costs are normally variable in nature and vary directly and proportionately with the number of units produced. They should not be included with standard fixed overhead costs. Indirect material costs are normally considered to be a variable overhead cost.

102. A Since production equipment is necessary for the organization to manufacture its inventory, the operation of this equipment is considered a value-added activity. Nonvalue-added activities represent costs that are not incurred in the production of inventory and do not add to the value of the production process, such as materials handling.

103. A Under activity-based costing, manufacturing costs are allocated to products based on the activities that cause these costs to occur. The primary difference between activity-based costing and traditional standard costing is that, under activity-based costing, multiple activities can be used to allocate different costs to inventory. In cases where different products are produced within a single facility, the use of activity-based costing becomes particularly advantageous.

104. A Regression analysis allows the fixed and variable components of costs to be determined through the fomula $Y = a + bx$. **Y** represents the total cost, **a** the fixed cost, **b** the variable cost per activity, and **x** the level of activity.

105. B For internal reporting purposes, normal spoilage is reflected in the standard cost of nonspoiled units. Normal spoilage costs are not separately calculated nor included in fixed overhead costs.

106. A Since the probability of defective materials and defective workmanship is independent, some units could contain defects of both types. As a result, the total number of spoiled units will be less than 25 in 1,000 and the probability of normal spoilage would be less than 0.025.

107. A The incremental costs associated with the special order are the variable production costs and one-half of the variable selling and administrative costs. Assuming that these costs could be recovered in the selling price charged to Isle's customer, Isle would break even on the contract. Fixed costs are not considered, since these costs are not expected to increase with the acceptance of the special order.

108. B The unfavorable direct labor efficiency variance indicates that the actual direct labor hours worked during 19X3 were greater than standard direct labor hours allowed.

109. B The only difference between net income under absorption costing and variable costing is in the treatment of fixed overhead costs. Under absorption costing, fixed overhead is allocated to units in ending inventory and units sold, while under variable costing, fixed overhead costs are expensed as incurred. Since some of the units produced during the period were included in ending inventory, some of the fixed costs would be included in inventory cost under absorption costing, but expensed under variable costing. As a result, variable costing would show a lower profit.

110. A Since material price variances are recorded when materials are taken from inventory, the sum of the direct materials price and usage variance represents the difference between the standard material costs of producing Aran and the actual material costs of producing Aran. The sum is a net $14,000 unfavorable, consisting of $16,000 unfavorable – $2,000 favorable, the total amount paid for direct materials used for the manufacture of Aran is greater than the standard cost allowed.

111. A The net present value of the operating savings is $12,000 × 5.65 or $67,800. Since the lease investment would require an initial outlay of $60,000, the net present value is $67,800 – $60,000 or $7,800.

112. B The internal rate of return is that interest rate where the present value of expected future cash inflows equals the present value of the cash outflow and the net present value is zero. Since the cost of capital is used to discount the future cash outflows, and since the net present value is positive, the internal rate of return is greater than the cost of capital.

113. B The payback method is considered more appropriate when cash inflows are relatively constant throughout the year and easy to project. Isle's customers' demand for Bute possesses both of these characteristics.

114. B The economic order quantity is adversely affected by uncertain, seasonal demand. Seasonal demand may result in excessive materials being maintained during slack periods and insufficient materials being available during peak production periods. The economic order quantity would be most useful in purchasing raw materials for the production of Bute.

115. A Isle earns a contribution margin of $176,000/$800,000 or 22% on sales of Bute. The contribution margin earned on sales of Cilly is $144,000/$500,000 or 28.8%. Selling a greater amount of Bute and a lesser amount of Cilly would increase the standard dollar breakeven point.

116. C The return on investment for Aran is $0/$1,000,000 or 0%. For Bute it is $41,000/$800,000 or 5.125%. For Cilly it is $36,000/$400,000 or 9%.

117. C When overhead is allocated to products based on expected demand, any instances where expected demand differs greatly from actual demand would result in a large amount of underapplied or overapplied overhead. Since the demand for Cilly is highly seasonal, the amount of overhead applied is likely to differ greatly from actual overhead costs.

118. $1.50 Variable costs vary directly and proportionately with changes in activity. At 80,000 units, Aran's standard cost per unit for variable selling and administrative costs is $120,000/80,000 units or $1.50. Since 75,000 units appear to be in the relevant range of production of Aran, the standard cost per unit for variable selling and administrative costs would also equal $1.50.

119. $140,000 Fixed costs do not vary over levels of activity within the relevant range. At 80,000 units, the fixed selling and administrative costs are $140,000. Since 75,000 units appear to be in the relevant range of production of Aran, the budgeted fixed selling and administrative costs would also equal $140,000.

120. $2,100,000 Assuming that the actual sales mix is achieved, the total breakeven point in sales dollars can be determined by dividing total fixed costs by the contribution margin percentage. Total fixed costs are $1,000,000 − $160,000 or $840,000. The contribution margin percentage is $1,000,000/$2,500,000 or 40%. The breakeven point in sales dollars equals $840,000/0.40 or $2,100,000.

121. $40,000 Direct labor employees would normally be responsible for the use of direct materials and the amount of direct labor hours worked. The total amount of Aran's direct material and labor variances that could be regarded as the responsibility of direct labor employees would be the sum of the direct materials usage variance, $16,000 unfavorable, and the direct labor efficiency variance, $24,000 unfavorable, or $40,000 unfavorable.

122. $440,000 In a graphical analysis, the point at which the total cost line intersects the vertical axis represents the total costs at zero units of activity. This is also the total fixed cost. Aran's total fixed manufacturing costs are $440,000.

1. B Neutrality, along with representational faithfulness and verifiability are the ingredients of reliability, one of the primary qualitative characteristics. The other primary qualitative characteristic is relevance, which includes timeliness, feedback value, and predictive value as the three ingredients.

2. D In the hierarchy of generally accepted accounting principles, the first category includes items that are considered to have the most authoritative support. These items are FASB Statements of Financial Accounting Standards, FASB Interpretations, Accounting Principle Board Opinions, and AICPA Accounting Research Bulletins.

3. D The immediate recognition of a loss contingency involves application of both the matching concept and the concept of conservatism. It is an application of matching in that a loss contingency is recognized, when possible, in the same period in which the event or circumstance that will result in the loss occurred. There is not, however, a direct relationship between the cost and a revenue or benefit. The concept of conservatism applies more directly. It requires that uncertainty and risks inherent in business situations are adequately considered, making it necessary to evaluate the existence of loss contingencies and the probability that they will have an effect on the financial statements.

4. C A company is encouraged, but not required, to provide information about the effect of changing prices. This information will generally be provided in the form of supplementary schedules accompanying the financial statements.

5. A Liquidity and financial flexibility are most easily measured by evaluating a company's assets and the ease with which they can be converted into cash or used for financing purposes. The balance sheet would be most useful in making such an evaluation.

6. D A deferred tax asset or liability is classified similarly to the asset or liability creating the temporary difference. At December 31, 19X3, Thorn will report a noncurrent deferred tax liability of $75,000 related to the accelerated tax depreciation, and a current deferred tax asset of $25,000 related to the additional costs in inventory for tax purposes.

7. C Cash flow per share should not be disclosed with a statement of cash flows. Such information leads users to believe that it represents the amount that may be distributed in the form of dividends and is considered misleading.

8. A The foreign currency translation adjustment is a stockholders' equity valuation account. As a result, Trey's income is $3,600,000 – $2,600,000 or $1,000,000 and income tax expense, at 30% is $300,000. The prepaid taxes should be reclassified to an expense. In addition, the $500,000 due from a customer involves a current asset of $250,000 for the installments due in the next year, and a noncurrent asset of $250,000 for those due later. Total current assets will be $550,000 + $1,650,000 – $250,000 or $1,950,000.

9. C The retained earnings balance of $630,000 will be increased by revenues of $3,600,000 and decreased by expenses of $2,600,000 and taxes of $300,000 for a net increase of $700,000. The resulting balance will be $1,330,000.

10. B An investment in bonds that is to be held to maturity is initially recorded at cost. Any difference between the cost and the face value is amortized as a discount or premium using the effective interest method. As a result, at any balance sheet date, the amount reported will be the cost, net of amortization, or the amortized cost.

11. C The consignment inventory should be reported as inventory, not as a receivable, reducing net accounts receivable by $26,000 to $94,000. The amount to be included in inventory should be the cost. Since profit is 30% of cost, the cost is $20,000 and the profit that has not yet been earned is $6,000. This will increase inventory to $80,000 resulting in total current assets of $70,000 + $94,000 + $80,000 or $244,000.

12. A An entry to write off a specific uncollectible account is recorded with a debit, or decrease, to the allowance and a credit, or decrease, to accounts receivable.

13. D Inventory will include the $90,000 in transit to Herc since it was shipped FOB shipping point prior to the end of the year. The goods awaiting shipment were not yet picked up by the common carrier and should also be included in inventory as of the end of the year. As a result, the correct amount to be reported as inventory will be $1,500,000 + $90,000 + $120,000 or $1,710,000.

14. B Under the lower of cost or market approach, if the original price were lower than the replacement price of inventory, the amount to be reported would be the original price, not the replacement price. In order for the replacement price to be used, however, it must be below the ceiling, which is the net realizable value, and above the floor, which is the net realizable value minus a normal profit.

15. A Since the preferred stock is cumulative, it must be assumed that preferred stockholders will receive a dividend of 10% of par value or $10,000 before any earnings are available to common stockholders. The common stockholders will then be entitled to the remaining $50,000 in earnings. Moss will be entitled to 20% of the preferred amount, or $2,000, and 80% of the common amount, or $40,000, for a total of $42,000.

16. B Although Well owns only 10% of the stock of Rea, being the largest single shareholder and having officers on Rea's board of directors gives Wells the ability to exercise significant influence over the activities of Rea. As a result, the equity method should be used. Under the equity method, the investment of $400,000 will be increased by 10% of Rea's income, or $50,000, and decreased by 10% of the dividends, or $15,000, for a net investment of $435,000.

17. B The excess $200,000 paid upon acquiring Shef would be recorded as goodwill. Costs incurred to maintain goodwill, however, including the $80,000 incurred in 19X3 would be reported as expense. Since the estimated useful life of the goodwill is 40 years as a result of the additional expenditures, amortization will be computed at $5,000 per year, giving a carrying value of $195,000 at 12/31/X3.

18. D With a debit to interest expense of $85,000 and a credit to cash of $68,000, the amount required to balance the transaction would be a credit of $17,000 to accrued interest. Combined with the balance of $15,000 at 12/31/X2, accrued interest at 12/31/X3 would be $32,000.

19. B At the date of acquisition, 2 months had elapsed during the current tax year. As a result, Day would have reported a real estate tax liability of $4,000. In September and October, Day would record real estate taxes, with an increase to the liability, of $2,000 per month or an additional $4,000. When the taxes were paid on 11/1/X3, the liability would be debited for $8,000 and prepaid taxes would be debited for $4,000.

20. A The minimum lease payments include the periodic amount required to be paid, excluding executory costs, along with any guaranteed residual value. The present value of the minimum lease payments is calculated to determine the cost of the asset and the lease obligation.

21. D Regardless of when revenues are collected, they are recognized as they are earned. Since customers are paying $540 for insect control services for the entire year, the amount should be reported as income evenly over the contract year as the services are performed.

22. B Since the $1,000,000 will be paid in installments of $50,000 without interest, the amount to be reported as a liability will be the present value. The present value of the $950,000 to be paid beginning on 1/2/X5 is apparently $418,250, the amount paid for the annuity, while the present value of the $50,000 to be paid on 1/2/X4 is $50,000. As a result, the current portion of the note will be $50,000, while the noncurrent portion will be reported at $418,250.

23. C Since the prize was awarded on 12/31/X3, it would be recognized as expense in 19X2. The amount will be equal to the present value of the payments to be made, including the $50,000 to be paid imminently and the $418,250, which is the present value of the future payments, for a total of $468,250.

24. B Interest for the 6 months ended 6/30/X4 would be $469,500 × 10% × 6/12 or $23,475. The interest to be paid for the period would be $500,000 × 9% × 6/12 or $22,500. The difference of $975 would amortize the discount, increasing the carrying value of the bond to $469,500 + $975 or $470,475.

25. B The balance of $118,000 for advances at 12/31/X2 would be increased by the $184,000 received with orders in 19X3. This total of $302,000 would be reduced by advances applied of $164,000 and by advances on orders canceled of $50,000, which would be either refunded or retained and taken into income. As a result, the ending balance in the liability for customer advances would be $302,000 – $214,000, or $88,000.

26. A Loss contingencies, including those that will occur if a foreign government expropriates company assets, are accrued only when it is probable that the loss will occur and the amount can be reasonably estimated. When the loss is only reasonably possible, it is disclosed but not accrued.

27. D A warranty associated with a product is offered in order to improve the salability of the product. As a result, warranty costs are estimated and recognized in the period of sale, according to the matching concept, rather than at the time that the warranty services are provided.

28. A When stock is issued in a nonmonetary exchange, it is recorded as if it were sold for the fair value of the stock, if known. Since the fair value of the stock is known to be $140 per share, the issuance will be reported at $140,000 with $5,000 reported as the par value of the common stock, and $135,000 reported as additional paid-in capital.

29. A The preferred stock was originally issued for $550,000. When converted into common stock, each of the 5,000 shares was converted into 3 shares of common, resulting in an issuance of 15,000 shares of common. At a par value of $25 per share, the amount credited to common stock would be $375,000 and the remaining $175,000 would be a credit to additional paid-in capital.

30. A A dividend is initially recorded on the date on which it is declared, with a debit to retained earnings and a credit to dividends payable. The date of record is significant to determine who will receive the dividend. Payment is reported with a debit to dividends payable and a credit to cash.

31. B A stock split increases the number of shares outstanding without increasing the amount reported for common stock. It is not considered a dividend. As a result of the stock split, Long had 200,000 shares outstanding when the $.50 per share dividend was declared. Long would report dividends of $100,000.

32. C A sale of treasury stock for more than its cost would be recorded with a debit to cash for the proceeds, a credit to treasury stock for the cost, and a credit to additional paid-in capital for the excess.

33. B When a company grants stock options to an employee, compensation is measured as the difference between the fair value of the shares on the measurement date, usually the grant date, and the option price. At the date of grant, the shares had a market price of $50. With an option price of $40, the total compensation is $10 per share or $10,000. All of the compensation would be recognized in 19X3 since the options become exercisable at the end of the year.

34. A The minimum pension liability is the unfunded ABO or $140,000. The company already has an accrual for pension cost of $80,000, indicating that an additional liability of $60,000 must be recorded. The debit would ordinarily be to deferred pension cost, an intangible asset. If the additional liability, however, exceeds the unrecognized prior service cost, the excess is reported in a contra equity account. In this case, the excess is $60,000 – $45,000 or $15,000.

35. C Under the bonus method, an amount paid to a retiring partner in excess of the partner's capital balance represents a bonus that the remaining partners are paying to the retiring partner. This bonus will be recorded with a credit to cash and a debit to the remaining partners' capital accounts.

36. A The owner's equity will be reported on the basis of the amount paid, $350,000. It will be increased for income of $60,000 and decreased for drawings of $20,000. As a result, capital would have a balance of $390,000.

37. C A quasireorganization does not have any impact on a corporation's relationship with creditors and does not involve a distribution of stock of a newly created subsidiary. It generally involves a decrease in the recorded amount of overvalued assets and the elimination of a deficit in retained earnings.

38. B Leaf will receive a total of 5 payments of $5,009 each, or $25,045 for the note. Since the amount paid for the note was $19,485, the difference of $5,560, would be recognized as interest income over the term of the note.

39. D An investor recognizes a stock dividend by increasing the number of shares held without increasing the total carrying value of the investment. This is true whether the investment is accounted for under the cost or the equity method.

40. A The amount to be reported as royalty revenue for 19X3 would be the royalties earned during the calendar year. This would include the revenues earned for the period from 1/1 to 6/30, paid on September 15 at $17,000. The royalties for the period from 7/1 to 12/31 will equal the amount to be paid on March 15, at 15% of $60,000, or $9,000. Total royalty revenue for 19X3 would be $17,000 + $9,000 or $26,000.

41. D When a lease calls for unequal payments, including the offer of free rent for a portion of the lease period, the rental income should still be recognized on a straight-line basis. In order to do this, all of the rents to be received under the lease are spread over the entire term of the lease. Since this lease is for 5 years, the total of the lease payments will be spread over the 5-year period. In the first year, when no payments are received, the lessor will recognize rental income equal to 1/5 of the total and report it as rent receivable.

42. A Upon calling the 600 bonds at 102, Dome will pay $612,000 to retire the bonds. The carrying value of the bonds is the face of $600,000 plus the unamortized premium of $65,000 for a total of $665,000. The difference is an extraordinary gain on early extinguishment of debt equal to $53,000.

43. C An understatement in beginning inventory results in an understatement of cost of goods available for sale and cost of goods sold. Likewise, an overstatement in ending inventory results in an understatement of cost of goods sold. As a result, cost of goods sold is understated by $26,000 + $52,000 or $78,000.

44. D Research and development costs incurred by another company on behalf of Orr will be recognized as R and D expense by Orr. In addition, costs incurred for design, construction, and testing of preproduction prototypes and models, and costs incurred for testing in search of new products or process alternatives are both considered R and D costs that would also be expensed in the period incurred. The amount to be reported as R and D expense will be $150,000 + $200,000 + $175,000 or $525,000.

45. B   With accounts receivable of $350,000 and a net realizable value of $325,000, Inge should have a credit balance in the allowance for uncollectible accounts of $25,000. The beginning balance was $30,000. This will be reduced by accounts written off of $18,000 and increased by accounts recovered of $2,000, resulting in a balance of $14,000 before recording bad debt expense. To get a balance of $25,000, the entry to record expense will be for $11,000.

46. A   When the cash surrender value of a life insurance policy increases, the difference between the period's insurance premium and the increase in the cash surrender value is considered insurance expense. In most cases, the entire premium is recorded as insurance expense. The increase in the cash surrender value is subsequently recorded with a decrease to the expense.

47. C   The cost of printing catalogs to be used for a sales promotion campaign in January 19X4 would be reported as prepaid advertising expense in 19X3. This would reduce advertising expense by $15,000. The cost of radio advertisements should be reported as advertising expense in 19X3, when the ads aired, regardless of the fact that they were billed and paid in 19X4. This will increase advertising expense by $9,000. As a result, advertising expense for 19X3 will be $146,000 – $15,000 + $9,000 or $140,000.

48. B   If net income is $360,000 after income tax and after bonus, and the tax rate is 40%, net income before income tax but after the bonus would be $360,000/60% or $600,000. Since the

bonus is 10% of income after the bonus but before income tax, the bonus will be 10% of $600,000 or $60,000.

49. D   The deferred income tax liability will be equal to the cumulative temporary difference of $20,000 multiplied by the 40% tax rate that applies to 19X3 and subsequent periods. As a result, the amount of the deferred tax liability will be $8,000.

50. A   The current portion of income tax expense is equal to taxable income of $129,000, multiplied by the current tax rate of 40%, or $51,600.

51. C   There do not appear to be any temporary differences, indicating that income tax expense will consist of a current portion only. This will be equal to taxable income of $280,000 multiplied by the tax rate of 30% or $84,000.

52. A   A loss from discontinued operations is reported in its estimated amount in the period in which the decision to dispose of the segment is made. Since Wand committed to disposing of Kam in 19X3, the entire loss, including the $100,000 incurred from operations in 19X3, the $50,000 estimated to be incurred from operations in 19X4, and the $25,000 estimated as the ultimate loss on disposal of the assets will be combined to give a loss of $175,000 from discontinued operations.

53. D   A transaction that is both unusual in nature and infrequent of occurrence is an extraordinary item. As such, it should be presented, net of tax, after discontinued operations and before the cumulative effect of a change in accounting principles.

54. D   A change in accounting estimate is reported by applying the new estimate in the preparation of financial information in the period of the change and in future periods. Prior periods are not adjusted and no pro forma amounts need be disclosed.

55. C   An adjustment to record warranty expense that was mistakenly not accrued in a previous period is a correction of an error that is reported as a prior period adjustment to beginning retained earnings. A change from straight-line to accelerated depreciation is a change in accounting principle and the cumulative effect is reported on the income statement after extraordinary items. Only the $50,000 warranty expense adjustment is a prior period adjustment.

56. A   When preparing consolidated financial statements, a purchase by a subsidiary of some of the parent company's stock is considered similar to a purchase of treasury stock. As such, no gain or loss would be recognized.

57. A   Park apparently sells goods at a gross profit margin equal to 60% of the sales price. Since 20% of the goods sold to Small for $500,000, or $100,000 worth, remain in Small's inventory, the intercompany profits included in inventory would be $60,000. Park's sales are overstated by the $500,000 in intercompany sales. These intercompany items would be eliminated with a debit to sales of $500,000, a credit to inventory of $60,000, and a credit to cost of sales of $440,000. As a result, consolidated cost of goods sold would actually be $800,000 + $700,000 – $440,000 or $1,060,000.

58. D   Under the cash basis of accounting, revenues would be equal to amounts collected. Eagle would have collected the cash sales of $80,000 minus the returns of $4,000 for a net amount of $76,000. In addition, there was a beginning balance in accounts receivable of $40,000. This would be increased by sales of $120,000 and decreased by discounts of $6,000 to give an ending balance $154,000 before recording collections. With an actual ending balance of $30,000, collections must be $124,000 giving cash basis revenues of $76,000 + $124,000 or $200,000.

59. C   All of the items indicated as possible answers to this question would be disclosed along with the financial statements. The disclosure related to significant accounting policies, however, is intended to indicate the choices the company made in selecting the accounting principles applied in the preparation of the financial statements. This would include the criteria used when deciding which investments are to be treated as cash equivalents.

60. C   The operating profit of a business segment is equal to that segment's sales reduced by traceable costs and allocable common costs. Allocable common costs include indirect operating expenses incurred at the corporate level, but do not include interest expense or general expenses incurred at the corporate level.

61. A   All costs of preparing an asset for its intended use will be capitalized, provided the resulting capitalized amount does not exceed the asset's fair value. This will include freight-in paid for goods held for resale.

62. A All costs of preparing an asset for its intended use will be capitalized, provided the resulting capitalized amount does not exceed the asset's fair value. This will also include in-transit insurance on goods held for resale that was purchased FOB shipping point. Under those terms, the goods belong to the purchaser as soon as they are in the possession of the common carrier and insurance is a normal cost associated with obtaining the goods.

63. B Interest on a note payable related to goods held for resale cannot be capitalized. It is considered an ordinary cost of doing business and will be recognized as an expense as incurred.

64. A The installation of equipment is generally considered a necessary part of preparing the equipment for use. As a result, the cost of installation would be capitalized.

65. A The initial testing of newly purchased equipment is also considered a necessary part of preparing the equipment for use. It must be tested in order to make certain that any necessary adjustments are made so that the equipment can be used effectively and efficiently. This cost is also capitalized.

66. B The cost of a service contract on equipment for the current year is related to the maintenance and repair related services that will be received during the year. As a result, the cost will be recognized as expense over the year for which the service contract applies.

67. The cost of the land and building acquired will be equal to the cash paid of $800,000 plus the mortgage assumed in the amount of $200,000 for a total of $1,000,000. Although the property tax assessment is not generally considered a fair measure of value, it is often used to allocate cost between land and building. Since 60% of the assessed value is allocated to building, 60% of the purchase price, or **$600,000,** will be recorded as its cost.

68. Link will capitalize the lease using the lessee's incremental borrowing rate of 9%. Even though the 8% rate implicit in the lease is lower than the lessee's 9% rate, the implicit rate is not known to the lessee and may not be used. Link will capitalize the asset by calculating the present value of the minimum lease payments at 9%. The amount will be $100,000 × 5.03 or **$503,000.**

69. The exchange of undeveloped land is a like kind exchange that does not involve an earnings process. Since Link is paying but not receiving cash, Link will recognize losses, but not gains. Link is giving up cash of $50,000 plus land with a carrying value of $320,000 in exchange for land with a fair value of $500,000. The $130,000 gain will not be recognized and Link will record the land at **$370,000.**

70. Although the exchange of undeveloped land is also a like kind exchange for Club, the receipt of $50,000 indicates that some gain will be recognized on the basis of the portion of the sale that would be considered a cash sale. Club is receiving $50,000 in cash and land with a fair value of $450,000, or $500,000 in total, for land with a carrying value of $350,000, resulting in a gain of $150,000. The cash received represents 10% of the total proceeds, indicating that 10% of the gain, or $15,000, will be recognized by Club. Club will record this transaction with a debit to cash of $50,000, a credit to land of $350,000, a credit to a gain of $15,000, and a debit to the new land account for the amount required to balance the entry, **$315,000.**

71. Under the straight-line method, the $864,000 cost of the equipment is reduced by the salvage value of $144,000 to establish the depreciable basis of $720,000. This will be spread evenly over the 8 year estimated life resulting in depreciation of **$90,000** per year.

72. Under the double-declining balance method, salvage value is ignored. The straight-line rate, which is 1/8 or 12.5%, will be doubled to give the appropriate rate of 25%. This will be multiplied by the carrying value of the equipment to give the current period's depreciation expense. For 19X2, depreciation will be 25% × the cost of $864,000 or $216,000. This reduces the carrying value to $648,000, which will be multiplied by 25% to give depreciation expense for 19X3 of **$162,000.**

73. Under sum-of-the-years'-digits, the depreciable basis of $864,000 – $144,000, or $720,000 is multiplied by a ratio. The numerator will be the year number in reverse order, 8 for 19X2, and 7 for 19X3. The denominator will be equal to the sum-of-the-years'-digits, which can be calculated as $n(n+1)/2$ or $8 \times 9/2$ or 36. As a result, depreciation in 19X3 will be 7/36 × $720,000 or **$140,000.**

74. Under the units of production approach, salvage value is also taken into consideration and depreciation is calculated based on the depreciable basis of $864,000 – $144,000 or $720,000. This amount is divided by the total estimated production during the life of the asset, 1,800,000, indicating that depreciation will be $720,000/1,800,000 units or $.40 per unit. Since Half produced 300,000 units in 19X3, depreciation will be 300,000 × $.40 or **$120,000.**

75. At the beginning of the year, there is a credit balance in income taxes payable of $150,000. No income tax expense has been recorded, and there is an ending debit balance of $35,000. This indicates that the income taxes payable of $150,000 must have been paid, and prepaid income taxes of $35,000 have also been paid, for total payments of $185,000. Payments for income taxes represent an operating activity. Under the indirect method, however, only the change in income taxes payable would be included on the statement of cash flows. Payments for income taxes would be reported as a supplementary disclosure. **$185,000 D**

76. There is interest expense in the amount of $46,000. In addition, however, there is a decrease in the premium on bonds payable in the amount of $79,000. A portion of this, $75,000, relates to premium that was eliminated upon the retirement of bonds, and the remaining $4,000 represents amortization. Amortization of bond premium decreases interest expense. As a result, payments for interest were $46,000 + $4,000 or $50,000. Interest payments represent an operating activity. Under the indirect method, however, only a change in interest receivable or payable would be included on the statement of cash flows. Payments for interest would be reported as a supplementary disclosure. **$50,000 D**

77. The bonds that were redeemed had a face value of $500,000 and unamortized premium of $75,000 for a total carrying value of $575,000. Before tax considerations, there was a gain on extinguishment of bonds on $90,000, indicating that the amount paid to redeem the bonds was $90,000 less than the carrying value or $485,000. Amounts paid to redeem bonds represent a financing activity. **$485,000 C**

78. Probe issued 80,000 shares of stock with a par value of $2.50 per share, accounting for the $200,000 increase in the common stock account. Since there were no other transactions involving common stock other than the payment of dividends, the $55,000 increase in additional paid-in capital must have also resulted from the issuance of the stock. The proceeds from the issuance must be $200,000 + $55,000 or $255,000. Proceeds from the issuance of stock represents a financing activity. **$255,000 C**

79. A decrease in retained earnings of $80,000 implies that there was an $80,000 dividend declared during 19X3. The beginning balance in the dividend payable account of $10,000 would be increased by the $80,000 dividend to give an ending balance of $90,000. Since the ending balance was only $25,000, the amount paid must have been $90,000 – $25,000 or $65,000. Payments of dividends represent a financing activity. **$65,000 C**

80. The equipment sold had a cost of $50,000. Accumulated depreciation had a beginning balance of $280,000 and depreciation expense for the period was $88,000, implying that there should have been an ending balance in accumulated depreciation of $368,000. Since the actual ending balance was $345,000, the accumulated depreciation on the equipment sold must have been the difference of $23,000, indicating that the carrying value of the equipment sold was $27,000. There was a loss on the sale of equipment of $7,000, which implies that the sales price must have been $20,000. Proceeds from the sale of equipment represent an investing activity. **$20,000 B**

4.

Probe Co.
INCOME STATEMENT
For the Year Ended December 31, 19X3

Sales		$2,420,000
Cost of sales		1,863,000
Gross profit		557,000
Selling and administrative expenses	$220,000	
Depreciation	88,000	308,000
Operating income		249,000
Other income (expenses):		
Interest income	14,000	
Interest expense	(46,000)	
Loss on sale of equipment	(7,000)	39,000
Income before income tax and extraordinary item		210,000
Income tax:		
Current	45,000 [1]	
Deferred	12,000 [2]	57,000
Income before extraordinary item		153,000
Extraordinary item:		
Gain on extinguishment of debt, net of income		
taxes of $27,000		63,000
Net income		216,000

Earnings per share		
Earnings before extraordinary item	1.275	[3]
Extraordinary item	.525	Optional
Net income	$1.800	

[1] Current income tax expense:

Income before income tax and extraordinary item	$210,000
Differences between financial statement and taxable income	(60,000)
Income subject to tax	150,000
Income tax rate	× 30%
Income tax excluding extraordinary item	$45,000

[2] Deferred income tax expense:

Cumulative temporary differences—12/31/X3	$180,000
Income tax rate	× 30%
Deferred tax liability—12/31/X3	54,000
Deferred tax liability—12/31/X2	42,000
Deferred tax expense for 19X3	$12,000

[3] Earnings per share:

Weighted average number of shares outstanding for 19X3:

January thru March (60,000 × 3)	180,000
April thru December (140,000 × 9)	1,260,000
Total	1,440,000
	÷ 12
	120,000

Income before extraordinary item		153,000
Earnings per share	(153,000 ÷ 120,000)	1.275

5.   a.

To: Mr. Brown, Controller, Emco

From: Wyatt, CPA

As you requested, I have summarized some of the issues we discussed regarding the recognition of revenue, including some of the special considerations associated with revenue recognition when a right to return exists.

In general, revenues are recognized in the period in which they are realized or realizable and in which they are earned. Revenues are realized or realizable when goods or services are exchanged for cash or claims to cash. Revenues are earned when goods have been delivered or services have been performed and the earnings process is substantially complete.

When a right to return exists, revenues will be recognized at the time of sale when all of the following conditions are met:

- The price to the buyer is substantially fixed or determinable on the date of sale.

- The buyer has paid the seller, or the buyer is obligated to pay the seller and the obligation to pay is not contingent on the resale of the product.

- The buyer's obligation to the seller will not change in the case of theft or physical damage to the product.

- The buyer is not simply a sales division of the seller, but has economic substance that is separate from the seller.

- The seller does not have significant obligations to cause the resale of the product by the buyer.

- The amount of future returns can be reasonably estimated.

If any of these conditions have not been met, the seller may not recognize revenues until either the conditions have been met, or the return privilege has substantially expired. Since Emco is unable to estimate the amount of future returns, Emco must either postpone recognition of revenues until the right to return substantially expires, or Emco is able to accumulate enough information to reasonably estimate the amount of future returns.

When revenues are recognized in a situation where a right of return exists, the seller must evaluate the impact of the right of return similarly to any other contingency. The estimated amount of future returns will be accrued with a reduction to sales revenues and cost of sales.

b.

To: Mr. Brown, Controller, Emco

From: Wyatt, CPA

As you requested, I have summarized some of the issues we discussed regarding the recognition of revenue, including some of the special considerations associated with revenue recognition when a right to return exists. I have also described some of the reporting goals and requirements of FAS No. 106, Employers' Accounting for Postretirement Benefits Other Than Pensions.

The principal focus of FAS 106, Employers' Accounting for Postretirement Benefits Other Than Pensions, is postretirement health care benefits. The statement, however, applies to all postretirement benefits. Other benefits covered by FAS 106 may include life insurance and welfare benefits such as tuition assistance, day care, legal services, and housing subsidies.

The cost of postretirement benefits other than pensions is accrued on the basis of estimates. The use of estimates is superior than implying, by failing to accrue, that no cost or obligation exists prior to the payment of benefits.

The primary recipients of postretirement benefits other than pensions are current and former employees, their beneficiaries, and covered dependents.

TEST TWO

INSTRUCTIONS FOR COMPUTER-ASSISTED FEEDBACK

A special feature of this book is the computer-assisted feedback you can receive. Simply enter your solutions to the questions on the grids at the back of the book and complete the essays and problems on the response sheets. Kaplan will analyze your exam and send you detailed feedback on how you performed. The feedback will highlight your strengths and weaknesses in each subject area of the test. You can do Test One early to get feedback on where to focus your study effort and take this test later to check on your progress.

1. Be sure that on each answer grid you have entered your **name** and the **test ID.** Each of the answer grids you send in should have a different test ID. The test ID can be found can be found on the first page of each the four sections of the test.

2. **Do not fold the answer grids.** Enclose them in an envelope at least 8 1/2 by 11 inches and send to the address below. Affix extra postage for oversized mail (at least 43 cents is needed). Please include a self-addressed envelope.

> KAPLAN
> Computer-Assisted Feedback
> 1221 East 14th Street
> Brooklyn, NY 11230

3. Send your essay response sheets to the address below. Please include a self-addressed envelope.

> KAPLAN
> CPA Team
> 888 Seventh Avenue
> New York, NY 10106

TEST 2: QUESTIONS

BUSINESS LAW & PROFESSIONAL RESPONSIBILITES

Test ID: 4200

INSTRUCTIONS

1. Question Numbers 1, 2, and 3 should be answered on the scannable grid, which is at the back of this book. You should attempt to answer all objective items. There is no penalty for incorrect responses. Since the objective items are computer graded, your comments and calculations associated with them are not considered. Be certain that you have entered your answers on the scannable grid before the examination time is up. The objective portion of your examination will not be graded if you fail to record your answers on the scannable grid.

2. Question Numbers 4 and 5 should be answered using the essay response pages at the back of this book. If you have not completed answering a question on a page, fill in the appropriate spaces in the wording on the bottom of the page: **"QUESTION NUMBER ___ CONTINUES ON PAGE ___."** If you have completed answering a question, fill in the appropriate space in the wording on the bottom of the page: **"QUESTION NUMBER ___ ENDS ON THIS PAGE."** Always begin the start of an answer to a question on the top of a new page (which may be the back side of a sheet of paper).

3. Although the primary purpose of the examination is to test your knowledge and application of the subject matter, selected essay responses will be graded for writing skills.

	Point Value	Estimated Minutes	
		Minimum	Maximum
No. 1	60	90	100
No. 2	10	10	15
No. 3	10	10	15
No. 4	10	15	25
No. 5	10	15	25
Totals	**100**	**140**	**180**

The point values for each question, and estimated time allotments based primarily on point value, are as follows:

Number 1 (Estimated time—90 to 100 minutes)

Select the **best** answer for each of the following items. Use a No. 2 Pencil to blacken the appropriate ovals on the Multiple-Choice Section of your scannable grid using response items #1 through #60. **Mark only one answer for each item. Answer all items.**

1. According to the ethical standards of the profession, which of the following acts is generally prohibited?

A. Purchasing a product from a third party and reselling it to a client.
B. Writing a financial management newsletter promoted and sold by a publishing company.
C. Accepting a commission for recommending a product to an audit client.
D. Accepting engagements obtained through the efforts of third parties.

2. According to the ethical standards of the profession, which of the following acts is generally prohibited?

A. Issuing a modified report explaining a failure to follow a governmental regulatory agency's standards when conducting an attest service for a client.
B. Revealing confidential client information during a quality review of a professional practice by a team from the state CPA society.
C. Accepting a contingent fee for representing a client in an examination of the client's federal tax return by an IRS agent.
D. Retaining client records after an engagement is terminated prior to completion and the client has demanded their return.

3. According to the standards of the profession, which of the following activities may be required in exercising due care?

	Consulting with experts	Obtaining specialty accreditation
A.	Yes	Yes
B.	Yes	No
C.	No	Yes
D.	No	No

4. According to the standards of the profession, which of the following activities would most likely **not** impair a CPA's independence?

A. Providing extensive advisory services for a client.
B. Contracting with a client to supervise the client's office personnel.
C. Signing a client's checks in emergency situations.
D. Accepting a luxurious gift from a client.

5. Under the Statements on Standards for Consulting Services, which of the following statements best reflects a CPA's responsibility when undertaking a consulting services engagement? The CPA must

A. Not seek to modify any agreement made with the client.
B. Not perform any attest services for the client.
C. Inform the client of significant reservations concerning the benefits of the engagement.
D. Obtain a written understanding with the client concerning the time for completion of the engagement.

6. According to the standards of the profession, which of the following sources of information should a CPA consider before signing a client's tax return?

I. Information actually known to the CPA from the tax return of another client.

II. Information provided by the client that appears to be correct based on the client's returns from prior years.

   A. I only.
   B. II only.
   C. Both I and II.
   D. Neither I nor II.

7. According to the standards of the profession, which of the following statements is (are) correct regarding the action to be taken by a CPA who discovers an error in a client's previously filed tax return?

I. Advise the client of the error and recommend the measures to be taken.

II. Withdraw from the professional relationship regardless of whether or not the client corrects the error.

   A. I only.
   B. II only.
   C. Both I and II.
   D. Neither I nor II.

8. Under the "Ultramares" rule, to which of the following parties will an accountant be liable for negligence?

	Parties in Privity	Foreseen Parties
A.	Yes	Yes
B.	Yes	No
C.	No	Yes
D.	No	No

9. When performing an audit, a CPA will most likely be considered negligent when the CPA fails to

   A. Detect all of a client's fraudulent activities.
   B. Include a negligence disclaimer in the client engagement letter.
   C. Warn a client of known internal control weaknesses.
   D. Warn a client's customers of embezzlement by the client's employees.

10. Which of the following is the best defense a CPA firm can assert in a suit for common law fraud based on its unqualified opinion on materially false financial statements?

   A. Contributory negligence on the part of the client.
   B. A disclaimer contained in the engagement letter.
   C. Lack of privity.
   D. Lack of scienter.

11. Under the anti-fraud provisions of Section 10(b) of the Securities Exchange Act of 1934, a CPA may be liable if the CPA acted

   A. Negligently.
   B. With independence.
   C. Without due diligence.
   D. Without good faith.

12. Under Section 11 of the Securities Act of 1933, which of the following standards may a CPA use as a defense?

	Generally accepted accounting principles	Generally accepted fraud-detection standards
A.	Yes	Yes
B.	Yes	No
C.	No	Yes
D.	No	No

13. Ocean and Associates, CPAs, audited the financial statements of Drain Corporation. As a result of Ocean's negligence in conducting the audit, the financial statements included material misstatements. Ocean was unaware of this fact. The financial statements and Ocean's unqualified opinion were included in a registration statement and prospectus for an original public offering of stock by Drain. Sharp purchased shares in the offering. Sharp received a copy of the prospectus prior to the purchase but did not read it. The shares declined in value as a result of the misstatements in Drain's financial statements becoming known. Under which of the following Acts is Sharp most likely to prevail in a lawsuit against Ocean?

	Securities Exchange Act of 1934, Section 10(b) Rule 10b-5	Securities Act of 1933, Section II
A.	Yes	Yes
B.	Yes	No
C.	No	Yes
D.	No	No

14. Which of the following statements is correct regarding a CPA's working papers? The working papers must be

A. Transferred to another accountant purchasing the CPA's practice even if the client hasn't given permission.
B. Transferred permanently to the client if demanded.
C. Turned over to any government agency that requests them.
D. Turned over pursuant to a valid federal court subpoena.

15. Thorp, CPA, was engaged to audit Ivor Co.'s financial statements. During the audit, Thorp discovered that Ivor's inventory contained stolen goods. Ivor was indicted and Thorp was subpoenaed to testify at the criminal trial. Ivor claimed accountant-client privilege to prevent Thorp from testifying. Which of the following statements is correct regarding Ivor's claim?

A. Ivor can claim an accountant-client privilege only in states that have enacted a statute creating such a privilege.
B. Ivor can claim an accountant-client privilege only in federal courts.
C. The accountant-client privilege can be claimed only in civil suits.
D. The accountant-client privilege can be claimed only to limit testimony to audit subject matter.

16. Generally, under the Uniform Partnership Act, a partnership has which of the following characteristics?

	Unlimited Duration	Obligation for Payment of Federal Income Tax
A.	Yes	Yes
B.	Yes	No
C.	No	Yes
D.	No	No

17. Which of the following statements is (are) usually correct regarding general partners' liability?

I. All general partners are jointly and severally liable for partnership torts.

II. All general partners are liable only for those partnership obligations they actually authorized.

    A. I only.
    B. II only.
    C. Both I and II.
    D. Neither I nor II.

18. Which of the following statements is correct regarding the division of profits in a general partnership when the written partnership agreement provides only that losses be divided equally among the partners? Profits are to be divided

    A. Based on the partners' ratio of contribution to the partnership.
    B. Based on the partners' participation in day- to-day management.
    C. Equally among the partners.
    D. Proportionately among the partners.

19. Which of the following statements best describes the effect of the assignment of an interest in a general partnership?

    A. The assignee becomes a partner.
    B. The assignee is responsible for a proportionate share of past and future partnership debts.
    C. The assignment automatically dissolves the partnership.
    D. The assignment transfers the assignor's interest in partnership profits and surplus.

20. Park and Graham entered into a written partnership agreement to operate a retail store. Their agreement was silent as to the duration of the partnership. Park wishes to dissolve the partnership. Which of the following statements is correct?

    A. Park may dissolve the partnership at any time.
    B. Unless Graham consents to a dissolution, Park must apply to a court and obtain a decree ordering the dissolution.
    C. Park may **not** dissolve the partnership unless Graham consents.
    D. Park may dissolve the partnership only after notice of the proposed dissolution is given to all partnership creditors.

21. Which of the following facts is (are) generally included in a corporation's articles of incorporation?

	Name of Registered Agent	Number of Authorized Shares
A.	Yes	Yes
B.	Yes	No
C.	No	Yes
D.	No	No

22. Which of the following statements best describes an advantage of the corporate form of doing business?

    A. Day-to-day management is strictly the responsibility of the directors.
    B. Ownership is contractually restricted and is **not** transferable.
    C. The operation of the business may continue indefinitely.
    D. The business is free from state regulation.

23. To which of the following rights is a stockholder of a public corporation entitled?

A. The right to have annual dividends declared and paid.
B. The right to vote for the election of officers.
C. The right to a reasonable inspection of corporate records.
D. The right to have the corporation issue a new class of stock.

24. Carr Corp. declared a 7% stock dividend on its common stock. The dividend

A. Must be registered with the SEC pursuant to the Securities Act of 1933.
B. Is includable in the gross income of the recipient taxpayers in the year of receipt.
C. Has no effect on Carr's earnings and profits for federal income tax purposes.
D. Requires a vote of Carr's stockholders.

25. Which of the following statements is a general requirement for the merger of two corporations?

A. The merger plan must be approved unanimously by the stockholders of both corporations.
B. The merger plan must be approved unanimously by the boards of both corporations.
C. The absorbed corporation must amend its articles of incorporation.
D. The stockholders of both corporations must be given due notice of a special meeting, including a copy or summary of the merger plan.

26. Which of the following statements is (are) correct regarding debtors' rights?

I. State exemption statutes prevent all of a debtor's personal property from being sold to pay a federal tax lien.

II. Federal social security benefits received by a debtor are exempt from garnishment by creditors.

A. I only.
B. II only.
C. Both I and II.
D. Neither I nor II.

27. Which of the following liens generally require(s) the lienholder to give notice of legal action before selling the debtor's property to satisfy the debt?

	Mechanic's Lien	Artisan's Lien
A.	Yes	Yes
B.	Yes	No
C.	No	Yes
D.	No	No

28. Which of the following rights does one cosurety generally have against another cosurety?

A. Exoneration.
B. Subrogation.
C. Reimbursement.
D. Contribution.

29. Which of the following acts always will result in the total release of a compensated surety?

A. The creditor changes the manner of the principal debtor's payment.
B. The creditor extends the principal debtor's time to pay.
C. The principal debtor's obligation is partially released.
D. The principal debtor's performance is tendered.

30. When a principal debtor defaults and a surety pays the creditor the entire obligation, which of the following remedies gives the surety the best method of collecting from the debtor?

A. Exoneration.
B. Contribution.
C. Subrogation.
D. Attachment.

31. Under the Federal Insurance Contributions Act (FICA), which of the following acts will cause an employer to be liable for penalties?

	Failure to supply taxpayer identification numbers	Failure to make timely FICA deposits
A.	Yes	Yes
B.	Yes	No
C.	No	Yes
D.	No	No

32. Taxes payable under the Federal Unemployment Tax Act (FUTA) are

A. Calculated as a fixed percentage of all compensation paid to an employee.
B. Deductible by the employer as a business expense for federal income tax purposes.
C. Payable by employers for all employees.
D. Withheld from the wages of all covered employees.

33. Which of the following claims is(are) generally covered under workers' compensation statutes?

	Occupational Disease	Employment Aggravated Pre-Existing Disease
A.	Yes	Yes
B.	Yes	No
C.	No	Yes
D.	No	No

34. Generally, which of the following statements concerning workers' compensation laws is correct?

A. The amount of damages recoverable is based on comparative negligence.
B. Employers are strictly liable without regard to whether or **not** they are at fault.
C. Workers' compensation benefits are **not** available if the employee is negligent.
D. Workers' compensation awards are payable for life.

35. Under the Age Discrimination in Employment Act, which of the following remedies is(are) available to a covered employee?

	Early Retirement	Back Pay
A.	Yes	Yes
B.	Yes	No
C.	No	Yes
D.	No	No

36. Which of the following Acts prohibit(s) an employer from discriminating among employees based on sex?

	Equal Pay Act	Title VII of the Civil Rights Act
A.	Yes	Yes
B.	Yes	No
C.	No	Yes
D.	No	No

37. Under the Fair Labor Standards Act, which of the following pay bases may be used to pay covered, nonexempt employees who earn, on average, the minimum hourly wage?

	Hourly	Weekly	Monthly
A.	Yes	Yes	Yes
B.	Yes	Yes	No
C.	Yes	No	Yes
D.	No	Yes	Yes

38. Under the Fair Labor Standards Act, if a covered, nonexempt employee works consecutive weeks of 45, 42, 38, and 33 hours, how many hours of overtime must be paid to the employee?

A. 0
B. 7
C. 18
D. 20

39. Under the Employee Retirement Income Security Act of 1974 (ERISA), which of the following areas of private employer pension plans is (are) regulated?

	Employee Vesting	Plan Funding
A.	Yes	Yes
B.	Yes	No
C.	No	Yes
D.	No	No

40. Which of the following employee benefits is (are) exempt from the provisions of the National Labor Relations Act?

	Sick Pay	Vacation Pay
A.	Yes	Yes
B.	Yes	No
C.	No	Yes
D.	No	No

41. Under the Sales Article of the UCC, a firm offer will be created only if the

A. Offer states the time period during which it will remain open.
B. Offer is made by a merchant in a signed writing.
C. Offeree gives some form of consideration.
D. Offeree is a merchant.

42. Under the Sales Article of the UCC, when a written offer has been made without specifying a means of acceptance but providing that the offer will remain open only for ten days, which of the following statements represent(s) a valid acceptance of the offer?

I. An acceptance sent by regular mail the day before the ten-day period expires that reaches the offeror on the eleventh day.

II. An acceptance faxed the day before the ten-day period expires that reaches the offeror on the eleventh day, due to a malfunction of the offeror's printer.

A. I only.
B. II only.
C. Both I and II.
D. Neither I nor II.

43. Under the Sales Article of the UCC, the warranty of title

A. Provides that the seller cannot disclaim the warranty if the sale is made to a bona fide purchaser for value.
B. Provides that the seller deliver the goods free from any lien of which the buyer lacked knowledge when the contract was made.
C. Applies only if it is in writing and signed by the seller.
D. Applies only if the seller is a merchant.

44. To establish a cause of action based on strict liability in tort for personal injuries that result from the use of a defective product, one of the elements the injured party must prove is that the seller

    A. Was aware of the defect in the product.
    B. Sold the product to the injured party.
    C. Failed to exercise due care.
    D. Sold the product in a defective condition.

45. Under the Sales Article of the UCC, which of the following factors is most important in determining who bears the risk of loss in a sale of goods contract?

    A. The method of shipping the goods.
    B. The contract's shipping terms.
    C. Title to the goods.
    D. How the goods were lost.

46. Under the Sales Article of the UCC, in an F.O.B. place of shipment contract, the risk of loss passes to the buyer when the goods

    A. Are identified to the contract.
    B. Are placed on the seller's loading dock.
    C. Are delivered to the carrier.
    D. Reach the buyer's loading dock.

47. Under the Sales Article of the UCC, which of the following rights is (are) available to the buyer when a seller commits an anticipatory breach of contract?

	Demand assurance of performance	Cancel the contract	Collect punitive damages
A.	Yes	Yes	Yes
B.	Yes	Yes	No
C.	Yes	No	Yes
D.	No	Yes	Yes

48. Under the Sales Article of the UCC, and unless otherwise agreed to, the seller's obligation to the buyer is to

    A. Deliver the goods to the buyer's place of business.
    B. Hold conforming goods and give the buyer whatever notification is reasonably necessary to enable the buyer to take delivery.
    C. Deliver all goods called for in the contract to a common carrier.
    D. Set aside conforming goods for inspection by the buyer before delivery.

49. Under the Sales Article of the UCC, which of the following statements regarding liquidate damages is (are) correct?

    I. The injured party may collect any amount of liquidated damages provided for in the contract.

    II. The seller may retain a deposit of up to $500 when a buyer defaults even if there is no liquidated-damages provision in the contract.

    A. I only.
    B. II only.
    C. Both I and II.
    D. Neither I nor II.

50. Under the Sales Article of the UCC, which of the following rights is available to a seller when a buyer materially breaches a sales contract?

	Right to cancel the contract	Right to recover damages
A.	Yes	Yes
B.	Yes	No
C.	No	Yes
D.	No	No

51. Long, Fall, and Pear own a building as joint tenants with the right of survivorship. Long gave Long's interest in the building to Green by executing and delivering a deed to Green. Neither Fall nor Pear consented to this transfer. Fall and Pear subsequently died. After their deaths, Green's interest in the building would consist of

A. A 1/3 interest as a joint tenant.
B. A 1/3 interest as a tenant in common.
C. No interest because Fall and Pear did **not** consent to the transfer.
D. Total ownership due to the deaths of Fall and Pear.

52. A method of transferring ownership of real property that most likely would be considered an arm's-length transaction is transfer by

A. Inheritance.
B. Eminent domain.
C. Adverse possession.
D. Sale.

53. Which of the following provisions must be included to have an enforceable written residential lease?

	A description of the leased premises	A due date for the payment of rent/
A.	Yes	Yes
B.	Yes	No
C.	No	Yes
D.	No	No

54. Which of the following elements must be contained in a valid deed?

	Purchase price	Description of the land
A.	Yes	Yes
B.	Yes	No
C.	No	Yes
D.	No	No

55. Rich purchased property from Sklar for $200,000. Rich obtained a $150,000 loan from Marsh Bank to finance the purchase, executing a promissory note and a mortgage. By recording the mortgage, Marsh protects its

A. Rights against Rich under the promissory note.
B. Rights against the claims of subsequent bona fide purchasers for value.
C. Priority against a previously filed real estate tax lien on the property.
D. Priority against all parties having earlier claims to the property.

56. Which of the following factors help determine whether an item of personal property is a fixture?

I. Degree of the item's attachment to the property.

II. Intent of the person who had the item installed.

A. I only.
B. II only.
C. Both I and II.
D. Neither I nor II.

57. Which of the following activities is (are) regulated under the Federal Water Pollution Control Act (Clean Water Act)?

	Discharge of heated water by nuclear power plants	Dredging of wetlands
A.	Yes	Yes
B.	Yes	No
C.	No	Yes
D.	No	No

58. Which of the following methods of obtaining personal property will give the recipient ownership of the property?

	Lease	Finding abandoned property
A.	Yes	Yes
B.	Yes	No
C.	No	Yes
D.	No	No

59. A common carrier bailee generally would avoid liability for loss of goods entrusted to its care if the goods are

A. Stolen by an unknown person.
B. Negligently destroyed by an employee.
C. Destroyed by the derailment of the train carrying them due to railroad employee negligence.
D. Improperly packed by the party shipping them.

60. Which of the following statements correctly describes the requirement of insurable interest relating to property insurance? An insurable interest

A. Must exist when any loss occurs.
B. Must exist when the policy is issued and when any loss occurs.
C. Is created only when the property is owned in fee simple.
D. Is created only when the property is owned by an individual.

Number 2 (Estimated time—10 to 15 minutes)

Question Number 2 consists of two parts. Each part consists of five items. Select the **best** answer for each item. Use a No. 2 pencil to blacken the appropriate ovals on OOF Section #3 of your scannable grid to indicate your answers. **Answer all items.**

a. Items 61 through 65 are based on the following:

Lace Computer Sales Corp. orally contracted with Banks, an independent consultant, for Banks to work part time as Lace's agent to perform Lace's customers' service calls. Banks, a computer programmer and software designer, was authorized to customize Lace's software to the customers' needs, on a commission basis, but was specifically told not to sell Lace's computers.

On September 15, Banks made a service call on Clear Co. to repair Clear's computer. Banks had previously called on Clear, customized Lace's software for Clear, and collected cash payments for the work performed. During the call, Banks convinced Clear to buy an upgraded Lace computer for a price much lower than Lace would normally charge. Clear had previously purchased computers from other Lace agents and had made substantial cash down payments to the agents. Clear had no knowledge that the price was lower than normal. Banks received a $1,000 cash down payment and promised to deliver the computer the next week. Banks never turned in the down payment and left town. When Clear called the following week to have the computer delivered, Lace refused to honor Clear's order.

Required:

Items 61 through 65 relate to the relationships between the parties. For each item, select from List I whether only statement I is correct, whether only statement II is correct, or whether both statements I and II are correct, or whether neither statement I nor II is correct. Blacken the corresponding ovals on OOF Section #3, response items #1 through #5.

LIST I			
(A)	I only.	(C)	Both I and II.
(B)	II only.	(D)	Neither I nor II.

61. I. Lace's agreement with Banks had to be in writing for it to be a valid agency agreement.

   II. Lace's agreement with Banks empowered Banks to act as Lace's agent.

62. I. Clear was entitled to rely on Banks's implied authority to customize Lace's software.

   II. Clear was entitled to rely on Banks's express authority when buying the computer.

63. I. Lace's agreement with Banks was automatically terminated by Banks's sale of the computer.

   II. Lace must notify Clear before Banks's apparent authority to bind Lace will cease.

64. I. Lace is **not** bound by the agreement made by Banks with Clear.

   II. Lace may unilaterally amend the agreement made by Banks to prevent a loss on the sale of the computer to Clear.

65. I. Lace, as a disclosed principal, is solely contractually liable to Clear.

   II. Both Lace and Banks are contractually liable to Clear.

b. Items 66 through 70 are based on the following:

Under the provisions of Glenn's testamentary trust, after payment of all administrative expenses and taxes, the entire residuary estate was to be paid to Strong and Lake as trustees. The trustees were authorized to invest the trust assets, and directed to distribute income annually to Glenn's children for their lives, then distribute the principal to Glenn's grandchildren, per capita. The trustees were also authorized to make such principal payments to the income beneficiaries that the trustees determined to be reasonable for the beneficiaries' welfare. Glenn died in 19X2. On Glenn's death there were two surviving children, aged 21 and 30, and one two-year-old grandchild.

On June 15, 19X5, the trustees made the following distributions from the trust:

- Paid the 19X2, 19X3, and 19X4 trust income to Glenn's children. This amount included the proceeds from the sale of stock received by the trust as a stock dividend.

- Made a $10,000 principal payment for medical school tuition to one of Glenn's children.

- Made a $5,000 principal payment to Glenn's grandchild.

Required:

Items 66 through 70 relate to the above fact pattern. For each item, select from List II whether only statement I is correct, whether only statement II is correct, whether both statements I and II are correct, or whether neither statement I nor II is correct. Blacken the corresponding ovals on OOF Section #3, response items #6 through #10.

LIST II

(A)	I only.	(C)	Both I and II.
(B)	II only.	(D)	Neither I nor II.

66. I. Glenn's trust was valid because it did **not** violate the rule against perpetuities.

II. Glenn's trust was valid even though it permitted the trustees to make principal payments to income beneficiaries.

67. I. Glenn's trust would be terminated if both of Glenn's children were to die.

II. Glenn's trust would be terminated because of the acts of the trustees.

68. I. Strong and Lake violated their fiduciary duties by making any distributions of principal.

II. Strong and Lake violated their fiduciary duties by failing to distribute the trust income annually.

69. I. Generally, stock dividends are considered income and should be distributed.

II. Generally, stock dividends should be allocated to principal and remain as part of the trust.

70. I. The $10,000 principal payment was an abuse of the trustees' authority.

II. The $5,000 principal payment was valid because of its payment to a nonincome beneficiary.

Number 3 (Estimated time—10 to 15 minutes)

Question Number 3 consists of two parts. Each part consists of five items. Select the **best** answer for each item. Use a No. 2 pencil to blacken the appropriate ovals on OOF Section #3 of your scannable grid to indicate your answers. Answer all items.

A. *Items 71 through 75 are based on the following:*

On June 1, 19X5, Rusk Corp. was petitioned involuntarily into bankruptcy. At the time of the filing, Rusk had the following creditors:

- Safe Bank, for the balance due on the secured note and mortgage on Rusk's warehouse.

- Employee salary claims.

- 19X4 federal income taxes due.

- Accountant's fees outstanding.

- Utility bills outstanding.

Prior to the bankruptcy filing, but while insolvent, Rusk engaged in the following transactions:

- On February 1, 19X5, Rusk repaid all corporate directors' loans made to the corporation.

- On May 1, 19X5, Rusk purchased raw materials for use in its manufacturing business and paid cash to the supplier.

Required:

Items 71 through 75 relate to Rusk's creditors and the February 1 and May 1 transactions. For each item, select from List I whether only statement I is correct, whether only statement II is correct, whether both statements I and II are correct, or whether neither statement I nor II is correct. Blacken the corresponding ovals on OOF Section #3, response items #11 through #15.

LIST I		
(A) I only.	(C)	Both I and II.
(B) II only.	(D)	Neither I nor II.

71. I. Safe Bank's claim will be the first paid of the listed claims because Safe is a secured creditor.

    II. Safe Bank will receive the entire amount of the balance of the mortgage due as a secured creditor regardless of the amount received from the sale of the warehouse.

72. I. The employee salary claims will be paid in full after the payment of any secured party.

    II. The employee salary claims up to $4,000 per claimant will be paid before payment of any general creditors' claims.

73. I. The claim for 19X4 federal income taxes due will be paid as a secured creditor claim.

    II. The claim for 19X4 federal income taxes due will be paid prior to the general creditor claims.

74. I. The February 1 repayments of the directors' loans were preferential transfers even though the payments were made more than 90 days before the filing of the petition.

    II. The February 1 repayments of the directors' loans were preferential transfers because the payments were made to insiders.

75. I. The May 1 purchase and payment was **not** a preferential transfer because it was a transaction in the ordinary course of business.

    II. The May 1 purchase and payment was a preferential transfer because it occurred within 90 days of the filing of the petition.

b. Items 76 through 80 *are based on the following:*

Coffee Corp., a publicly held corporation, wants to make an $8,000,000 exempt offering of its shares as a private placement offering under Regulation D, Rule 506, of the Securities Act of 1933. Coffee has more than 500 shareholders and assets in excess of $1 billion, and has its shares listed on a national securities exchange.

Required:

Items 76 through 80 relate to the application of the provisions of the Securities Act of 1933 and the Securities Exchange Act of 1934 to Coffee Corp. and the offering. For each item, select from List II whether only statement I is correct, whether only statement II is correct, whether both statements I and II are correct, or whether neither statement I nor II is correct. Blacken the corresponding ovals on OOF Section #3, response items #16 through #20.

LIST II		
(A) I only.	(C)	Both I and II.
(B) II only.	(D)	Neither I nor II.

76. I. Coffee Corp. may make the Regulation D, Rule 506, exempt offering.

    II. Coffee Corp., because it is required to report under the Securities Exchange Act of 1934, may **not** make an exempt offering

77. I. Shares sold under a Regulation D, Rule 506, exempt offering may be purchased only by accredited investors.

II. Shares sold under a Regulation D, Rule 506, exempt offering may be purchased by any number of investors provided there are **no** more than 35 nonaccredited investors.

78. I. An exempt offering under Regulation D, Rule 506, must **not** be for more than $10,000,000.

II. An exempt offering under Regulation D, Rule 506, has **no** dollar limit.

79. I. Regulation D, Rule 506, requires that all investors in the exempt offering be notified that for nine months after the last sale **no** resale may be made to a nonresident.

II. Regulation D, Rule 506, requires that the issuer exercise reasonable care to assure that purchasers of the exempt offering are buying for investment and are **not** underwriters.

80. I. The SEC must be notified by Coffee Corp. within 5 days of the first sale of the exempt offering securities.

II. Coffee Corp. must include an SEC notification of the first sale of the exempt offering securities in Coffee's next filed Quarterly Report (Form 10-Q).

Number 4 (Estimated time—15 to 25 minutes)

On July 5, 19X5, Korn sent Wilson a written offer to clear Wilson's parking lot whenever it snowed through December 31, 19X5. Korn's offer stated that Wilson had until October 1 to accept.

On September 28, 19X5, Wilson mailed Korn an acceptance with a request that the agreement continue through March, 19X6. Wilson's acceptance was delayed and didn't reach Korn until October 3.

On September 29, 19X5, Korn saw weather reports indicating the snowfall for the season would be much heavier than normal. This would substantially increase Korn's costs to perform under the offer.

On September 30, 19X5, Korn phoned Wilson to insist that the terms of the agreement be changed. When Wilson refused, Korn orally withdrew the offer and stated that Korn would not perform.

Required:

a. State and explain the points of law that Korn would argue to show that there was **no** valid contract.

b. State and explain the points of law that Wilson would argue to show that there was a valid contract.

c. Assuming that a valid contract existed:

1. Determine whether Korn breached the contract and the nature of the breach and

2. State the common law remedies available to Wilson.

Number 5 (Estimated time—15 to 25 minutes)

On October 30, 19X5, Dover, CPA, was engaged to audit the financial records of Crane Corp., a tractor manufacturer. During the review of notes receivable, Dover reviewed a promissory note given to Crane by Jones Corp., one of its customers, in payment for a tractor. The note appears below.

(Face)

```
                                    July 18, 19X5
Sixty (60) days from date, the undersigned
promises to
Pay to the order of      Jones Corp.
Twenty Thousand and 00/100 ($20,000)...dollars
at West Bank

                        OVAL CORP.
                        G.J. Small
                        By: G.J. Small, Pres.
```

(Back)

```
        Jones Corp. Without Recourse
                R. Mall
        By: R. Mall, Pres.


            Crane Corp.
            For Collection


            Payment Refused
```

On the note's due date, Crane deposited the note for collection and was advised by the bank that Oval had refused payment. After payment was refused, Crane contacted Oval. Oval told Crane that Jones fraudulently induced Oval into executing the note and that Jones knew about Oval's claim before Jones endorsed the note to Crane.

Dover also reviewed a security agreement signed by Harper, a customer, given to Crane to finance Harper's purchase of a tractor for use in Harper's farming business. On October 1, 19X5, Harper made a down payment and gave Crane a purchase money security interest for the balance of the price of the tractor. Harper executed a financing statement that was filed on October 10, 19X5. The tractor had been delivered to Harper on October 5,19X5. On October 8, 19X5, Harper gave Acorn Trust a security agreement covering all of Harper's business equipment, including the tractor. Harper executed a financing statement that Acorn filed on October 9, 19X5.

Required:

As the auditor on this engagement, write a memo to the partner-in-charge identifying, explaining, and stating your conclusions about the legal issues pertaining to the note and the security interest.

The memo should address the following:

- Whether Crane is a holder in due course

- Whether Oval will be required to pay the note

- Whether Jones is liable to pay the note

- When Crane's security interest was perfected and whether it had priority over Acorn's security interest

TEST 2: QUESTIONS

AUDIT

Test ID: 3200

INSTRUCTIONS

1. Question Numbers 1, 2, and 3 should be answered on the scannable grid, which is at the back of this book. You should attempt to answer all objective items. There is no penalty for incorrect responses. Since the objective items are computer graded, your comments and calculations associated with them are not considered. Be certain that you have entered your answers on the scannable grid before the examination time is up. The objective portion of your examination will not be graded if you fail to record your answers on the scannable grid. You will not be given additional time to record your answers.

2. Question Numbers 4 and 5 should be answered using the essay response sheets at the back of this book. If you have not completed answering a question on a page, fill in the appropriate spaces in the wording on the bottom of the page. **"QUESTION NUMBER ___ CONTINUES ON PAGE ___."** If you have completed answering a question, fill in the appropriate space in the wording on the bottom of the page. **"QUESTION NUMBER ___ ENDS ON THIS PAGE."** Always begin the start of an answer to a question on the top of a new page (which may be the back side of a sheet of paper).

3. Although the primary purpose of the examination is to test your knowledge and application of the subject matter, selected essay responses will be graded for writing skills.

The point values for each question, and estimated time allotments based primarily on point value, are as follows:

	Point Value	Estimated Minutes Minimum	Estimated Minutes Maximum
No. 1	60	140	150
No. 2	10	15	25
No. 3	10	15	25
No. 4	10	25	35
No. 5	10	25	35
Totals	**100**	**220**	**270**

Number 1 (Estimated time—140 to 150 minutes)

Select the **best** answer for each of the following items. Use a No. 2 pencil to blacken ovals on the Multiple-Choice Section of your scannable grid, response items #1 through #90. **Mark only one answer for each item. Answer all items.**

1. In assessing the objectivity of internal auditors, an independent auditor should

   A. Evaluate the quality control program in effect for the internal auditors.

   B. Examine documentary evidence of the work performed by the internal auditors.

   C. Test a sample of the transactions and balances that the internal auditors examined.

   D. Determine the organizational level to which the internal auditors report.

2. In planning an audit, the auditor's knowledge about the design of relevant internal control policies and procedures should be used to

   A. Identify the types of potential misstatements that could occur.

   B. Assess the operational efficiency of the internal control.

   C. Determine whether controls have been circumvented by collusion.

   D. Document the assessed level of control risk.

3. Able Co. uses an online sales order processing system to process its sales transactions. Able's sales data are electronically sorted and subjected to edit checks. A direct output of the edit checks most likely would be a

   A. Report of all missing sales invoices.

   B. File of all rejected sales transactions.

   C. Printout of all user code numbers and passwords.

   D. List of all voided shipping documents.

4. Which of the following auditor concerns most likely could be so serious that the auditor concludes that a financial statement audit **cannot** be conducted?

   A. The entity has **no** formal written code of conduct.

   B. The integrity of the entity's management is suspect.

   C. Procedures requiring segregation of duties are subject to management override.

   D. Management fails to modify prescribed controls for changes in conditions.

5. Management philosophy and operating style most likely would have a significant influence on the entity's control environment when

   A. The internal auditor reports directly to management.

   B. Management is dominated by one individual.

   C. Accurate management job descriptions delineate specific duties.

   D. The audit committee actively oversees the financial reporting process.

6. Which of the following is a management control method that most likely could improve management's ability to supervise company activities effectively?

   A. Monitoring compliance with internal control requirements imposed by regulatory bodies.

   B. Limiting direct access to assets by physical segregation and protective devices.

   C. Establishing budgets and forecasts to identify variances from expectations.

   D. Supporting employees with the resources necessary to discharge their responsibilities.

*Items **7 and 8** are based on the following flowchart of a client's revenue cycle:*

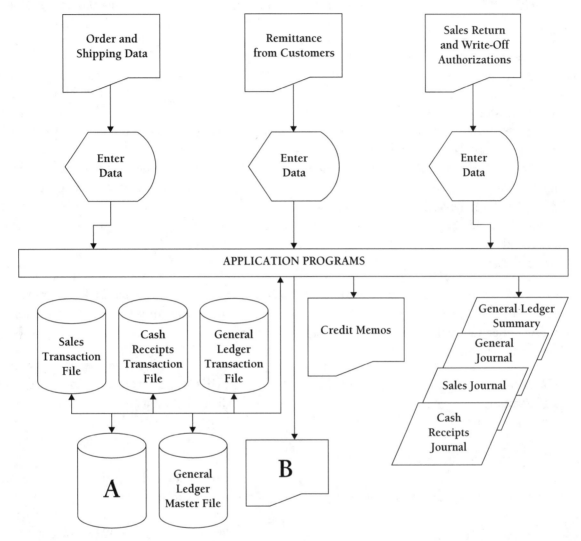

7. Symbol A most likely represents

- A. Remittance advice file.
- B. Receiving report file.
- C. Accounts receivable master file.
- D. Cash disbursements transaction file.

8. Symbol B most likely represents

- A. Customer orders.
- B. Receiving reports.
- C. Customer checks.
- D. Sales invoices.

9. In an audit of financial statements in accordance with generally accepted auditing standards, an auditor is required to

- A. Document the auditor's understanding of the entity's internal control.
- B. Search for significant deficiencies in the operation of the internal control.
- C. Perform tests of controls to evaluate the effectiveness of the entity's accounting system.
- D. Determine whether control procedures are suitably designed to prevent or detect material misstatements.

10. Which of the following is an example of a validity check?

A. The computer ensures that a numerical amount in a record does **not** exceed some predetermined amount.

B. As the computer corrects errors and data are successfully resubmitted to the system, the causes of the errors are printed out.

C. The computer flags any transmission for which the control field value did **not** match that of an existing file record.

D. After data for a transaction are entered, the computer sends certain data back to the terminal for comparison with data originally sent.

11. Which of the following types of evidence would an auditor most likely examine to determine whether internal control policies and procedures are operating as designed?

A. Gross margin information regarding the client's industry.

B. Confirmations of receivables verifying account balances.

C. Client records documenting the use of EDP programs.

D. Anticipated results documented in budgets or forecasts.

12. Which of the following internal controls most likely would reduce the risk of diversion of customer receipts by an entity's employees?

A. A bank lockbox system.
B. Prenumbered remittance advices.
C. Monthly bank reconciliations.
D. Daily deposit of cash receipts.

13. In obtaining an understanding of an entity's internal control policies and procedures that are relevant to audit planning, an auditor is required to obtain knowledge about the

A. Design of the policies and procedures pertaining to the internal control elements.

B. Effectiveness of the policies and procedures that have been placed in operation.

C. Consistency with which the policies and procedures are currently being applied.

D. Control procedures related to each principal transaction class and account balance.

14. Which of the following control procedures most likely could prevent EDP personnel from modifying programs to bypass programmed controls?

A. Periodic management review of computer utilization reports and systems documentation.

B. Segregation of duties within EDP for computer programming and computer operations.

C. Participation of user department personnel in designing and approving new systems.

D. Physical security of EDP facilities in limiting access to EDP equipment.

15. Which of the following is a control procedure that most likely could help prevent employee payroll fraud?

    A. The personnel department promptly sends employee termination notices to the payroll supervisor.

    B. Employees who distribute payroll checks forward unclaimed payroll checks to the absent employees' supervisors.

    C. Salary rates resulting from new hires are approved by the payroll supervisor.

    D. Total hours used for determination of gross pay are calculated by the payroll supervisor.

16. Which of the following controls would a company most likely use to safeguard marketable securities when an independent trust agent is **not** employed?

    A. The investment committee of the board of directors periodically reviews the investment decisions delegated to the treasurer.

    B. Two company officials have joint control of marketable securities, which are kept in a bank safe-deposit box.

    C. The internal auditor and the controller independently trace all purchases and sales of marketable securities from the subsidiary ledgers to the general ledger.

    D. The chairman of the board verifies the marketable securities, which are kept in a bank safe-deposit box, each year on the balance sheet date.

17. The diagram below depicts an auditor's estimated maximum deviation rate compared with the tolerable rate, and also depicts the true population deviation rate compared with the tolerable rate.

Auditor's Estimate Based on Sample Results	True State of Population	
	Deviation rate is less than tolerable rate	Deviation rate exceeds tolerable rate
Maximum deviation rate is less than tolerable rate	I.	III.
Maximum deviation rate exceeds tolerable rate	II.	IV.

As a result of tests of controls, the auditor assesses control risk too low and thereby decreases substantive testing. This is illustrated by situation

    A. I.

    B. II.

    C. III.

    D. IV.

18. In assessing control risk, an auditor ordinarily selects from a variety of techniques, including

    A. Inquiry and analytical procedures.

    B. Reperformance and observation.

    C. Comparison and confirmation.

    D. Inspection and verification.

19. The risk of incorrect acceptance and the likelihood of assessing control risk too low relate to the

    A. Allowable risk of tolerable misstatement.
    B. Preliminary estimates of materiality levels.
    C. Efficiency of the audit.
    D. Effectiveness of the audit.

20. Which of the following statements is correct concerning an auditor's assessment of control risk?

    A. Assessing control risk may be performed concurrently during an audit with obtaining an understanding of the entity's internal control.
    B. Evidence about the operation of control procedures in prior audits may **not** be considered during the current year's assessment of control risk.
    C. The basis for an auditor's conclusions about the assessed level of control risk need **not** be documented unless control risk is assessed at the maximum level.
    D. The lower the assessed level of control risk, the less assurance the evidence must provide that the control procedures are operating effectively.

21. An auditor assesses control risk because it

    A. Is relevant to the auditor's understanding of the control environment.
    B. Provides assurance that the auditor's materiality levels are appropriate.
    C. Indicates to the auditor where inherent risk may be the greatest.
    D. Affects the level of detection risk that the auditor may accept.

22. Assessing control risk at below the maximum level most likely would involve

    A. Performing more extensive substantive tests with larger sample sizes than originally planned.
    B. Reducing inherent risk for most of the assertions relevant to significant account balances.
    C. Changing the timing of substantive tests by omitting interim-date testing and performing the tests at year end.
    D. Identifying specific internal control policies and procedures relevant to specific assertions.

23. After assessing control risk at below the maximum level, an auditor desires to seek a further reduction in the assessed level of control risk. At this time, the auditor would consider whether

    A. It would be efficient to obtain an understanding of the entity's accounting system.
    B. The entity's internal control policies and procedures have been placed in operation.
    C. The entity's internal control policies and procedures pertain to any financial statement assertions.
    D. Additional evidential matter sufficient to support a further reduction is likely to be available.

24. When assessing control risk below the maximum level, an auditor is required to document the auditor's

	Understanding of the entity's control environment	Basis for concluding that control risk is below the maximum level
A.	Yes	No
B.	No	Yes
C.	Yes	Yes
D.	No	No

25. An auditor who uses statistical sampling for attributes in testing internal controls should reduce the planned reliance on a prescribed control when the

A. Sample rate of deviation plus the allowance for sampling risk equals the tolerable rate.

B. Sample rate of deviation is less than the expected rate of deviation used in planning the sample.

C. Tolerable rate less the allowance for sampling risk exceeds the sample rate of deviation.

D. Sample rate of deviation plus the allowance for sampling risk exceeds the tolerable rate.

26. In addition to evaluating the frequency of deviations in tests of controls, an auditor should also consider certain qualitative aspects of the deviations. The auditor most likely would give broader consideration to the implications of a deviation if it was

A. The only deviation discovered in the sample.

B. Identical to a deviation discovered during the prior year's audit.

C. Caused by an employee's misunderstanding of instructions.

D. Initially concealed by a forged document.

27. When there are numerous property and equipment transactions during the year, an auditor who plans to assess control risk at a low level usually performs

A. Tests of controls and extensive tests of property and equipment balances at the end of the year.

B. Analytical procedures for current year property and equipment transactions.

C. Tests of controls and limited tests of current year property and equipment transactions.

D. Analytical procedures for property and equipment balances at the end of the year.

28. An auditor suspects that a client's cashier is misappropriating cash receipts for personal use by lapping customer checks received in the mail. In attempting to uncover this embezzlement scheme, the auditor most likely would compare the

   A. Dates checks are deposited per bank statements with the dates remittance credits are recorded.
   B. Daily cash summaries with the sums of the cash receipts journal entries.
   C. Individual bank deposit slips with the details of the monthly bank statements.
   D. Dates uncollectible accounts are authorized to be written off with the dates the write-offs are actually recorded.

29. In testing controls over cash disbursements, an auditor most likely would determine that the person who signs checks also

   A. Reviews the monthly bank reconciliation.
   B. Returns the checks to accounts payable.
   C. Is denied access to the supporting documents.
   D. Is responsible for mailing the checks.

30. For effective internal control, the accounts payable department generally should

   A. Stamp, perforate, or otherwise cancel supporting documentation after payment is mailed.
   B. Ascertain that each requisition is approved as to price, quantity, and quality by an authorized employee.
   C. Obliterate the quantity ordered on the receiving department copy of the purchase order.
   D. Establish the agreement of the vendor's invoice with the receiving report and purchase order.

31. In determining the effectiveness of an entity's policies and procedures relating to the existence or occurrence assertion for payroll transactions, an auditor most likely would inquire about and

   A. Observe the segregation of duties concerning personnel responsibilities and payroll disbursement.
   B. Inspect evidence of accounting for prenumbered payroll checks.
   C. Recompute the payroll deductions for employee fringe benefits.
   D. Verify the preparation of the monthly payroll account bank reconciliation.

32. In obtaining an understanding of a manufacturing entity's internal control concerning inventory balances, an auditor most likely would

   A. Analyze the liquidity and turnover ratios of the inventory.
   B. Perform analytical procedures designed to identify cost variances.
   C. Review the entity's descriptions of inventory policies and procedures.
   D. Perform test counts of inventory during the entity's physical count.

33. Which of the following factors is (are) considered in determining the sample size for a test of controls?

	Expected Deviation Rate	Tolerable Deviation Rate
A.	Yes	Yes
B.	No	No
C.	No	Yes
D.	Yes	No

34. A weakness in internal control over recording retirements of equipment may cause an auditor to

A. Inspect certain items of equipment in the plant and trace those items to the accounting records.
B. Review the subsidiary ledger to ascertain whether depreciation was taken on each item of equipment during the year.
C. Trace additions to the "other assets" account to search for equipment that is still on hand but no longer being used.
D. Select certain items of equipment from the accounting records and locate them in the plant.

35. An auditor's letter issued on reportable conditions relating to an entity's internal control observed during a financial statement audit should

A. Include a brief description of the tests of controls performed in searching for reportable conditions and material weaknesses.
B. Indicate that the reportable conditions should be disclosed in the annual report to the entity's shareholders.
C. Include a paragraph describing management's assertion concerning the effectiveness of the internal control.
D. Indicate that the audit's purpose was to report on the financial statements and **not** to provide assurance on the internal control.

36. Brown, CPA, has accepted an engagement to examine and report on Crow Company's written assertion about the effectiveness of Crow's internal control. In what form may Crow present its written assertion?

I. In a separate report that will accompany Brown's report.

II. In a representation letter to Brown.

A. I only.
B. II only.
C. Either I or II.
D. Neither I nor II.

37. Computer Services Company (CSC) processes payroll transactions for schools. Drake, CPA, is engaged to report on CSC's policies and procedures placed in operation as of a specific date. These policies and procedures are relevant to the schools' internal control, so Drake's report will be useful in providing the schools' independent auditors with information necessary to plan their audits. Drake's report expressing an opinion on CSC's policies and procedures placed in operation as of a specific date should contain a (an)

A. Description of the scope and nature of Drake's procedures.
B. Statement that CSC's management has disclosed to Drake all design deficiencies of which it is aware.
C. Opinion on the operating effectiveness of CSC's policies and procedures.
D. Paragraph indicating the basis for Drake's assessment of control risk.

38. An auditor may achieve audit objectives related to particular assertions by

A. Performing analytical procedures.
B. Adhering to a system of quality control.
C. Preparing auditor working papers.
D. Increasing the level of detection risk.

39. The confirmation of customers' accounts receivable rarely provides reliable evidence about the completeness assertion because

A. Many customers merely sign and return the confirmation without verifying its details.
B. Recipients usually respond only if they disagree with the information on the request.
C. Customers may **not** be inclined to report understatement errors in their accounts.
D. Auditors typically select many accounts with low recorded balances to be confirmed.

40. Which of the following sets of information does an auditor usually confirm on one form?

A. Accounts payable and purchase commitments.
B. Cash in bank and collateral for loans.
C. Inventory on consignment and contingent liabilities.
D. Accounts receivable and accrued interest receivable.

41. An auditor's analytical procedures most likely would be facilitated if the entity

A. Segregates obsolete inventory before the physical inventory count.
B. Uses a standard cost system that produces variance reports.
C. Corrects material weaknesses in internal control before the beginning of the audit.
D. Develops its data from sources solely within the entity.

42. To measure how effectively an entity employs its resources, an auditor calculates inventory turnover by dividing average inventory into

A. Net sales.
B. Cost of goods sold.
C. Operating income.
D. Gross sales.

43. How would increases in tolerable misstatement and assessed level of control risk affect the sample size in a substantive test of details?

	Increase in Tolerable Misstatement	Increase in Assessed Level of Control Risk
A.	Increase sample size	Increase sample size
B.	Increase sample size	Decrease sample size
C.	Decrease sample size	Increase sample size
D.	Decrease sample size	Decrease sample size

44. An advantage of statistical sampling over nonstatistical sampling is that statistical sampling helps an auditor to

A. Eliminate the risk of nonsampling errors.
B. Reduce the level of audit risk and materiality to a relatively low amount.
C. Measure the sufficiency of the evidential matter obtained.
D. Minimize the failure to detect errors and irregularities.

45. The usefulness of the standard bank confirmation request may be limited because the bank employee who completes the form may

- A. Not believe that the bank is obligated to verify confidential information to a third party.
- B. Sign and return the form without inspecting the accuracy of the client's bank reconciliation.
- C. Not have access to the client's cutoff bank statement.
- D. Be unaware of all the financial relationships that the bank has with the client.

46. An auditor most likely would limit substantive audit tests of sales transactions when control risk is assessed as low for the existence or occurrence assertion concerning sales transactions and the auditor has already gathered evidence supporting

- A. Opening and closing inventory balances.
- B. Cash receipts and accounts receivable.
- C. Shipping and receiving activities.
- D. Cutoffs of sales and purchases.

47. Which of the following procedures would an auditor most likely perform in searching for unrecorded liabilities?

- A. Trace a sample of accounts payable entries recorded just before year-end to the unmatched receiving report file.
- B. Compare a sample of purchase orders issued just after year-end with the year-end accounts payable trial balance.
- C. Vouch a sample of cash disbursements recorded just after year-end to receiving reports and vendor invoices.
- D. Scan the cash disbursements entries recorded just before year-end for indications of unusual transactions.

48. An auditor traced a sample of purchase orders and the related receiving reports to the purchases journal and the cash disbursements journal. The purpose of this substantive audit procedure most likely was to

- A. Identify unusually large purchases that should be investigated further.
- B. Verify that cash disbursements were for goods actually received.
- C. Determine that purchases were properly recorded.
- D. Test whether payments were for goods actually ordered.

49. Which of the following explanations most likely would satisfy an auditor who questions management about significant debits to the accumulated depreciation accounts?

- A. The estimated remaining useful lives of plant assets were revised upward.
- B. Plant assets were retired during the year.
- C. The prior year's depreciation expense was erroneously understated.
- D. Overhead allocations were revised at year-end.

50. Which of the following circumstances most likely would cause an auditor to suspect an employee payroll fraud scheme?

- A. There are significant unexplained variances between standard and actual labor cost.
- B. Payroll checks are disbursed by the same employee each payday.
- C. Employee time cards are approved by individual departmental supervisors.
- D. A separate payroll bank account is maintained on an imprest basis.

51. The objective of tests of details of transactions performed as substantive tests is to

   A. Comply with generally accepted auditing standards.

   B. Attain assurance about the reliability of the accounting system.

   C. Detect material misstatements in the financial statements.

   D. Evaluate whether management's policies and procedures operated effectively.

52. A primary advantage of using generalized audit software packages to audit the financial statements of a client that uses an EDP system is that the auditor may

   A. Access information stored on computer files while having a limited understanding of the client's hardware and software features.

   B. Consider increasing the use of substantive tests of transactions in place of analytical procedures.

   C. Substantiate the accuracy of data through self-checking digits and hash totals.

   D. Reduce the level of required tests of controls to a relatively small amount.

53. The work of internal auditors may affect the independent auditor's

   I. Procedures performed in obtaining an understanding of the internal control.

   II. Procedures performed in assessing the risk of material misstatement.

   III. Substantive procedures performed in gathering direct evidence.

   A. I and II only.

   B. I and III only.

   C. II and III only.

   D. I, II, and III.

54. Which of the following statements is correct concerning an auditor's use of the work of a specialist?

   A. The auditor need **not** obtain an understanding of the methods and assumptions used by the specialist.

   B. The auditor may **not** use the work of a specialist in matters material to the fair presentation of the financial statements.

   C. The reasonableness of the specialist's assumptions and their applications are strictly the auditor's responsibility.

   D. The work of a specialist who has a contractual relationship with the client may be acceptable under certain circumstances.

55. Which of the following is an audit procedure that an auditor most likely would perform concerning litigation, claims, and assessments?

   A. Request the client's lawyer to evaluate whether the client's pending litigation, claims, and assessments indicate a going concern problem.

   B. Examine the legal documents in the client's lawyer's possession concerning litigation, claims, and assessments to which the lawyer has devoted substantive attention.

   C. Discuss with management its policies and procedures adopted for evaluating and accounting for litigation, claims, and assessments.

   D. Confirm directly with the client's lawyer that all litigation, claims, and assessments have been recorded or disclosed in the financial statements.

56. Which of the following procedures would an auditor most likely perform to obtain evidence about the occurrence of subsequent events?

- A. Confirming a sample of material accounts receivable established after year-end.
- B. Comparing the financial statements being reported on with those of the prior period.
- C. Investigating personnel changes in the accounting department occurring after year-end.
- D. Inquiring as to whether any unusual adjustments were made after year-end.

57. Which of the following matters would an auditor most likely include in a management representation letter?

- A. Communications with the audit committee concerning weaknesses in the internal control.
- B. The completeness and availability of minutes of stockholders' and directors' meetings.
- C. Plans to acquire or merge with other entities in the subsequent year.
- D. Management's acknowledgment of its responsibility for the detection of employee fraud.

58. Which of the following auditing procedures most likely would assist an auditor in identifying related party transactions?

- A. Inspecting correspondence with lawyers for evidence of unreported contingent liabilities.
- B. Vouching accounting records for recurring transactions recorded just after the balance sheet date.
- C. Reviewing confirmations of loans receivable and payable for indications of guarantees.
- D. Performing analytical procedures for indications of possible financial difficulties.

59. Cooper, CPA, believes there is substantial doubt about the ability of Zero Corp. to continue as a going concern for a reasonable period of time. In evaluating Zero's plans for dealing with the adverse effects of future conditions and events, Cooper most likely would consider, as a mitigating factor, Zero's plans to

- A. Discuss with lenders the terms of all debt and loan agreements.
- B. Strengthen internal controls over cash disbursements.
- C. Purchase production facilities currently being leased from a related party.
- D. Postpone expenditures for research and development projects.

60. The permanent (continuing) file of an auditor's working papers most likely would include copies of the

- A. Lead schedules.
- B. Attorney's letters.
- C. Bank statements.
- D. Debt agreements.

61. Harris, CPA, has been asked to audit and report on the balance sheet of Fox Co. but not on the statements of income, retained earnings, or cash flows. Harris will have access to all information underlying the basic financial statements. Under these circumstances, Harris may

A. Not accept the engagement because it would constitute a violation of the profession's ethical standards.
B. Not accept the engagement because it would be tantamount to rendering a piecemeal opinion.
C. Accept the engagement because such engagements merely involve limited reporting objectives.
D. Accept the engagement but should disclaim an opinion because of an inability to apply the procedures considered necessary.

62. Which of the following statements is a basic element of the auditor's standard report?

A. The disclosures provide reasonable assurance that the financial statements are free of material misstatement.
B. The auditor evaluated the overall internal control.
C. An audit includes assessing significant estimates made by management.
D. The financial statements are consistent with those of the prior period.

63. An auditor may **not** issue a qualified opinion when

A. An accounting principle at variance with GAAP is used.
B. The auditor lacks independence with respect to the audited entity.
C. A scope limitation prevents the auditor from completing an important audit procedure.
D. The auditor's report refers to the work of a specialist.

64. An auditor most likely would express an unqualified opinion and would **not** add explanatory language to the report if the auditor

A. Wishes to emphasize that the entity had significant transactions with related parties.
B. Concurs with the entity's change in its method of computing depreciation.
C. Discovers that supplementary information required by FASB has been omitted.
D. Believes that there is a remote likelihood of a material loss resulting from an uncertainty.

65. An auditor would express an unqualified opinion with an explanatory paragraph added to the auditor's report for

	An unjustified accounting change	A material weakness in the internal control
A.	Yes	Yes
B.	Yes	No
C.	No	Yes
D.	No	No

66. Under which of the following circumstances would a disclaimer of opinion **not** be appropriate?

A. The auditor is unable to determine the amounts associated with an employee fraud scheme.
B. Management does **not** provide reasonable justification for a change in accounting principles.
C. The client refuses to permit the auditor to confirm certain accounts receivable or apply alternative procedures to verify their balances.
D. The chief executive officer is unwilling to sign the management representation letter.

67. Digit Co. uses the FIFO method of costing for its international subsidiary's inventory and LIFO for its domestic inventory. Under these circumstances, the auditor's report on Digit's financial statements should express an

A. Unqualified opinion.
B. Opinion qualified because of a lack of consistency.
C. Opinion qualified because of a departure from GAAP.
D. Adverse opinion.

68. The fourth standard of reporting requires the auditor's report to contain either an expression of opinion regarding the financial statements taken as a whole or an assertion to the effect that an opinion cannot be expressed. The objective of the fourth standard is to prevent

A. An auditor from expressing different opinions on each of the basic financial statements.
B. Restrictions on the scope of the audit, whether imposed by the client or by the inability to obtain evidence.
C. Misinterpretations regarding the degree of responsibility the auditor is assuming.
D. An auditor from reporting on one basic financial statement and **not** the others.

69. In which of the following circumstances would an auditor **not** express an unqualified opinion?

A. There has been a material change between periods in accounting principles.
B. Quarterly financial data required by the SEC has been omitted.
C. The auditor wishes to emphasize an unusually important subsequent event.
D. The auditor is unable to obtain audited financial statements of a consolidated investee.

70. An explanatory paragraph following the opinion paragraph of an auditor's report describes an uncertainty as follows:

As discussed in Note X to the financial statements, the Company is a defendant in a lawsuit alleging infringement of certain patent rights and claiming damages. Discovery proceedings are in progress. The ultimate outcome of the litigation cannot presently be determined. Accordingly, no provision for any liability that may result upon adjudication has been made in the accompanying financial statements.

What type of opinion should the auditor express under these circumstances?

    A. Adverse.
    B. Qualified due to a scope limitation.
    C. Qualified due to a GAAP violation.
    D. Unqualified.

71. Which of the following phrases would an auditor most likely include in the auditor's report when expressing a qualified opinion because of inadequate disclosure?

    A. Subject to the departure from generally accepted accounting principles, as described above.
    B. With the foregoing explanation of these omitted disclosures.
    C. Except for the omission of the information discussed in the preceding paragraph.
    D. Does **not** present fairly in all material respects.

72. Kane, CPA, concludes that there is substantial doubt about Lima Co.'s ability to continue as a going concern for a reasonable period of time. If Lima's financial statements adequately disclose its financial difficulties, Kane's auditor's report is required to include an explanatory paragraph that specifically uses the phrase(s)

	"Possible discontinuance of operations"	"Reasonable period of time, **not** to exceed one year"
A.	Yes	Yes
B.	Yes	No
C.	No	Yes
D.	No	No

73. Mead, CPA, had substantial doubt about Tech Co.'s ability to continue as a going concern when reporting on Tech's audited financial statements for the year ended June 30, 19X4. That doubt has been removed in 19X5. What is Mead's reporting responsibility if Tech is presenting its financial statements for the year ended June 30, 19X5, on a comparative basis with those of 19X4?

    A. The explanatory paragraph included in the 19X4 auditor's report should **not** be repeated.
    B. The explanatory paragraph included in the 19X4 auditor's report should be repeated in its entirety.
    C. A different explanatory paragraph describing Mead's reasons for the removal of doubt should be included.
    D. A different explanatory paragraph describing Tech's plans for financial recovery should be included.

74. In the first audit of a new client, an auditor was able to extend auditing procedures to gather sufficient evidence about consistency. Under these circumstances, the auditor should

  A. Not report on the client's income statement.
  B. Not refer to consistency in the auditor's report.
  C. State that the consistency standard does not apply.
  D. State that the accounting principles have been applied consistently.

75. When reporting on comparative financial statements, an auditor ordinarily should change the previously issued opinion on the prior-year's financial statements if the

  A. Prior year's financial statements are restated to conform with generally accepted accounting principles.
  B. Auditor is a predecessor auditor who has been requested by a former client to reissue the previously issued report.
  C. Prior year's opinion was unqualified and the opinion on the current year's financial statements is modified due to a lack of consistency.
  D. Prior year's financial statements are restated following a pooling of interests in the current year.

76. Jewel, CPA, audited Infinite Co.'s prior-year financial statements. These statements are presented with those of the current year for comparative purposes without Jewel's auditor's report, which expressed a qualified opinion. In drafting the current year's auditor's report, Crain, CPA, the successor auditor, should

  I. Not name Jewel as the predecessor auditor.

  II. Indicate the type of report issued by Jewel.

  III. Indicate the substantive reasons for Jewel's qualification.

    A. I only.
    B. I and II only.
    C. II and III only.
    D. I, II, and III.

77. The introductory paragraph of an auditor's report contains the following sentences:

We did not audit the financial statements of EZ Inc., a wholly owned subsidiary, which statements reflect total assets and revenues constituting 27 percent and 29 percent, respectively, of the related consolidated totals. Those statements were audited by other auditors whose report has been furnished to us, and our opinion, insofar as it relates to the amounts included for EZ Inc., is based solely on the report of the other auditors.

These sentences

  A. Indicate a division of responsibility.
  B. Assume responsibility for the other auditor.
  C. Require a departure from an unqualified opinion.
  D. Are an improper form of reporting.

78. March, CPA, is engaged by Monday Corp., a client, to audit the financial statements of Wall Corp., a company that is not March's client. Monday expects to present Wall's audited financial statements with March's auditor's report to 1st Federal Bank to obtain financing in Monday's attempt to purchase Wall. In these circumstances, March's auditor's report would usually be addressed to

A. Monday Corp., the client that engaged March.
B. Wall Corp., the entity audited by March.
C. 1st Federal Bank.
D. Both Monday Corp. and 1st Federal Bank.

79. Financial statements of a nonpublic entity that have been reviewed by an accountant should be accompanied by a report stating that a review

A. Provides only limited assurance that the financial statements are fairly presented.
B. Includes examining, on a test basis, information that is the representation of management.
C. Consists principally of inquiries of company personnel and analytical procedures applied to financial data.
D. Does **not** contemplate obtaining corroborating evidential matter or applying certain other procedures ordinarily performed during an audit.

80. Financial statements of a nonpublic entity compiled without audit or review by an accountant should be accompanied by a report stating that

A. The scope of the accountant's procedures has **not** been restricted in testing the financial information that is the representation of management.
B. The accountant assessed the accounting principles used and significant estimates made by management.
C. The accountant does **not** express an opinion or any other form of assurance on the financial statements.
D. A compilation consists principally of inquiries of entity personnel and analytical procedures applied to financial data.

81. A CPA's report on agreed-upon procedures related to management's assertion about an entity's compliance with specified requirements should contain

A. A statement of limitations on the use of the report.
B. An opinion about whether management's assertion is fairly stated.
C. Negative assurance that control risk has **not** been assessed.
D. An acknowledgment of responsibility for the sufficiency of the procedures.

82. When an accountant examines projected financial statements, the accountant's report should include a separate paragraph that

    A. Describes the limitations on the usefulness of the presentation.

    B. Provides an explanation of the differences between an examination and an audit.

    C. States that the accountant is responsible for events and circumstances up to one year after the report's date.

    D. Disclaims an opinion on whether the assumptions provide a reasonable basis for the projection.

83. Field is an employee of Gold Enterprises. Hardy, CPA, is asked to express an opinion on Field's profit participation in Gold's net income. Hardy may accept this engagement only if

    A. Hardy also audits Gold's complete financial statements.

    B. Gold's financial statements are prepared in conformity with GAAP.

    C. Hardy's report is available for distribution to Gold's other employees.

    D. Field owns controlling interest in Gold.

84. Which of the following statements is correct about an auditor's required communication with an entity's audit committee?

    A. Any matters communicated to the entity's audit committee also are required to be communicated to the entity's management.

    B. The auditor is required to inform the entity's audit committee about significant errors discovered by the auditor and subsequently corrected by management.

    C. Disagreements with management about the application of accounting principles are required to be communicated in writing to the entity's audit committee.

    D. Weaknesses in the internal control previously reported to the entity's audit committee are required to be communicated to the audit committee after each subsequent audit until the weaknesses are corrected.

85. Which of the following events occurring after the issuance of an auditor's report most likely would cause the auditor to make further inquiries about the previously issued financial statements?

    A. An uninsured natural disaster occurs that may affect the entity's ability to continue as a going concern.

    B. A contingency is resolved that had been disclosed in the audited financial statements.

    C. New information is discovered concerning undisclosed lease transactions of the audited period.

    D. A subsidiary is sold that accounts for 25% of the entity's consolidated net income.

86. A registration statement filed with the SEC contains the reports of two independent auditors on their audits of financial statements for different periods. The predecessor auditor who audited the prior-period financial statements generally should obtain a letter of representation from the

A. Successor independent auditor.
B. Client's audit committee.
C. Principal underwriter.
D. Securities and Exchange Commission.

87. An auditor is engaged to report on selected financial data that are included in a client-prepared document containing audited financial statements. Under these circumstances, the report on the selected data should

A. Be limited to data derived from the audited financial statements.
B. Be distributed only to senior management and the board of directors.
C. State that the presentation is a comprehensive basis of accounting other than GAAP.
D. Indicate that the data are **not** fairly stated in all material respects.

88. In auditing a not-for-profit entity that receives governmental financial assistance, the auditor has a responsibility to

A. Issue a separate report that describes the expected benefits and related costs of the auditor's suggested changes to the entity's internal control.
B. Assess whether management has identified laws and regulations that have a direct and material effect on the entity's financial statements.
C. Notify the governmental agency providing the financial assistance that the audit is **not** designed to provide any assurance of detecting errors and irregularities.

D. Render an opinion concerning the entity's continued eligibility for the governmental financial assistance.

89. In auditing compliance with requirements governing major federal financial assistance programs under the Single Audit Act, the auditor's consideration of materiality differs from materiality under generally accepted auditing standards. Under the Single Audit Act, materiality is

A. Calculated in relation to the financial statements taken as a whole.
B. Determined separately for each major federal financial assistance program.
C. Decided in conjunction with the auditor's risk assessment.
D. Ignored, because all account balances, regardless of size, are fully tested.

90. Which of the following statements represents a quality control requirement under government auditing standards?

A. A CPA who conducts government audits is required to undergo an annual external quality control review when an appropriate internal quality control system is **not** in place.
B. A CPA seeking to enter into a contract to perform an audit should provide the CPA's most recent external quality control review report to the party contracting for the audit.
C. An external quality control review of a CPA's practice should include a review of the working papers of each government audit performed since the prior external quality control review.
D. A CPA who conducts government audits may **not** make the CPA's external quality control review report available to the public.

Number 2 (Estimated time—15 to 25 minutes)

Question Number 2 consists of 15 items. Select the **best** answer for each item. Use a No. 2 pencil to blacken the appropriate ovals on OOF Section #1 of your scannable grid, response items #1 through #15. **Answer all items.**

Required:

Items 91 through 105 represent a series of unrelated statements, questions, excerpts, and comments taken from various parts of an auditor's working paper file. Below the items is a list of the likely sources of the statements, questions, excerpts, and comments. Select, as the best answer for each item, the most likely source. Select only one source for each item. A source may be selected once, more than once, or not at all.

91. There are no material transactions that have not been properly recorded in the accounting records underlying the financial statements.

92. In connection with an audit of our financial statements, management has prepared, and furnished to our auditors, a description and evaluation of certain contingencies.

93. Provision has been made for any material loss to be sustained in the fulfillment of, or from the inability to fulfill, any sales commitments.

94. Fees for our services are based on our regular per diem rates, plus travel and other out-of-pocket expenses.

95. The objective of our audit is to express an unqualified opinion on the financial statements, although it is possible that facts or circumstances encountered may preclude us from expressing an unqualified opinion.

96. There have been no irregularities involving employees that could have a material effect on the financial statements.

97. Are you aware of any facts or circumstances that may indicate a lack of integrity by any member of senior management?

98. If a difference of opinion on a practice problem existed between engagement personnel and a specialist or other consultant, was the difference resolved in accordance with firm policy and appropriately documented?

99. Although we have not conducted a comprehensive, detailed search of our records, no other deposit or loan accounts have come to our attention except as noted below.

100. At the conclusion of our audit, we will request certain written representations from you about the financial statements and related matters.

101. We have no plans or intentions that may materially affect the carrying value or classification of assets and liabilities.

102. As discussed in Note 14 to the financial statements, the Company has had numerous dealings with businesses controlled by, and people who are related to, the officers of the Company.

103. There were unreasonable delays by management in permitting the commencement of the audit and in providing needed information.

104. If this statement is not correct, please write promptly, using the enclosed envelope, and give details of any differences directly to our auditors.

105. The Company has suffered recurring losses from operations and has a net capital deficiency that raises substantial doubt about its ability to continue as a going concern.

LIST OF SOURCES

(A) Partner's engagement review program.

(B) Communication with predecessor auditor.

(C) Auditor's engagement letter.

(D) Management representation letter.

(E) Standard financial institution confirmation request.

(F) Auditor's communication with the audit committee.

(G) Auditor's report.

(H) Letter for underwriters.

(I) Audit inquiry letter to legal counsel.

(J) Accounts receivable confirmation.

Number 3 (Estimated time—15 to 25 minutes)

Question Number 3 consists of 15 items. Select the **best** answer for each item. Use a No. 2 pencil to blacken the appropriate ovals on OOF Multiple-Response Section of your scannable grid, response items #1 through #15. **Answer all items.**

Required:

Items 106 through 120 represent a series of unrelated procedures that an accountant may consider performing in separate engagements to review the financial statements of a nonpublic entity (a review) and to compile the financial statements for a nonpublic entity (a compilation). Select, as the best answer for each item, whether the procedure is Required (A) or Not Required (B) for both review and compilation engagements. Make two selections for each item. In answering for a review engagement, blacken the correct oval in the first column of response items #1 through #15. For a compilation, blacken the correct ovals in the second column.

Procedures

106. The accountant should establish an understanding with the entity regarding the nature and limitations of the services to be performed.

107. The accountant should make inquiries concerning actions taken at the board of directors' meetings.

108. The accountant, as the entity's successor accountant, should communicate with the predecessor accountant to obtain access to the predecessor's working papers.

109. The accountant should obtain a level of knowledge of the accounting principles and practices of the entity's industry.

110. The accountant should obtain an understanding of the entity's internal control.

111. The accountant should perform analytical procedures designed to identify relationships that appear to be unusual.

112. The accountant should make an assessment of control risk.

113. The accountant should send a letter of inquiry to the entity's attorney to corroborate the information furnished by management concerning litigation.

114. The accountant should obtain a management representation letter from the entity.

115. The accountant should study the relationships of the financial statement elements that would be expected to conform to a predictable pattern.

116. The accountant should communicate to the entity's senior management illegal employee acts discovered by the accountant that are clearly inconsequential.

117. The accountant should make inquiries about events subsequent to the date of the financial statements that would have a material effect on the financial statements.

118. The accountant should modify the accountant's report if there is a change in accounting principles that is adequately disclosed.

119. The accountant should submit a hard copy of the financial statements and accountant's report when the financial statements and accountant's report are submitted on a computer disk.

120. The accountant should perform specific procedures to evaluate whether there is substantial doubt about the entity's ability to continue as a going concern.

Number 4 (Estimated time—25 to 50 minutes)

Recently there has been a significant number of highly publicized cases of alleged or actual management fraud involving the misstatement of financial statements. Although most client managements possess unquestioned integrity, a very small number, given sufficient incentive and opportunity, may be predisposed to fraudulently misstate reported financial condition and operating results.

Required:

a. What distinguishes management fraud from a defalcation?

b. What are an auditor's responsibilities under generally accepted auditing standards to detect management fraud?

c. What are the characteristics of management fraud that an auditor should consider to fulfill the auditor's responsibilities under generally accepted auditing standards related to detecting management fraud?

d. Three factors that heighten an auditor's concern about the existence of management fraud include (1) an intended public placement of securities in the near future, (2) management remuneration dependent on operating results, and (3) a weak internal control environment evidenced by lack of concern for basic controls and disregard of the auditor's recommendations.

What other factors should heighten an auditor's concern about the existence of management fraud?

Number 5 (Estimated time—25 to 35 minutes)

Most of an auditor's work in forming an opinion on financial statements consists of obtaining and evaluating evidential matter concerning the financial statement assertions.

Required:

a. What is the definition of "financial statement assertions"?

Do not list the assertions.

b. What is the relationship between audit objectives and financial statement assertions?

c. What should an auditor consider in developing the audit objectives of a particular engagement?

d. What is the relationship between audit objectives and audit procedures?

e. What are an auditor's primary considerations when selecting particular substantive tests to achieve audit objectives?

TEST 2: QUESTIONS

ACCOUNTING & REPORTING—
Taxation, Managerial, and Governmental and Not-for-Profit Organizations

Test ID: 1200

INSTRUCTIONS

1. All questions should be answered on the scannable grid, which is at the back of this book. You should attempt to answer all objective items. There is no penalty for incorrect responses. Work space to solve the objective answers is provided. Be certain that you have entered all your answers on the scannable grid. The objective portion of your examination will not be graded if you fail to record your answers on the scannable grid.

2. At examination time, you will receive an AICPA-approved calculator to help you work through the problems in this section of the CPA Exam.

	Point Value	Estimated Minutes Minimum	Estimated Minutes Maximum
No. 1	60	120	130
No. 2	5	5	10
No. 3	20	25	40
No. 4	5	5	10
No. 5	10	15	20
Totals	**100**	**170**	**210**

The point values for each question, and estimated time allotments based primarily on point value, are as follows:

Number 1 (Estimated time—120 to 130 minutes)

Select the **best** answer for each of the following items. Use a No. 2 pencil to blacken ovals on the Multiple-Choice Section of your scannable grid, response items #1 through #75. **Mark only one answer for each item. Answer all items.**

Items 1 through 38 are in the areas of federal taxation. The answers should be based on the Internal Revenue Code and Tax Regulations in effect for the tax period specified in the item. If *no* tax period is specified, use the *current* Internal Revenue Code and Tax Regulations.

1. In 19X4, Starke Corp., an accrual-basis calendar year corporation, reported book income of $380,000. Included in that amount was $50,000 municipal bond interest income, $170,000 for federal income tax expense, and $2,000 interest expense on the debt incurred to carry the municipal bonds. What amount should Starke's taxable income be as reconciled on Starke's Schedule M-1 of Form 1120, U.S. Corporation Income Tax Return?

   A. $330,000
   B. $500,000
   C. $502,000
   D. $550,000

2. Lake Corp., an accrual-basis calendar year corporation, had the following 19X4 receipts:

19X5 advanced rental payments where the lease ends in 19X6	$125,000
Lease cancellation payment from a 5-year lease tenant	50,000

Lake had no restrictions on the use of the advanced rental payments and renders no services. What amount of income should Lake report on its 19X4 tax return?

   A. $0
   B. $50,000
   C. $125,000
   D. $175,000

3. A C corporation's net capital losses are

   A. Carried forward indefinitely until fully utilized.
   B. Carried back 3 years and forward 5 years.
   C. Deductible in full from the corporation's ordinary income.
   D. Deductible from the corporation's ordinary income only to the extent of $3,000.

Please use this area for work space.

4. In 19X4, Best Corp., an accrual-basis calendar year C corporation, received $100,000 in dividend income from the common stock that it held in an unrelated domestic corporation. The stock was not debt-financed, and was held for over a year. Best recorded the following information for 19X4:

Loss from Best's operations	($10,000)
Dividends received	100,000
Taxable income (before dividends-received deduction)	$90,000

Best's dividends-received deduction on its 19X4 tax return was

A. $100,000
B. $80,000
C. $70,000
D. $63,000

5. Data Corp., a calendar year corporation, purchased and placed into service office equipment during November 19X4. No other equipment was placed into service during 19X4. Under the general MACRS depreciation system, what convention must Data use?

A. Full-year.
B. Half-year.
C. Mid-quarter.
D. Mid-month.

6. Capital assets include

A. A corporation's accounts receivable from the sale of its inventory.
B. Seven-year MACRS property used in a corporation's trade or business.
C. A manufacturing company's investment in U.S. Treasury bonds.
D. A corporate real estate developer's unimproved land that is to be subdivided to build homes, which will be sold to customers.

7. Baker Corp., a calendar year C corporation, realized taxable income of $36,000 from its regular business operations for calendar year 19X4. In addition, Baker had the following capital gains and losses during 19X4:

Short-term capital gain	$8,500
Short-term capital loss	(4,000)
Long-term capital gain	1,500
Long-term capital loss	(3,500)

Baker did not realize any other capital gains or losses since it began operations. What is Baker's total taxable income for 19X4?

A. $46,000
B. $42,000
C. $40,500
D. $38,500

Please use this area for work space.

8. In 19X4, Cable Corp., a calendar year C corporation, contributed $80,000 to a qualified charitable organization. Cable's 19X4 taxable income before the deduction for charitable contributions was $820,000 after a $40,000 dividends-received deduction. Cable also had carryover contributions of $10,000 from the prior year. In 19X4, what amount can Cable deduct as charitable contributions?

   A. $90,000
   B. $86,000
   C. $82,000
   D. $80,000

9. If a corporation's charitable contributions exceed the limitation for deductibility in a particular year, the excess

   A. Is **not** deductible in any future or prior year.
   B. May be carried back or forward for one year at the corporation's election.
   C. May be carried forward to a maximum of five succeeding years.
   D. May be carried back to the third preceding year.

10. In 19X4, Stewart Corp. properly accrued $5,000 for an income item on the basis of a reasonable estimate. In 19X5, after filing its 19X4 federal income tax return, Stewart determined that the exact amount was $6,000. Which of the following statements is correct?

   A. No further inclusion of income is required as the difference is less than 25% of the original amount reported and the estimate had been made in good faith.
   B. The $1,000 difference is includible in Stewart's 19X5 income tax return.
   C. Stewart is required to notify the IRS within 30 days of the determination of the exact amount of the item.
   D. Stewart is required to file an amended return to report the additional $1,000 of income.

11. The uniform capitalization method must be used by

   I. Manufacturers of tangible personal property.

   II. Retailers of personal property with $2 million dollars in average annual gross receipts for the 3 preceding years.

   A. I only.
   B. II only.
   C. Both I and II.
   D. Neither I nor II.

Please use this area for work space.

12. Kane Corp. is a calendar year domestic personal holding company. Which deduction(s) must Kane make from 19X4 taxable income to determine undistributed personal holding company income prior to the dividend-paid deduction?

	Federal income taxes	Net long-term capital gain less related federal income taxes
A.	Yes	Yes
B.	Yes	No
C.	No	Yes
D.	No	No

13. Bank Corp. owns 80% of Shore Corp.'s outstanding capital stock. Shore's capital stock consists of 50,000 shares of common stock issued and outstanding. Shore's 19X4 net income was $140,000. During 19X4, Shore declared and paid dividends of $60,000. In conformity with generally accepted accounting principles, Bank recorded the following entries in 19X4:

	Debit	Credit
Investment in Shore Corp. common stock	$112,000	
Equity in earning of subsidiary		$112,000
Cash	48,000	
Investment in Shore Corp. common stock		48,000

In its 19X4 consolidated tax return, Bank should report dividend revenue of

A. $48,000
B. $14,400
C. $9,600
D. $0

Please use this area for work space.

---

14. Dart Corp., a calendar year domestic C corporation, is not a personal holding company. For purposes of the accumulated earnings tax, Dart has accumulated taxable income for 19X4. Which step(s) can Dart take to eliminate or reduce any 19X4 accumulated earnings tax?

I. Demonstrate that the "reasonable needs" of its business require the retention of all or part of the 19X4 accumulated taxable income.

II. Pay dividends by March 15, 19X5.

    A. I only.
    B. II only.
    C. Both I and II.
    D. Neither I nor II.

15. Eastern Corp., a calendar year corporation, was formed January 3, 19X4, and on that date placed five-year property in service. The property was depreciated under the general MACRS system. Eastern did not elect to use the straightline method. The following information pertains to Eastern:

Eastern's 19X4 taxable income	$300,000
Adjustment for the accelerated depreciation taken on 19X4 five-year property	1,000
19X4 tax-exempt interest from specified private activity bonds issued after August 7, 19X6	5,000

What was Eastern's 19X4 alternative minimum taxable income before the adjusted current earnings (ACE) adjustment?

    A. $306,000
    B. $305,000
    C. $304,000
    D. $301,000

Please use this area for work space.

16. A civil fraud penalty can be imposed on a corporation that underpays tax by

A. Omitting income as a result of inadequate recordkeeping.
B. Failing to report income it erroneously considered **not** to be part of corporate profits.
C. Filing an incomplete return with an appended statement, making clear that the return is incomplete.
D. Maintaining false records and reporting fictitious transactions to minimize corporate tax liability.

17. A corporation may reduce its regular income tax by taking a tax credit for

A. Dividends-received exclusion.
B. Foreign income taxes.
C. State income taxes.
D. Accelerated depreciation.

18. The accumulated earnings tax can be imposed

A. On both partnerships and corporations.
B. On companies that make distributions in excess of accumulated earnings.
C. On personal holding companies.
D. Regardless of the number of stockholders in a corporation.

19. The following information pertains to Dahl Corp.:

Accumulated earnings and profits at January 1,19X4	$120,000
Earnings and profits for the year ended December 31,19X4	160,000
Cash distributions to individual stockholders during 19X4	360,000

What is the total amount of distributions taxable as dividend income to Dahl's stockholders in 19X4?

A. $0
B. $160,000
C. $280,000
D. $360,000

Please use this area for work space.

20. Ridge Corp., a calendar year C corporation, made a nonliquidating cash distribution to its shareholders of $1,000,000 with respect to its stock. At that time, Ridge's current and accumulated earnings and profits totaled $750,000 and its total paid-in capital for tax purposes was $10,000,000. Ridge had no corporate shareholders. Ridge's cash distribution

I. Was taxable as $750,000 in ordinary income to its shareholders.

II. Reduced its shareholders' adjusted bases in Ridge stock by $250,000.

  A. I only.
  B. II only.
  C. Both I and II.
  D. Neither I nor II.

21. Clark and Hunt organized Jet Corp. with authorized voting common stock of $400,000. Clark contributed $60,000 cash. Both Clark and Hunt transferred other property in exchange for Jet stock as follows:

Other Property

	Adjusted Basis	Fair Market Value	Percentage of Jet Stock Acquired
Clark	$ 50,000	$100,000	40%
Hunt	120,000	240,000	60%

What was Clark's basis in Jet stock?

  A. $0
  B. $100,000
  C. $110,000
  D. $160,000

22. Ace Corp. and Bate Corp. combine in a qualifying reorganization and form Carr Corp., the only surviving corporation. This reorganization is tax-free to the

	Shareholders	Corporation
A.	Yes	Yes
B.	Yes	No
C.	No	Yes
D.	No	No

Please use this area for work space.

23. Bass Corp., a calendar year C corporation, made qualifying 19X4 estimated tax deposits based on its actual 19X3 tax liability. On March 15, 19X5, Bass filed a timely automatic extension request for its 19X4 corporate income tax return. Estimated tax deposits and the extension payment totaled $7,600. This amount was 95% of the total tax shown on Bass' final 19X4 corporate income tax return. Bass paid $400 additional tax on the final 19X4 corporate income tax return filed before the extended due date. For the 19X4 calendar year, Bass was subject to pay

I. Interest on the $400 tax payment made in 19X5.

II. A tax delinquency penalty.

A. I only.
B. II only.
C. Both I and II.
D. Neither I nor II.

24. Edge Corp., a calendar year C corporation, had a net operating loss and zero tax liability for its 19X4 tax year. To avoid the penalty for underpayment of estimated taxes, Edge could compute its first quarter 19X5 estimated income tax payment using the

	Annualized Income Method	Preceding-Year Method
A.	Yes	Yes
B.	Yes	No
C.	No	Yes
D.	No	No

25. A corporation's tax year can be reopened after all statutes of limitations have expired if

I. The tax return has a 50% nonfraudulent omission from gross income.

II. The corporation prevails in a determination allowing a deduction in an open tax year that was taken erroneously in a closed tax year.

A. I only.
B. II only.
C. Both I and II.
D. Neither I nor II.

Please use this area for work space.

26. A penalty for understated corporate tax liability can be imposed on a tax preparer who fails to

A. Audit the corporate records.
B. Examine business operations.
C. Copy all underlying documents.
D. Make reasonable inquiries when taxpayer information appears incorrect.

27. Barker acquired a 50% interest in Kode Partnership by contributing $20,000 cash and a building with an adjusted basis of $26,000 and a fair market value of $42,000. The building was subject to a $10,000 mortgage which was assumed by Kode. The other partners contributed cash only. The basis of Barker's interest in Kode is

A. $36,000
B. $41,000
C. $52,000
D. $62,000

28. At partnership inception, Black acquires a 50% interest in Decorators Partnership by contributing property with an adjusted basis of $250,000. Black recognizes a gain if

I. The fair market value of the contributed property exceeds its adjusted basis.

II. The property is encumbered by a mortgage with a balance of $100,000.

A. I only.
B. II only.
C. Both I and II.
D. Neither I nor II.

29. Evan, a 25% partner in Vista Partnership, received a $20,000 guaranteed payment in 19X4 for deductible services rendered to the partnership. Guaranteed payments were not made to any other partner. Vista's 19X4 partnership income consisted of:

Net business income before guaranteed payments	$80,000
Net long-term capital gains	10,000

What amount of income should Evan report from Vista Partnership on her 19X4 tax return?

A. $37,500
B. $27,500
C. $22,500
D. $20,000

Please use this area for work space.

30. On January 4, 19X4, Smith and White contributed $4,000 and $6,000 in cash, respectively, and formed the Macro General Partnership. The partnership agreement allocated profits and losses 40% to Smith and 60% to White. In 19X4, Macro purchased property from an unrelated seller for $10,000 cash and a $40,000 mortgage note that was the general liability of the partnership. Macro's liability

A. Increases Smith's partnership basis by $16,000.
B. Increases Smith's partnership basis by $20,000.
C. Increases Smith's partnership basis by $24,000.
D. Has **no** effect on Smith's partnership basis.

31. Hart's adjusted basis in Best Partnership was $9,000 at the time he received the following nonliquidating distributions of partnership property:

Cash		$ 5,000
Land		
Adjusted basis	7,000	
Fair market value	10,000	

What was the amount of Hart's basis in the land?

A. $0
B. $4,000
C. $7,000
D. $10,000

32. Stone's basis in Ace Partnership was $70,000 at the time he received a nonliquidating distribution of partnership capital assets. These capital assets had an adjusted basis of $65,000 to Ace, and a fair market value of $83,000. Ace had no unrealized receivables, appreciated inventory, or properties which had been contributed by its partners. What was Stone's recognized gain or loss on the distribution?

A. $18,000 ordinary income.
B. $13,000 capital gain.
C. $5,000 capital loss.
D. $0.

--- Please use this area for work space. ---

33. On January 3, 19X4, the partners' interests in the capital, profits, and losses of Able Partnership were:

	% of Capital, Profits and Losses
Dean	25%
Poe	30%
Ritt	45%

On February 4, 19X4, Poe sold her entire interest to an unrelated party. Dean sold his 25% interest in Able to another unrelated party on December 20, 19X4. No other transactions took place in 19X4. For tax purposes, which of the following statements is correct with respect to Able?

    A. Able terminated as of February 4, 19X4.
    B. Able terminated as of December 20, 19X4.
    C. Able terminated as of December 31, 19X4.
    D. Able did not terminate.

34. Curry's sale of her partnership interest causes a partnership termination. The partnership's business and financial operations are continued by the other members. What is (are) the effect(s) of the termination?

    I. There is a deemed distribution of assets to the remaining partners and the purchaser.

    II. There is a hypothetical recontribution of assets to a new partnership.

    A. I only.
    B. II only.
    C. Both I and II.
    D. Neither I nor II.

35. A distribution to an estate's sole beneficiary for the 19X4 calendar year equaled $15,000, the amount currently required to be distributed by the will. The estate's 19X4 records were as follows:

Estate Income
    $40,000   Taxable interest
Estate Disbursements
    $34,000   Expenses attributable to taxable interest

What amount of the distribution was taxable to the beneficiary?

    A. $40,000
    B. $15,000
    C. $6,000
    D. $0

Please use this area for work space.

---

36. Steve and Kay Briar, U.S. citizens, were married for the entire 19X4 calendar year. In 19X4, Steve gave a $30,000 cash gift to his sister. The Briars made no other gifts in 19X4. They each signed a timely election to treat the $30,000 gift as made one-half by each spouse. Disregarding the unified credit and estate tax consequences, what amount of the 19X4 gift is taxable to the Briars?

    A. $30,000
    B. $20,000
    C. $10,000
    D. $0

37. The organizational test to qualify a public service charitable entity as tax exempt requires the articles of organization to

   I. Limit the purpose of the entity to the charitable purpose.

  II. State that an information return should be filed annually with the Internal Revenue Service.

    A. I only.
    B. II only.
    C. Both I and II.
    D. Neither I nor II.

38. Which of the following activities regularly conducted by a tax exempt organization will result in unrelated business income?

   I. Selling articles made by handicapped persons as part of their rehabilitation, when the organization is involved exclusively in their rehabilitation.

  II. Operating a grocery store almost fully staffed by emotionally handicapped persons as part of a therapeutic program.

    A. I only.
    B. II only.
    C. Both I and II.
    D. Neither I nor II.

Please use this area for work space.

Items 39 through 56 are in the area of Managerial Accounting.

39. Sender, Inc. estimates parcel mailing costs using data shown on the chart below.

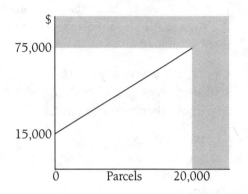

What is Sender's estimated cost for mailing 12,000 parcels?

A. $36,000
B. $45,000
C. $51,000
D. $60,000

40. Mien Co. is budgeting sales of 53,000 units of product Nous for October 19X5. The manufacture of one unit of Nous requires 4 kilos of chemical Loire. During October 19X5, Mien plans to reduce the inventory of Loire by 50,000 kilos and increase the finished goods inventory of Nous by 6,000 units. There is no Nous work-in-process inventory. How many kilos of Loire is Mien budgeting to purchase in October 19X5?

A. 138,000
B. 162,000
C. 186,000
D. 238,000

41. The basic difference between a master budget and a flexible budget is that a master budget is

A. Only used before and during the budget period and a flexible budget is used only after the budget period.
B. For an entire production facility and a flexible budget is applicable to single departments only.
C. Based on one specific level of production and a flexible budget can be prepared for any production level within a relevant range.
D. Based on a fixed standard and a flexible budget allows management latitude in meeting goals.

Please use this area for work space.

42. For the next 2 years, a lease is estimated to have an operating net cash inflow of $7,500 per annum, before adjusting for $5,000 per annum tax basis lease amortization, and a 40% tax rate. The present value of an ordinary annuity of $1 per year at 10% for 2 years is $1.74. What is the lease's after-tax present value using a 10% discount factor?

    A. $2,610
    B. $4,350
    C. $9,570
    D. $11,310

43. Product Cott has sales of $200,000, a contribution margin of 20%, and a margin of safety of $80,000. What is Cott's fixed cost?

    A. $16,000
    B. $24,000
    C. $80,000
    D. $96,000

44. Break-even analysis assumes that over the relevant range

    A. Unit revenues are nonlinear.
    B. Unit variable costs are unchanged.
    C. Total costs are unchanged.
    D. Total fixed costs are nonlinear.

45. Gram Co. develops computer programs to meet customers' special requirements. How should Gram categorize payments to employees who develop these programs?

	Direct Costs	Value-Adding Costs
A.	Yes	Yes
B.	Yes	No
C.	No	No
D.	No	Yes

46. The Forming Department is the first of a two-stage production process. Spoilage is identified when the units have completed the Forming process. Costs of spoiled units are assigned to units completed and transferred to the second department in the period spoilage is identified. The following information concerns Forming's conversion costs in May 19X5:

	Units	Conversion Costs
Beginning work-in-process (50% complete)	2,000	$10,000
Units started during May	8,000	$75,000
Spoilage—normal	500	
Units completed & transferred	7,000	
Ending work-in-process (80% complete)	2,500	

_____ Please use this area for work space. _____

Using the weighted average method, what was Forming's conversion cost transferred to the second production department?

A. $59,850
B. $64,125
C. $67,500
D. $71,250

47. The standard direct material cost to produce a unit of Lem is 4 meters of material at $2.50 per meter. During May 19X5, 4,200 meters of material costing $10,080 were purchased and used to produce 1,000 units of Lem. What was the material price variance for May 19X5?

A. $400 favorable.
B. $420 favorable.
C. $80 unfavorable.
D. $480 unfavorable.

48. For purposes of allocating joint costs to joint products, the sales price at point of sale, reduced by cost to complete after split-off, is assumed to be equal to the

A. Joint costs.
B. Total costs.
C. Net sales value at split-off.
D. Sales price less a normal profit margin at point of sale.

49. Parat College allocates support department costs to its individual schools using the step method. Information for May 19X5 is as follows:

	Support Departments	
	Maintenance	Power
Costs incurred	$99,000	$54,000
Service percentages provided to:		
Maintenance	–	10%
Power	20%	–
School of Education	30%	20%
School of Technology	50%	70%
	100%	100%

What is the amount of May 19X5 support department costs allocated to the School of Education?

A. $40,500
B. $42,120
C. $46,100
D. $49,125

50. The following selected data pertain to the Darwin Division of Beagle Co. for 19X4:

Sales	$400,000
Operating income	$40,000
Capital turnover	4
Imputed interest rate	10%

Please use this area for work space.

What was Darwin's 19X4 residual income?

A. $0
B. $4,000
C. $10,000
D. $30,000

51. Key Co. changed from a traditional manufacturing operation with a job order costing system to a just-in-time operation with a backflush costing system. What is(are) the expected effect(s) of these changes on Key's inspection costs and recording detail of costs tracked to jobs in process?

	Inspection Costs	Detail of Costs Tracked to Jobs
A.	Decrease	Decrease
B.	Decrease	Increase
C.	Increase	Decrease
D.	Increase	Increase

52. The economic order quantity formula assumes that

A. Periodic demand for the good is known.
B. Carrying costs per unit vary with quantity ordered.
C. Costs of placing an order vary with quantity ordered.
D. Purchase costs per unit differ due to quantity discounts.

53. Under frost-free conditions, Cal Cultivators expects its strawberry crop to have a $60,000 market value. An unprotected crop subject to frost has an expected market value of $40,000. If Cal protects the strawberries against frost, then the market value of the crop is still expected to be $60,000 under frost-free conditions and $90,000 if there is a frost. What must be the probability of a frost for Cal to be indifferent to spending $10,000 for frost protection?

A. .167
B. .200
C. .250
D. .333

Please use this area for work space.

54. During 19X4, Deet Corp. experienced the following power outages:

Number of Outages Per Month	Number of Months
0	3
1	2
2	4
3	3
	12

Each power outage results in out-of-pocket costs of $400. For $500 per month, Deet can lease an auxiliary generator to provide power during outages. If Deet leases an auxiliary generator in 19X5, the estimated savings (or additional expenditures) for 19X5 would be

A. ($3,600)
B. ($1,200)
C. $1,600
D. $1,900

55. Based on potential sales of 500 units per year, a new product has estimated traceable costs of $990,000. What is the target price to obtain a 15% profit margin on sales?

A. $2,329
B. $2,277
C. $1,980
D. $1,935

56. Lynn Manufacturing Co. prepares income statements using both standard absorption and standard variable costing methods. For 19X4, unit standard costs were unchanged from 19X3. In 19X4, the only beginning and ending inventories were finished goods of 5,000 units. How would Lynn's ratios using absorption costing compare with those using variable costing?

	Current Ratio	Return on Stockholders' Equity
A.	Same	Same
B.	Same	Smaller
C.	Greater	Same
D.	Greater	Smaller

Please use this area for work space.

Items 57 through 75 are in the area of Accounting for Governmental and Not-for-Profit Organizations.

57. Which of the following fund types of a governmental unit has (have) income determination as a measurement focus?

	General Funds	Expendable Trust Funds
A.	Yes	Yes
B.	Yes	No
C.	No	No
D.	No	Yes

58. Fixed assets donated to a governmental unit should be recorded

A. At the donor's carrying amount.
B. At estimated fair value when received.
C. At the lower of the donor's carrying amount or estimated fair value when received.
D. As a memorandum entry only.

59. Which event(s) is (are) supportive of interperiod equity as a financial reporting objective of a governmental unit?

I. A balanced budget is adopted.

II. Residual equity transfers out equals residual equity transfers in.

A. I only.
B. II only.
C. Both I and II.
D. Neither I nor II.

60. Fund accounting is used by governmental units with resources that must be

A. Composed of cash or cash equivalents.
B. Incorporated into combined or combining financial statements.
C. Segregated for the purpose of carrying on specific activities or attaining certain objectives.
D. Segregated physically according to various objectives.

61. Vale City legally adopts a cash-basis budget. What basis should be used in Vale's combined statement of revenues, expenditures, and changes in fund balances–budget and actual?

A. Cash.
B. Modified accrual.
C. Accrual.
D. Modified cash.

Please use this area for work space.
---

62. What is the basic criterion used to determine the reporting entity for a governmental unit?

    A. Special financing arrangement.
    B. Geographic boundaries.
    C. Scope of public services.
    D. Financial accountability.

63. Which event(s) should be included in a statement of cash flows for a governmental entity?

  I. Cash inflow from issuing bonds to finance city hall construction.

  II. Cash outflow from a city utility representing payments in lieu of property taxes.

    A. I only.
    B. II only.
    C. Both I and II.
    D. Neither I nor II.

64. Fish Road property owners in Sea County are responsible for special assessment debt that arose from a storm sewer project. If the property owners default, Sea has no obligation regarding debt service, although it does bill property owners for assessments and uses the monies it collects to pay debt holders. What fund type should Sea use to account for these collection and servicing activities?

    A. Agency.
    B. Debt service.
    C. Expendable trust funds.
    D. Capital projects.

65. The revenues control account of a governmental unit is increased when

    A. The encumbrance account is decreased.
    B. Appropriations are recorded.
    C. Property taxes are recorded.
    D. The budget is recorded.

66. Tuston Township issued the following bonds during the year ended June 30, 19X5:

Bonds issued for the garbage collection enterprise fund that will service the debt	$700,000
Revenue bonds to be repaid from admission fees collected by the Township zoo enterprise fund	500,000

Please use this area for work space.

What amount of these bonds should be accounted for in Tuston's general long-term debt account group?

A. $1,200,000
B. $700,000
C. $500,000
D. $0

67. Frome City signed a 20-year office property lease for its general staff. Frome could terminate the lease at any time after giving one year's notice, but termination is considered a remote possibility. The lease meets the criteria for a capital lease. What is the effect of the lease on the asset amount in Frome's general fixed assets account group and the liability amount in Frome's general long-term debt account group?

	Asset Amount	Liability Amount
A.	Increase	Increase
B.	Increase	No effect
C.	No effect	Increase
D.	No effect	No effect

68. Polk County's solid waste landfill operation is accounted for in a governmental fund. Polk used available cash to purchase equipment that is included in the estimated current cost of closure and post-closure care of this operation. How would this purchase affect the asset amount in Polk's general fixed assets account group and the

liability amount in Polk's general long-term debt account group?

	Asset Amount	Liability Amount
A.	Increase	Increase
B.	Increase	No effect
C.	No effect	Increase
D.	No effect	No effect

69. Financial statements for which fund type generally report retained earnings?

A. Capital projects.
B. Enterprise.
C. Special revenue.
D. Expendable pension trust.

70. Lys City reports a compensated absences liability in its combined balance sheet. The salary rate used to calculate the liability should normally be the rate in effect

A. When the unpaid compensated absences were earned.
B. When the compensated absences are to be paid.
C. At the balance sheet date.
D. When the compensated absences were earned or are to be paid, or at the balance sheet date, whichever results in the lowest amount.

—————————— Please use this area for work space. ——————————

71. Which account should Spring Township credit when it issues a purchase order for supplies?

    A. Appropriations control.
    B. Vouchers payable.
    C. Encumbrance control.
    D. Reserve for encumbrances.

72. The estimated revenues control account of a governmental unit is debited when

    A. Actual revenues are recorded.
    B. Actual revenues are collected.
    C. The budget is recorded.
    D. The budget is closed at the end of the year.

73. The billings for transportation services provided to other governmental units are recorded by the internal service fund as

    A. Transportation appropriations.
    B. Operating revenues.
    C. Interfund exchanges.
    D. Intergovernmental transfers.

74. A large not-for-profit organization's statement of activities should report the net change for net assets that are

	Unrestricted	Permanently Restricted
A.	Yes	Yes
B.	Yes	No
C.	No	No
D.	No	Yes

75. Which of the following should normally be considered ongoing or central transactions for a not-for-profit hospital?

  I. Room-and-board fees from patients.

  II. Recovery-room fees.

    A. Neither I nor II.
    B. Both I and II.
    C. II only.
    D. I only.

—————————— Please use this area for work space. ——————————

Number 2 (Estimated time—5 to 10 minutes)

Question Number 2 consists of 6 items. Select the **best** answer for each item. Use a No. 2 pencil to blacken the appropriate ovals on your scannable grid. **Answer all items.**

Lan Corp., an accrual-basis calendar year repair-service corporation, began business on Monday, January 3, 19X4. Lan's valid S corporation election took effect retroactively on January 3, 19X4.

Required:

a. For **Items 76 through 79,** determine the amount, if any, using the fact pattern for each item. To record your answer, blacken the ovals on the OOF Numeric Section of your scannable grid using response items #9 through #12 (round the answer to the nearest hundred). If zeros precede your numerical answer, blacken the zeros in the ovals preceding your answer. **You cannot receive credit for your answers if you fail to blacken an oval in each column.** You may write the numbers in the boxed provided to facilitate blackening the ovals; however, the numbers written in the boxes will not be graded.

76. Assume the following facts:

Lan's 19X4 books recorded the following items:

Gross receipts	$7,260
Interest income on investments	50
Charitable contributions	1,000
Supplies	1,120

What amount of net business income should Lan report on its 19X4 Form 1120S, U.S. Income Tax Return for an S Corporation, Schedule K?

77. Assume the following facts:

As of January 3, 19X4, Taylor and Barr each owned 100 shares of the 200 issued shares of Lan stock. On January 31, 19X4, Taylor and Barr each sold 20 shares to Pike. No election was made to terminate the tax year. Lan had net business income of $14,520 for the year ended December 31, 19X4, and made no distributions to its shareholders. Lan's 19X4 calendar year had 363 days.

What amount of net business income should have been reported on Pike's 19X4 Schedule K-1 from Lan? (19X4 is a 363-day tax year.) Round the answer to the nearest hundred.

Please use this area for work space.

78. Assume the following facts:

Pike purchased 40 Lan shares on January 31, 19X4, for $4,000. Lan made no distributions to shareholders, and Pike's 19X4 Schedule K-1 from Lan reported:

Ordinary business loss	($1,000)
Municipal bond interest income	150

What was Pike's basis in his Lan stock at December 31, 19X4?

79. Assume the following facts:

On January 3, 19X4, Taylor and Barr each owned 100 shares of the 200 issued shares of Lan stock. Taylor's basis in Lan shares on that date was $10,000. Taylor sold all of his Lan shares to Pike on January 31, 19X4, and Lan made a valid election to terminate its tax year. Taylor's share of ordinary income from Lan prior to the sale was $2,000. Lan made a cash distribution of $3,000 to Taylor on January 30, 19X4.

What was Taylor's basis in Lan shares for determining gain or loss from the sale to Pike?

Required:

b. For **Items 80 and 81,** indicate if the statement is True (A) or False (B) regarding Lan's S corporation status. Blacken the ovals on OOF Section #2, response items #1 and #2.

80. Lan issues shares of both preferred and common stock to shareholders at inception on January 3, 19X4. This will **not** affect Lan's S corporation eligibility.

81. Lan, an S corporation since inception, has passive investment income for 3 consecutive years following the year a valid S corporation election takes effect. Lan's S corporation election is terminated as of the first day of the fourth year.

———————————————— Please use this area for work space. ————————————————

Number 3 (Estimated time—25 to 40 minutes)

Question Number 3 consists of 29 items. Select the **best** answer for each item. Use a No. 2 pencil to blacken the appropriate ovals on the OOF Numeric Response Section of your scannable grid. **Answer all items.**

Tom and Joan Moore, both CPAs, filed a joint 19X4 federal income tax return showing $70,000 in taxable income. During 19X4, Tom's daughter Laura, age 16, resided with Tom's former spouse. Laura had no income of her own and was not Tom's dependent.

Required:

a. For **Items 82 through 91,** determine the amount of income or loss, if any, that should be included on page one of the Moores' 19X4 Form 1040. To record your answer, blacken the ovals on the OOF Numeric Response Section of your scannable grid (round the answer to the nearest hundred). For questions 82 through 85, use response items #1 through #3 in the OOF Numeric Response Section. For questions 85 through 91, use response items #13 through #19. If zeros precede your numerical answer, blacken the zeros in the ovals preceding your answer. **You cannot receive credit for answers if you fail to blacken an oval in each column.** You may write the numbers in the boxes provided to facilitate blackening the ovals; however, the numbers written in the boxes will **not** be graded.

82. The Moores had no capital loss carryovers from prior years. During 19X4 the Moores had the following stock transactions, which resulted in a net capital loss:

	Date Acquired	Date Sold	Sales Price	Cost
Revco	2/1/X3	3/17/X4	$15,000	$24,000
Abbco	2/18/X4	4/1/X4	8,000	4,000

83. In 19X2, Joan received an acre of land as an *inter vivos* gift from her grandfather. At the time of the gift, the land had a fair market value of $50,000. The grandfather's adjusted basis was $60,000. Joan sold the land in 19X4 to an unrelated third party for $56,000.

84. The Moores received a $500 security deposit on their rental property in 19X4. They are required to return the amount to the tenant.

85. Tom's 19X4 wages were $53,000. In addition, Tom's employer provided group-term life insurance on Tom's life in excess of $50,000. The value of such excess coverage was $2,000.

Please use this area for work space.

86. During 19X4, the Moores received a $2,500 federal tax refund and a $1,250 state tax refund for 19X3 overpayments. In 19X3, the Moores were not subject to the alternative minimum tax and were not entitled to any credit against income tax. The Moores' 19X3 adjusted gross income was $80,000 and itemized deductions were $1,450 in excess of the standard deduction. The state tax deduction for 19X3 was $2,000.

87. In 19X4, Joan received $1,300 in unemployment compensation benefits. Her employer made a $100 contribution to the unemployment insurance fund on her behalf.

88. The Moores received $8,400 in gross receipts from their rental property during 19X4. The expenses for the residential rental property were:

Bank mortgage interest	$1,200
Real estate taxes	700
Insurance	500
MACRS depreciation	3,500

89. The Moores received a stock dividend in 19X4 from Ace Corp. They had the option to receive either cash or Ace stock with a fair market value of $900 as of the date of distribution. The par value of the stock was $500.

90. In 19X4, Joan received $3,500 as beneficiary of the death benefit which was provided by her brother's employer. Joan's brother did not have a nonforfeitable right to receive the money while living.

91. Tom received $10,000, consisting of $5,000 each of principal and interest, when he redeemed a Series EE savings bond in 19X4. The bond was issued in his name in 1987 and the proceeds were used to pay for Laura's college tuition. Tom had not elected to report the yearly increases in the value of the bond.

Required:

b. For **Item 92,** determine the amount of the adjustment, if any, to arrive at adjusted gross income. To record your answer, blacken the ovals on the OOF Numeric Response Section, response item #20. If zeros precede your numerical answer, blacken the zeros in the ovals preceding your answer. **You cannot receive credit for your answers if you fail to blacken an oval in each column.** You may write the numbers in the boxes provided to facilitate blackening the ovals; however, the numbers written in the boxes will **not** be graded.

Please use this area for work space.

---

92. As required by a 19X0 divorce agreement, Tom paid an annual amount of $8,000 in alimony and $10,000 in child support during 19X4.

Required:

  c. During 19X4, the following events took place. For **Items 93 to 104,** select the appropriate tax treatment and blacken the corresponding oval on OOF Section #1 of your scannable grid, response items #1 through #12. A tax treatment may be selected once, more than once, or not at all.

93. On March 23, 19X4, Tom sold 50 shares of Zip stock at a $1,200 loss. He repurchased 50 shares of Zip on April 15, 19X4.

94. Payment of a personal property tax based on the value of the Moores' car.

95. Used clothes were donated to church organization.

96. Premiums were paid covering insurance against Tom's loss of earnings.

97. Tom paid for subscriptions to accounting journals.

98. Interest was paid on a $10,000 home-equity line of credit secured by the Moores' residence. The fair market value of the home exceeded the mortgage by $50,000. Tom used the proceeds to purchase a sailboat.

99. Amounts were paid in excess of insurance reimbursement for prescription drugs.

100. Funeral expenses were paid by the Moores for Joan's brother.

101. Theft loss was incurred on Joan's jewelry in excess of insurance reimbursement. There were no 19X4 personal casualty gains.

102. Loss on the sale of the family's sailboat.

103. Interest was paid on the $300,000 acquisition mortgage on the Moores' home. The mortgage is secured by their home.

104. Joan performed free accounting services for the Red Cross. The estimated value of the services was $500.

Tax treatments can be found on the following page.

Please use this area for work space.

Relates to Items 93 to 104.

TAX TREATMENT
(A) Not deductible on Form 1040.
(B) Deductible in full in Schedule A-Itemized Deductions.
(C) Deductible in Schedule A-Itemized Deductions, subject to a threshold of 7.5% of adjusted gross income.
(D) Deductible in Schedule A-Itemized Deductions, subject to a limitation of 50% of adjusted gross income.
(E) Deductible in Schedule A-Itemized Deductions, subject to a $100 floor and a threshold of 10% of adjusted gross income.
(F) Deductible in Schedule A-Itemized Deductions, subject to a threshold of 2% of adjusted gross income.

Required:

d. For **Items 105 to 110,** indicate if the statement is True (A) or False (B) regarding the Moores' 19X4 tax return. Blacken the corresponding ovals on OOF Section #2 of your scannable grid, response items #3 through #8.

105. For 19X4, the Moores were subject to the phaseout of half their personal exemptions for regular tax because their adjusted gross income was $75,000.

106. The Moores' unreimbursed medical expenses for AMT had to exceed 10% of adjusted gross income.

107. The Moores' personal exemption amount for regular tax was not permitted for determining 19X4 AMT.

108. The Moores paid $1,200 in additional 19X4 taxes when they filed their return on Friday, April 14, 19X5. Their 19X4 federal tax withholdings equaled 100% of 19X3 tax liability. Therefore, they were not subject to the underpayment of tax penalty.

109. The Moores, both being under age 50, were subject to an early withdrawal penalty on their IRA withdrawals used for medical expenses.

110. The Moores were allowed an earned income credit against their 19X4 tax liability equal to a percentage of their wages.

Please use this area for work space.

Number 4 (Estimated time—5 to 10 minutes)

Question Number 4 consists of 6 items. Select the **best** answer for each item. Use a No. 2 pencil to blacken the appropriate ovals on OOF Section #3 of your scannable grid, response items #1 through #6. **Answer all items.**

Alpha Hospital, a large not-for-profit organization, has adopted an accounting policy that does not imply a time restriction on gifts of long-lived assets.

Required:

For **Items 111 through 116,** indicate, by blackening the corresponding ovals on OOF Section #3, response items #1 through #6, the manner in which the transaction affects Alpha's financial statements.

- A. Increase in unrestricted revenues, gains, and other support.
- B. Decrease in an expense.
- C. Increase in temporarily restricted net assets.
- D. Increase in permanently restricted net assets.
- E. No required reportable event.

111. Alpha's board designates $1,000,000 to purchase investments whose income will be used for capital improvements.

112. Income from investments in item 111 above, which was not previously accrued, is received.

113. A benefactor provided funds for building expansion.

114. The funds in item 113 above are used to purchase a building in the fiscal period following the period in which the funds were received.

115. An accounting firm prepared Alpha's annual financial statements without charge to Alpha.

116. Alpha received investments subject to the donor's requirement that investment income be used to pay for outpatient services.

Please use this area for work space.

Number 5 (Estimated time—15 to 20 minutes)

Question Number 5 consists of 10 items. Select the **best** answer for each item. Use a No. 2 pencil to blacken the appropriate ovals on your scannable grid to indicate your answers. **Answer all items.**

The following information relates to Dane City during its fiscal year ended December 31, 19X4:

- On October 31, 19X4, to finance the construction of a city hall annex, Dane issued 8% 10-year general obligation bonds at their face value of $600,000. Construction expenditures during the period equaled $364,000.

- Dane reported $109,000 from hotel room taxes, restricted for tourist promotion, in a special revenue fund. The fund paid $81,000 for general promotions and $22,000 for a motor vehicle.

- 19X4 general fund revenues of $104,500 were transferred to a debt service fund and used to repay $100,000 of 9% 15-year term bonds, and to pay $4,500 of interest. The bonds were used to acquire a citizens' center.

- At December 31, 19X4, as a consequence of past services, city firefighters had accumulated entitlements to compensated absences valued at $86,000. General fund resources available at December 31, 19X4,

are expected to be used to settle $17,000 of this amount, and $69,000 is expected to be paid out of future general fund resources.

- At December 31, 19X4, Dane was responsible for $83,000 of outstanding general fund encumbrances, including the $8,000 for supplies indicated below.

- Dane uses the purchases method to account for supplies. The following information relates to supplies:

Inventory	1/1/X4	$ 39,000
	12/31/X4	42,000
Encumbrances outstanding		
	1/1/X4	6,000
	12/31/X4	8,000
Purchase orders during 19X4		190,000
Amounts credited to vouchers payable during 19X4		181,000

Please use this area for work space.

Required:

For **Items 117 through 126,** determine the amounts based solely on the above information. To record your answer, blacken the ovals on the OOF Numeric Response Section of your scannable grid, response items #21 through #30. If zeros precede your numerical answer, blacken the zeros in the ovals preceding your answer. **You cannot receive credit for your answers if you fail to blacken an oval in each column.** You may write the numbers in the boxes provided to facilitate blackening the ovals; however, numbers written in the boxes will not be graded.

117. What is the amount of 19X4 general fund operating transfers out?

118. How much should be reported as 19X4 general fund liabilities from entitlements for compensated absences?

119. What is the 19X4 reserved amount of the general fund balance?

120. What is the 19X4 capital projects fund balance?

121. What is the 19X4 fund balance on the special revenue fund for tourist promotion?

122. What is the amount of 19X4 debt service fund expenditures?

123. What amount should be included in the general fixed assets account group for the cost of assets acquired in 19X4?

124. What amount stemming from 19X4 transactions and events decreased the liabilities reported in the general long-term debt account group?

125. Using the purchases method, what is the amount of 19X4 supplies expenditures?

126. What was the total amount of 19X4 supplies encumbrances?

_____ Please use this area for work space. _____

TEST 2: QUESTIONS

FINANCIAL ACCOUNTING & REPORTING—
Business Enterprises

Test ID: 2200

INSTRUCTIONS

1. Question Numbers 1, 2, and 3 should be answered on the scannable grid, at the back of this book. You should attempt to answer all objective items. There is no penalty for incorrect responses. Work space to solve the objective questions is provided. Since the objective items are computer graded, your comments and calculations associated with them are not considered. Be certain that you have entered your answers on the scannable grid before the examination time is up. The objective portion of your examination will not be graded if you fail to record your answers on the scannable grid.

2. Question Numbers 4 and 5 should be answered on the essay and problem response sheets at the back of this book. Support **all** answers with properly labeled and legible calculations that can be identified as sources of amounts used to derive your final answer. If you have not completed answering a question on a page, fill in the appropriate spaces in the wording on the bottom of the page. **"QUESTION NUMBER ___ CONTINUES ON PAGE ___ ."** If you have completed answering a question, fill in the appropriate space in the wording on the bottom of the page. **"QUESTION NUMBER ___ ENDS ON THIS PAGE."** Always begin the start of an answer to a question on the top of a new page (which may be the back side of a sheet of paper). Use the entire width of the page to answer requirements of a noncomputational nature. To answer requirements of a computational nature, you may wish to use only a portion of the page.

The point values for each question, and estimated time allotments based primarily on point value, are as follows:

	Point Value	Estimated Minutes Minimum	Estimated Minutes Maximum
No. 1	60	130	140
No. 2	10	15	25
No. 3	10	15	25
No. 4	10	30	40
No. 5	10	30	40
Totals	**100**	**220**	**270**

3. Although the primary purpose of the examination is to test your knowledge and application of the subject matter, selected essay responses will be graded for writing skills.

4. At exam time, you will be supplied with an AICPA-approved calculator to help you work through the problems in this section of the CPA exam.

Number 1 (Estimated time—130 to 140 minutes)

Select the **best** answer for each of the following items. Use a No. 2 pencil to blacken ovals on the Multiple-Choice Section of your scannable grid, response items #1 through #60, to indicate your answers. **Mark only one answer for each item. Answer all items.**

1. According to the FASB conceptual framework, the objectives of financial reporting for business enterprises are based on

A. Generally accepted accounting principles.
B. Reporting on management's stewardship.
C. The need for conservatism.
D. The needs of the users of the information.

2. According to the FASB conceptual framework, the usefulness of providing information in financial statements is subject to the constraint of

A. Consistency.
B. Cost-benefit.
C. Reliability.
D. Representational faithfulness.

3. What is the underlying concept governing the generally accepted accounting principles pertaining to recording gain contingencies?

A. Conservatism.
B. Relevance.
C. Consistency.
D. Reliability.

4. A development-stage enterprise should use the same generally accepted accounting principles that apply to established operating enterprises for

	Revenue Recognition	Deferral of Expenses
A.	Yes	Yes
B.	Yes	No
C.	No	No
D.	No	Yes

5. According to the FASB conceptual framework, which of the following attributes would **not** be used to measure inventory?

A. Historical cost.
B. Replacement cost.
C. Net realizable value.
D. Present value of future cash flows.

Please use this area for work space.

6. Conceptually, interim financial statements can be described as emphasizing

    A. Timeliness over reliability.
    B. Reliability over relevance.
    C. Relevance over comparability.
    D. Comparability over neutrality.

7. For which type of material related-party transactions does Statement of Financial Accounting Standard No. 57, *Related Party Disclosures*, require disclosure?

    A. Only those not reported in the body of the financial statements.
    B. Only those that receive accounting recognition.
    C. Those that contain possible illegal acts.
    D. All those other than compensation arrangements, expense allowances, and other similar items in the ordinary course of business.

8. Terra Co.'s total revenues for its three business segments were as follows:

Segment	Sales to Unaffiliated Customers	Intersegment Sales	Total Revenues
Lion	$70,000	$30,000	$100,000
Monk	22,000	4,000	26,000
Nevi	8,000	16,000	24,000
Combined	$100,000	$50,000	$150,000
Elimination	–	(50,000)	(50,000)
Consolidated	$100,000	$ –	$100,000

Which business segment(s) is (are) deemed to be reportable segments?

    A. None.
    B. Lion only.
    C. Lion and Monk only.
    D. Lion, Monk, and Nevi.

9. A company decided to change its inventory valuation method from FIFO to LIFO in a period of rising prices. What was the result of the change on ending inventory and net income in the year of the change?

	Ending Inventory	Net Income
A.	Increase	Increase
B.	Increase	Decrease
C.	Decrease	Decrease
D.	Decrease	Increase

Please use this area for work space.

10. Lang Co. uses the installment method of revenue recognition. The following data pertain to Lang's installment sales for the years ended December 31, 19X3 and 19X4:

	19X3	19X4
Installment receivables at year-end on 19X3 sales	$60,000	$30,000
Installment receivables at year-end on 19X4 sales	—	69,000
Installment sales	80,000	90,000
Cost of sales	40,000	60,000

What amount should Lang report as deferred gross profit in its December 31, 19X4, balance sheet?

A. $23,000
B. $33,000
C. $38,000
D. $43,000

11. In a sale-leaseback transaction, a gain resulting from the sale should be deferred at the time of the sale-leaseback and subsequently amortized when

I. The seller-lessee has transferred substantially all the risks of ownership.

II. The seller-lessee retains the right to substantially all of the remaining use of the property.

A. I only.
B. II only.
C. Both I and II.
D. Neither I nor II.

12. A six-year capital lease entered into on December 31, 19X4, specified equal minimum annual lease payments due on December 31 of each year. The first minimum annual lease payment, paid on December 31, 19X4, consists of which of the following?

	Interest Expense	Lease Liability
A.	Yes	Yes
B.	Yes	No
C.	No	Yes
D.	No	No

13. Lime Co.'s payroll for the month ended January 31, 19X5, is summarized as follows:

Total wages	$10,000
Federal income tax withheld	1,200

All wages paid were subject to FICA. FICA tax rates were 7% each for employee and employer. Lime remits payroll taxes on the 15th of the following month. In its financial statements for the month ended January 31, 19X5, what amounts should Lime report as total payroll tax liability and as payroll tax expense?

Please use this area for work space.

	Liability	Expense
A.	$1,200	$1,400
B.	$1,900	$1,400
C.	$1,900	$700
D.	$2,600	$700

***Items 14 and 15** are based on the following:*

The following information pertains to Hall Co.'s defined-benefit pension plan at December 31, 19X4:

Unfunded accumulated benefit obligation	$25,000
Unrecognized prior service cost	12,000
Net periodic pension cost	8,000

Hall made no contributions to the pension plan during 19X4.

14. At December 31, 19X4, what amount should Hall record as additional pension liability?

A. $5,000
B. $13,000
C. $17,000
D. $25,000

15. In its December 31, 19X4, statement of stockholders' equity, what amount should Hall report as excess of additional pension liability over unrecognized prior service cost?

A. $5,000
B. $13,000
C. $17,000
D. $25,000

16. On March 1, 19X3, Fine Co. borrowed $10,000 and signed a two-year note bearing interest at 12% per annum compounded annually. Interest is payable in full at maturity on February 28, 19X5. What amount should Fine report as a liability for accrued interest at December 31, 19X4?

A. $0
B. $1,000
C. $1,200
D. $2,320

Please use this area for work space.

17. Eagle Co. has cosigned the mortgage note on the home of its president, guaranteeing the indebtedness in the event that the president should default. Eagle considers the likelihood of default to be remote. How should the guarantee be treated in Eagle's financial statements?

A. Disclosed only.
B. Accrued only.
C. Accrued and disclosed.
D. Neither accrued nor disclosed.

18. Nest Co. issued 100,000 shares of common stock. Of these, 5,000 were held as treasury stock at December 31, 19X3. During 19X4, transactions involving Nest's common stock were as follows:

May 3	1,000 shares of treasury stock were sold.
August 6	10,000 shares of previously unissued stock were sold.
November 18	A 2-for-1 stock split took effect.

Laws in Nest's state of incorporation protect treasury stock from dilution. At December 31, 19X4, how many shares of Nest's common stock were issued and outstanding?

	Shares Issued	Outstanding
A.	220,000	212,000
B.	220,000	216,000
C.	222,000	214,000
D.	222,000	218,000

19. Cyan Corp. issued 20,000 shares of $5 per common stock at $10 per share. On December 31, 19X3, Cyan's retained earnings were $300,000. In March 19X4, Cyan reacquired 5,000 shares of its common stock at $20 per share. In June 19X4, Cyan sold 1,000 of these shares to its corporate officers for $25 per share. Cyan uses the cost method to record treasury stock. Net income for the year ended December 19X4 was $60,000. At December 31, 19X4, what amount should Cyan report as retained earnings?

A. $360,000
B. $365,000
C. $375,000
D. $380,000

20. Asp Co. was organized on January 2, 19X4, with 30,000 authorized shares of $10 par common stock. During 19X4 the corporation had the following capital transactions:

January 5	Issued 20,000 shares at $15 per share.
July 14	Purchased 5,000 shares at $17 per share.
December 27	Reissued the 5,000 shares held in treasury at $20 per share.

_____ Please use this area for work space. _____

Asp used the par value method to record the purchase and reissuance of the treasury shares. In its December 31, 19X4, balance sheet, what amount should Asp report as additional paid-in capital in excess of par?

A. $100,000
B. $125,000
C. $140,000
D. $150,000

21. A company issued rights to existing shareholders without consideration. The rights allowed the recipients to purchase unissued common stock for an amount in excess of par value. When the rights are issued, which of the following accounts will be increased?

	Common Stock	Additional Paid-In Capital
A.	Yes	Yes
B.	Yes	No
C.	No	No
D.	No	Yes

22. In September 19X0, West Corp. made a dividend distribution of one right for each of its 120,000 shares of outstanding common stock. Each right was exercisable for the purchase of 1/100 of a share of West's $50 variable rate preferred stock at an exercise price of $80 per share. On March 20, 19X4, none of the rights had been exercised, and West redeemed them by paying each stockholder $0.10 per right. As a result of this redemption, West's stockholders' equity was reduced by

A. $120
B. $2,400
C. $12,000
D. $36,000

23. During 19X4, Young and Zinc maintained average capital balances in their partnership of $160,000 and $100,000, respectively. The partners receive 10% interest on average capital balances, and residual profit or loss is divided equally. Partnership profit before interest was $4,000. By what amount should Zinc's capital account change for the year?

A. $1,000 decrease.
B. $2,000 increase.
C. $11,000 decrease.
D. $12,000 increase.

Please use this area for work space.

24. On February 1, 19X5, Tory began a service proprietorship with an initial cash investment of $2,000. The proprietorship provided $5,000 of services in February and received full payment in March. The proprietorship incurred expenses of $3,000 in February, which were paid in April. During March, Tory drew $1,000 against the capital account. In the proprietorship's financial statements for the two months ended March 31, 19X5, prepared under the cash basis method of accounting, what amount would be reported as capital?

    A. $1,000
    B. $3,000
    C. $6,000
    D. $7,000

25. The stockholders' equity section of Brown Co.'s December 31, 19X4, balance sheet consisted of the following:

Common stock, $30 par, 10,000
   shares authorized and outstanding $300,000
Additional paid-in capital   150,000
Retain earnings (deficit)   (210,000)

On January 2, 19X5, Brown put into effect a stockholder-approved quasi-reorganization by reducing the par value of the stock to $5 and eliminating the deficit against additional paid-in capital. Immediately after the quasi-reorganization, what amount should Brown report as additional paid-in capital?

    A. $(60,000)
    B. $150,000
    C. $190,000
    D. $400,000

***Items 26 through 28** are based on the following:*

Grant, Inc. acquired 30% of South Co.'s voting stock for $200,000 on January 2, 19X3. Grant's 30% interest in South gave Grant the ability to exercise significant influence over South's operating and financial policies. During 19X3, South earned $80,000 and paid dividends of $50,000. South reported earnings of $100,000 for the six months ended June 30, 19X4, and $200,000 for the year ended December 31, 19X4. On July 1, 19X4, Grant sold half of its stock in South for $150,000 cash. South paid dividends of $60,000 on October 1, 19X4.

Please use this area for work space.

26. Before income taxes, what amount should Grant include in its 19X3 income statement as a result of the investment?

   A. $15,000
   B. $24,000
   C. $50,000
   D. $80,000

27. In Grant's December 31, 19X3, balance sheet, what should be the carrying amount of this investment?

   A. $200,000
   B. $209,000
   C. $224,000
   D. $230,000

28. In its 19X4 income statement, what amount should Grant report as gain from the sale of half of its investment?

   A. $24,500
   B. $30,500
   C. $35,000
   D. $45,500

29. Glade Co. leases computer equipment to customers under direct-financing leases. The equipment has no residual value at the end of the lease and the leases do not contain bargain purchase options. Glade wishes to earn 8%

interest on a five-year lease of equipment with a fair value of $323,400. The present value of an annuity due of $1 at 8% for five years is 4.312. What is the total amount of interest revenue that Glade will earn over the life of the lease?

   A. $51,600
   B. $75,000
   C. $129,360
   D. $139,450

30. Rill Co. owns a 20% royalty interest in an oil well. Rill receives royalty payments on January 31 for the oil sold between the previous June 1 and November 30, and on July 31 for oil sold between the previous December 1 and May 31. Production reports show the following oil sales:

June 1, 19X3–November 30, 19X3	$300,000
December 1, 19X3–December 31, 19X3	50,000
December 1, 19X3–May 31, 19X4	400,000
June 1, 19X4–November 30, 19X4	325,000
December 1, 19X4–December 31, 19X4	70,000

What amount should Rill report as royalty revenue for 19X4?

   A. $140,000
   B. $144,000
   C. $149,000
   D. $159,000

Please use this area for work space.

31. It is proper to recognize revenue prior to the sale of merchandise when

I. The revenue will be reported as an installment sale.

II. The revenue will be reported under the cost recovery method.

    A. I only.
    B. II only.
    C. Both I and II.
    D. Neither I nor II.

32. Fogg Co., a U.S. company, contracted to purchase foreign goods. Payment in foreign currency was due one month after the goods were received at Fogg's warehouse. Between the receipt of goods and the time of payment, the exchange rates changed in Fogg's favor. The resulting gain should be included in Fogg's financial statements as a (an)

    A. Component of income from continuing operations.
    B. Extraordinary item.
    C. Deferred credit.
    D. Separate component of stockholders' equity.

33. Gray Co. was granted a patent on January 2, 19X1, and appropriately capitalized $45,000 of related costs. Gray was amortizing the patent over its estimated useful life of fifteen years. During 19X4, Gray paid $15,000 in legal costs in successfully defending an attempted infringement of the patent. After the legal action was completed, Gray sold the patent to the plaintiff for $75,000. Gray's policy is to take no amortization in the year of disposal. In its 19X4 income statement, what amount should Gray report as gain from sale of patent?

    A. $15,000
    B. $24,000
    C. $27,000
    D. $39,000

34. When should a lessor recognize in income a nonrefundable lease bonus paid by a lessee on signing an operating lease?

    A. When received.
    B. At the inception of the lease.
    C. At the expiration of the lease.
    D. Over the life of the lease.

Please use this area for work space.

---

35. Upon the death of an officer, Jung Co. received the proceeds of a life insurance policy held by Jung on the officer. The proceeds were not taxable. The policy's cash surrender value had been recorded on Jung's books at the time of payment. What amount of revenue should Jung report in its statements?

    A. Proceeds received.
    B. Proceeds received less cash surrender value.
    C. Proceeds received plus cash surrender value.
    D. None.

36. On its December 31, 19X4, balance sheet, Shin Co. had income taxes payable of $13,000 and a current deferred tax asset of $20,000 before determining the need for a valuation account. Shin had reported a current deferred tax asset of $15,000 at December 31, 19X3. No estimated tax payments were made during 19X4. At December 31, 19X4, Shin determined that it was more likely than not that 10% of the deferred tax asset would not be realized. In its 19X4 income statement, what amount should Shin report as total income tax expense?

    A. $8,000
    B. $8,500
    C. $10,000
    D. $13,000

Items 37 and 38 are based on the following:

Zeff Co. prepared the following reconciliation of its pretax financial statement income to taxable income for the year ended December 31, 19X4, its first year of operations:

Pretax financial income	$160,000
Nontaxable interest received on municipal securities	(5,000)
Long-term loss accrual in excess of deductible amount	10,000
Depreciation in excess of financial statement amount	(25,000)
Taxable income	$140,000

Zeff's tax rate for 19X4 is 40%.

37. In its 19X4 income statement, what amount should Zeff report as income tax expense–current portion?

    A. $52,000
    B. $56,000
    C. $62,000
    D. $64,000

Please use this area for work space.

---

38. In its December 31, 19X4, balance sheet, what should Zeff report as deferred income tax liability?

    A. $2,000
    B. $4,000
    C. $6,000
    D. $8,000

39. During January 19X3, Doe Corp. agreed to sell the assets and product line of its Hart division. The sale was completed on January 15, 19X4, and resulted in a gain on disposal of $900,000. Hart's operating losses were $600,000 for 19X3 and $50,000 for the period January 1 through January 15, 19X4. Disregarding income taxes, what amount of net gain (loss) should be reported in Doe's comparative 19X4 and 19X3 income statements?

	19X4	19X3
A.	$0	$250,000
B.	$250,000	$0
C.	$850,000	$(600,000)
D.	$900,000	$(650,000)

40. On April 30, 19X4, Deer Corp. approved a plan to dispose of a segment of its business. For the period January 1 through April 30, 19X4, the segment had revenues of $500,000 and expenses of $800,000. The assets of the segment were sold on October 15, 19X4, at a loss for which no tax benefit is available. In its income statement for the year ended December 31, 19X4, how should Deer report the segment's operations from January 1 to April 30, 19X4?

    A. $500,000 and $800,000 should be included with revenues and expenses, respectively, as part of continuing operations.
    B. $300,000 should be reported as part of the loss on disposal of a segment.
    C. $300,000 should be reported as an extraordinary loss.
    D. $300,000 should be reported as a loss from operations of a discontinued segment.

———— Please use this area for work space. ————

41. In open market transactions, Gold Corp. simultaneously sold its long-term investment in Iron Corp. bonds and purchased its own outstanding bonds. The broker remitted the net cash from the two transactions. Gold's gain on the purchase of its own bonds exceeded its loss on the sale of the Iron bonds. Gold should report the

A. Net effect of the two transactions as an extraordinary gain.
B. Net effect of the two transactions in income before extraordinary items.
C. Effect of its own bond transaction gain in income before extraordinary items, and report the Iron bond transaction as an extraordinary loss.
D. Effect of its own bond transaction as an extraordinary gain, and report the Iron bond transaction loss in income before extraordinary items.

42. During 19X4 both Raim Co. and Cane Co. suffered loses due to the flooding of the Mississippi River. Raim is located two miles from the river and sustains flood losses every two to three years. Cane, which has been located fifty miles from the river for the past twenty years, has never before had flood losses. How should the flood losses be reported in each company's 19X4 income statement?

	Raim	Cane
A.	As a component of income from continuing operations.	As an extraordinary item.
B.	As a component of income from continuing operations.	As a component of income from continuing operations.
C.	As an extraordinary item.	As a component of income from continuing operations.
D.	As an extraordinary item.	As an extraordinary item.

43. Lore Co. change from the cash basis of accounting to the accrual basis of accounting during 19X4. The cumulative effect of this change should be reported in Lore's 19X4 financial statements as a

A. Prior period adjustment resulting from the correction of an error.
B. Prior period adjustment resulting from the change in accounting principle.
C. Component of income before extraordinary item.
D. Component of income after extraordinary item.

Please use this area for work space.

44. Oak Co. offers a three-year warranty on its products. Oak previously estimated warranty costs to be 2% of sales. Due to a technological advance in production at the beginning of 19X4, Oak now believes 1% of sales to be a better estimate of warranty costs. Warranty costs of $80,000 and $96,000 were reported in 19X2 and 19X3, respectively. Sales for 19X4 were $5,000,000. What amount should be disclosed in Oak's 19X4 financial statements as warranty expense?

   A. $50,000
   B. $88,000
   C. $100,000
   D. $138,000

45. Ute Co. had the following capital structure during 19X3 and 19X4:

Preferred stock, $10 par, 4%
   cumulative, 25,000 shares issued
   and outstanding $ 250,000
Common stock, $5 par, 200,000
   shares issued and outstanding   1,000,000

Deferred stock is not considered a common stock equivalent. Ute reported net income of $500,000 for the year ended December 31, 19X4. Ute paid no preferred dividends during 19X3 and paid $16,000 in preferred dividends during 19X4. In its December 31, 19X4, income statement, what amount should Ute report as earnings per share?

   A. $2.42
   B. $2.45
   C. $2.48
   D. $2.50

46. West Co. had earnings per share of $15.00 for 19X4 before considering the effects of any convertible securities. No conversion or exercise of convertible securities occurred during 19X4. However, possible conversion of convertible bonds, not considered common stock equivalents, would have reduced earnings per share by $0.75. The effect of possible exercise of common stock options would have increased earnings per share by $0.10. What amount should West report as primary earnings per share for 19X4?

   A. $14.25
   B. $14.35
   C. $15.00
   D. $15.10

47. Mend Co. purchased a three-month U.S. Treasury bill. Mend's policy is to treat as cash equivalents all highly liquid investments with an original maturity of three months or less when purchased. How should this purchase be reported in Mend's statement of cash flows?

   A. As an outflow from operating activities.
   B. As an outflow from investing activities.
   C. As an outflow from financing activities.
   D. Not reported.

Please use this area for work space.

---

48. Which of the following is **not** disclosed on the statement of cash flows when prepared under the direct method, either on the face of the statement or in a separate schedule?

A. The major classes of gross cash receipts and gross cash payments.
B. The amount of income taxes paid.
C. A reconciliation of net income to net cash flow from operations.
D. A reconciliation of ending retained earnings to net cash flow from operations.

Items 49 through 51 are based on the following:

On January 2, 19X4, Pare Co. purchased 75% of Kidd Co.'s outstanding common stock. Selected balance sheet data at December 31, 19X4, is as follows:

	Pare	Kidd
Total assets	$420,000	$180,000
Liabilities	$120,000	$60,000
Common stock	100,000	50,000
Retained earnings	200,000	70,000
	$420,000	$180,000

During 19X4, Pare and Kidd paid cash dividends of $25,000 and $5,000, respectively to their shareholders. There were no other intercompany transactions.

49. In its December 31, 19X4, consolidated statement of retained earnings, what amount should Pare report as dividends paid?

A. $5,000
B. $25,000
C. $26,250
D. $30,000

50. In Pare's December 31, 19X4, consolidated balance sheet, what amount should be reported as minority interest in net assets?

A. $0
B. $30,000
C. $45,000
D. $105,000

51. In its December 31, 19X4, consolidated balance sheet, what amount should Pare report as common stock?

A. $50,000
B. $100,000
C. $137,500
D. $150,000

Please use this area for work space.

52. In a business combination, how should long-term debt of the acquired company generally be reported under each of the following methods?

	Polling of Interest	Purchase
A.	Fair value	Carrying amount
B.	Fair value	Fair value
C.	Carrying amount	Fair value
D.	Carrying amount	Carrying amount

53. In a business combination accounted for as a purchase, the appraised values of the identifiable assets acquired exceeded the acquisition price. How should the excess appraised value be reported?

A. As negative goodwill.
B. As additional paid-in capital.
C. As a reduction of the values assigned to noncurrent assets and a deferred credit for any unallocated portion.
D. As positive goodwill.

54. A business interest that constitutes a large part of an individual's total assets should be presented in a personal statement of financial condition as

A. A separate listing of the individual assets and liabilities at cost.
B. Separate line items of both total assets and total liabilities at cost.
C. A single amount equal to the proprietorship equity.
D. A single amount equal to the estimated current value of the business interest.

55. Quinn is preparing a personal statement of financial condition as of April 30, 19X5. Included in Quinn's assets are the following:

- 50% of the voting stock of Ink Corp. A stockholders' agreement restricts the sale of the stock and, under certain circumstances, requires Ink to repurchase the stock. Quinn's tax basis for the stock is $430,000, and at April 30, 19X5, the buyout value is $675,000.

- Jewelry with a fair value aggregating $70,000 based on an independent appraisal on April 30, 19X5, for insurance purposes. This jewelry was acquired by purchase and gift over a 10-year period and has a total tax basis of $40,000.

Please use this area for work space.

What is the total amount at which the Ink stock and jewelry should be reported in Quinn's April 30, 19X5, personal statement of financial condition?

A. $470,000
B. $500,000
C. $715,000
D. $745,000

56. In financial statements prepared on the income-tax basis, how should the nondeductible portion of expenses such as meals and entertainment be reported?

A. Included in the expense category in the determination of income.
B. Included in a separate category in the determination of income.
C. Excluded from the determination of income but included in the determination of retained earnings.
D. Excluded from the financial statements.

57. Financial statements prepared under which of the following methods include adjustments for both specific price changes and general price level changes?

A. Historical cost/nominal dollar.
B. Current cost/nominal dollar.
C. Current cost/constant dollar.
D. Historical cost/constant dollar.

58. What effect would the sale of a company's trading securities at their carrying amount for cash have on each of the following ratios?

	Current Ratio	Quick Ratio
A.	No effect	No effect
B.	Increase	Increase
C.	No effect	Increase
D.	Increase	No effect

59. Barr Co. has total debt of $420,000 and stockholders' equity of $700,000. Barr is seeking capital to fund an expansion. Barr is planning to issue an additional $300,000 in common stock, and is negotiating with a bank to borrow additional funds. The bank is requiring a debt-to-equity ratio of .75. What is the maximum additional amount Barr will be able to borrow?

A. $225,000
B. $330,000
C. $525,000
D. $750,000

Please use this area for work space.
---

60. The following data pertain to Cowl, Inc., for the year ended December 31, 19X4:

Net sales	$ 600,000
Net income	150,000
Total assets, January 1, 19X4	2,000,000
Total assets, December 31, 19X4	3,000,000

What was Cowl's rate of return on assets for 19X4?

    A. 5%
    B. 6%
    C. 20%
    D. 24%

Number 2 (Estimated time—15 to 25 minutes)

Question Number 2 consists of 10 items. Select the **best** answer for each item. Use a No. 2 pencil to blacken the appropriate ovals on your scannable grid to indicate your answers. **Answer all items.**

Items 61 through 64 are based on the following:

Camp Co. purchased various securities during 19X4 to be classified as held-to-maturity securities, trading securities, or available-for-sale securities.

Required:

Items 61 through 64 describe various securities purchased by Camp. For each item, select from the following list the appropriate category for each security and blacken the corresponding oval on OOF Section #3, response items #1 through #4. A category may be used once, more than once, or not at all.

CATEGORIES
Ⓐ   Held-to-maturity.
Ⓑ   Trading.
Ⓒ   Available-for-sale.

61. Debt securities bought and held for the purpose of selling in the near term.

62. U.S. Treasury bonds that Camp has both the positive intent and the ability to hold to maturity.

63. $3 million debt security bought and held for the purpose of selling in three years to finance payment of Camp's $2 million long-term note payable when it matures.

64. Convertible preferred stock that Camp does not intend to sell in the near term.

Please use this area for work space.

Items 65 through 70 *are based on the following:*

The following information pertains to Dayle, Inc.'s portfolio of marketable investments for the year ended December 31, 19X4:

	Cost	Fair value, 12/31/X3	19X4 activity Purchases	19X4 activity Sales	Fair value, 12/31/X4
Held-to-maturity securities					
Security ABC			$100,000		$95,000
Trading securities					
Security DEF	$150,000	$160,000			155,000
Available-for-sale securities					
Security GHI	190,000	165,000		$175,000	
Security JKL	170,000	175,000			160,000

Security ABC was purchased at par. All declines in fair value are considered to be temporary.

Required:

Items 65 through 70 describe amounts to be reported in Dayle's 19X4 financial statements. For each item, select from the following list the correct numerical response and blacken the corresponding oval on your scannable grid. For questions 65 through 67, use response items #1 through #3 in OOF Section #1. An amount may be selected once, more than once, or not at all. Ignore income tax considerations.

65. Carrying amount of security ABC at December 31, 19X4.

66. Carrying amount of security DEF at December 31, 19X4.

67. Carrying amount of security JKL at December 31, 19X4.

Items 68 through 70 require a second response. For each item, indicate whether a Gain (A) or a Loss (B) is to be reported. Use response items #1 through #3 in the OOF Multiple Response Section of your scannable grid. Amount answers should be filled in the first column of response items #1 through #3, and the Gain/Loss answers in the second column.

68. Recognized gain or loss on sale of security GHI.

———————————— Please use this area for work space. ————————————

69. Unrealized gain or loss to be reported in 19X4 income statement.

70. Unrealized gain or loss to be reported at December 31, 19X4, as a separate component of stockholders' equity.

ANSWER LIST			
Ⓐ	$0	Ⓕ	$95,000
Ⓑ	$5,000	Ⓖ	$100,000
Ⓒ	$10,000	Ⓗ	$150,000
Ⓓ	$15,000	Ⓘ	$155,000
Ⓔ	$25,000	Ⓙ	$160,000

Number 3 (Estimated time—15 to 25 minutes)

Question Number 3 consists of 13 items. Select the **best** answer for each item. Use a No. 2 pencil to blacken the appropriate ovals on the OOF Multiple Response Section of your scannable grid. **Answer all items.**

Items 71 through 77 are based on the following:

On January 2, 19X4, North Co. issued bonds payable with a face value of $480,000 at a discount. The bonds are due in 10 years and interest is payable semiannually every June 30 and December 31. On June 30, 19X4, and on December 31, 19X4, North made the semiannual interest payments due, and recorded interest expense and amortization of bond discount.

Please use this area for work space.

Required:

Items 71 through 77, contained in the partially completed amortization table below, represent information needed to complete the table. For each item, select from the following lists the correct numerical response and blacken the corresponding oval on the OOF Multiple Response Section of your scannable grid. A response may be selected once, more than once, or not at all. Place answers in OOF section #1, response items #.

	Cash	Interest Expense	Amortization	Discount	Carrying Amount
1/2/X4					**(73)**
6/30/X4	**(72)**	18,000	3,600	**(71)**	363,600
12/31/X4	$14,400	**(76)**	**(77)**		

Annual Interest Rates: Stated **(74)**
Effective **(75)**

RATES			
(A)	3.0%	(D)	6.0%
(B)	4.5%	(E)	9.0%
(C)	5.0%	(F)	10.0%

AMOUNTS			
(G)	$3,780	(L)	$18,360
(H)	$3,960	(M)	$116,400
(I)	$14,400	(N)	$360,000
(J)	$17,820	(O)	$367,000
(K)	$18,180		

Items 78 through 83 are based on the following:

Town, Inc. is preparing its financial statements for the year ended December 31, 19X4.

Required:

Items 78 through 83 represent various commitments and contingencies of Town at December 31, 19X4, and events subsequent to December 31, 19X4, but prior to the issuance of the 19X4 financial statements. For each item, select from the following list the reporting requirement and blacken the corresponding oval on OOF Section #3, response items #5 through #10. A reporting requirement may be selected once, more than once, or not at all.

—————————— Please use this area for work space. ——————————

REPORTING REQUIREMENT

(A) Disclosure only.

(B) Accrual only.

(C) Both accrual and disclosure.

(D) Neither accrual nor disclosure.

78. On December 1, 19X4, Town was awarded damages of $75,000 in a patent infringement suit it brought against a competitor. The defendant did not appeal the verdict, and payment was received in January 19X5.

79. A former employee of Town has brought a wrongful-dismissal suit against Town. Town's lawyers believe the suit to be without merit.

80. At December 31, 19X4, Town had outstanding purchase orders in the ordinary course of business for purchase of a raw material to be used in its manufacturing process. The market price is currently higher than the purchase price and is not anticipated to change within the next year.

81. A government contract completed during 19X4 is subject to renegotiation. Although Town estimates that it is reasonably possible that a refund of approximately $200,000–$300,000 may be required by the government, it does not wish to publicize this possibility.

82. Town has been notified by a governmental agency that it will be held responsible for the cleanup of toxic materials at a site where Town formerly conducted operations. Town estimates that it is probable that its share of remedial action will be approximately $500,000.

83. On January 5, 19X5, Town redeemed its outstanding bonds and issued new bonds with a lower rate of interest. The reacquisition price was in excess of the carrying amount of the bonds.

Please use this area for work space.

Number 4 (Estimated time—30 to 40 minutes)

The following information pertains to Baron Flowers, a calendar-year sole proprietorship, which maintained its books on the cash basis during the year.

Baron Flowers
TRIAL BALANCE
December 31, 19X4

Account Title	Cash Basis Dr.	Cash Basis Cr.	Adjustments Dr.	Adjustments Cr.	Accrual Basis* Dr.*	Accrual Basis* Cr.*
Cash	$ 25,600					
Accounts receivable, 12/31/X3	16,200					
Inventory, 12/31/X3	62,000					
Furniture & fixtures	118,200					
Land improvements	45,000					
Accumulated depreciation, 12/31/X3		$ 32,400				
Accounts payable, 12/31/X3		17,000				
Baron, Drawings						
Baron, Capital, 12/31/X3		124,600				
Sales		653,000				
Purchases	305,100					
Salaries	174,000					
Payroll taxes	12,400					
Insurance	8,700					
Rent	34,200					
Utilities	12,600					
Living expenses	13,000					
	$827,000	$827,000				

Baron has developed plans to expand into the wholesale flower market and is in the process of negotiating a bank loan to finance the expansion. The bank is requesting 19X4 financial statements prepared on the accrual basis of accounting from Baron. During the course of a review engagement, Muir, Baron's accountant, obtained the following additional information.

1. Amounts due from customers totaled $32,000 at December 31, 19X4.

2. An analysis of the above receivables revealed that an allowance for uncollectible accounts of $3,800 should be provided.

3. Unpaid invoices for flower purchases totaled $30,500 and $17,000 at December 31, 19X4, and December 31, 19X3, respectively.

4. The inventory totaled $72,800 based on a physical count of the goods at December 31, 19X4. The inventory was priced at cost, which approximates market value.

5. On May 1, 19X4, Baron paid $8,700 to renew its comprehensive insurance coverage for one year. The premium on the previous policy, which expired on April 30, 19X4, was $7,800.

6. On January 2, 19X4, Baron entered into a twenty-five year operating lease for the vacant lot adjacent to Baron's retail store for use as a parking lot. As agreed in the lease,

Baron paved and fenced in the lot at a cost of $45,000. The improvements were completed on April 1, 19X4, and have an estimated useful life of fifteen years. No provision for depreciation or amortization has been recorded. Depreciation on furniture and fixtures was $12,000 for 19X4.

7. Accrued expenses at December 31, 19X3 and 19X4, were as follows:

	19X3	19X4
Utilities	$ 900	$1,500
Payroll taxes	1,100	1,600
	$2,000	$3,100

8. Baron is being sued for $400,000. The coverage under the comprehensive insurance policy is limited to $250,000. Baron's attorney believes that an unfavorable outcome is probable and that a reasonable estimate of the settlement is $300,000.

9. The salaries account includes $4,000 per month paid to the proprietor. Baron also receives $250 per week for living expenses.

Please use this area for work space.

Required:

a. Using the worksheet on the following page, prepare the adjustments necessary to convert the trial balance of Baron Flowers to the accrual basis of accounting for the year ended December 31, 19X4. Formal journal entries are not required to support your adjustments. However, use the numbers given with the additional information to cross-reference the postings in the adjustment columns on the worksheet.

b. Write a brief memo to Baron explaining why the bank would require financial statements prepared on the accrual basis instead of the cash basis.

———————— Please use this area for work space. ————————

Baron Flowers
WORKSHEET TO CONVERT TRIAL BALANCE TO ACCRUAL BASIS
December 31, 19X4

Account Title	Cash Basis Dr.	Cash Basis Cr.	Adjustments Dr.	Adjustments Cr.	Accrual Basis* Dr.*	Accrual Basis* Cr*
Cash	$ 25,600					
Accounts receivable, 12/31/X3	16,200					
Inventory, 12/31/X3	62,000					
Furniture & fixtures	118,200					
Land improvements	45,000					
Accumulated depreciation, 12/31/X3		$ 32,400				
Accounts payable, 12/31/X3		17,000				
Baron, Drawings						
Baron, Capital, 12/31/X3		124,600				
Sales		653,000				
Purchases	305,100					
Salaries	174,000					
Payroll taxes	12,400					
Insurance	8,700					
Rent	34,200					
Utilities	12,600					
Living expenses	13,000					
	$827,000	$827,000				

Number 5 (Estimated time—30 to 40 minutes)

During 19X4, Broca Co. had the following transactions:

- On January 2, Broca purchased the net assets of Amp Co. for $360,000. The fair value of Amp's identifiable net assets was $172,000. Broca believes that, due to the popularity of Amp's consumer products, the life of the resulting goodwill is unlimited.

- On February 1, Broca purchased a franchise to operate a ferry service from the state government for $60,000 and an annual fee of 1% of ferry revenues. The franchise expires after five years. Ferry revenues were $20,000 during 19X4. Broca projects future revenues of $40,000 in 19X5, and $60,000 per annum for the three years thereafter.

- On April 5, Broca was granted a patent that had been applied for by Amp. During 19X4, Broca incurred legal costs of $51,000 to register the patent and an additional $85,000 to successfully prosecute a patent infringement suit against a competitor. Broca estimates the patent's economic life to be ten years.

Broca's accounting policy is to amortize all intangibles on the straight-line basis over the maximum period permitted by generally accepted accounting principles, taking a full year's amortization in the year of acquisition.

Required:

a. 1. Describe the characteristics of intangible assets. Discuss the accounting for the purchase or internal development of intangible assets with an indeterminable life, such as goodwill.

2. Over what period should intangible assets be amortized? How should this period be determined? Discuss the justification for amortization of intangible assets with indeterminable lives.

3. Describe the financial statement disclosure requirements relating to Broca's intangible assets and expenses. Do not write the related footnotes.

b. Prepare a schedule showing the intangibles section of Broca's balance sheet at December 31, 19X4, and a schedule showing the related expenses that would appear on Broca's 19X4 income statement. Show supporting computations.

Please use this area for work space.

TEST 2: SOLUTIONS

BUSINESS LAW &
PROFESSIONAL RESPONSIBILITIES

1. **C** Rule 503 provides if a member receives a commission from a third party for referral to a client of products or services of others, the member will not be considered in violation of rule 503 due to his or her receipt of such commission if the member remits the entire commission to the client. The rule prohibits a member from recommending any product or service to a client when the firm performs an audit or review of financial statements.

2. **D** Rule 501 provides retention of client records after a demand is made for them is an act discreditable to the possession in violation of rule 501. The fact that the statutes of the state in which a member practices may grant the member a lien on certain records in his or her profession does not change this ethical standard. A client's record consist of any accounting or other records belonging to the client that were provided to the member by or on behalf of the client. If an engagement is terminated prior to completion, the member is required to return only client records.

3. **B** A CPA should engage only in those services that he or she reasonably expects to complete with professional competency and should exercise due care in carrying out those services. (See ET Section 201, General Standards, Rule 201 A, B).

4. **A** Rule 101 provides a member shall be independent in performance of professional service. Engaging in consulting services, by itself, does not impair the independence required of the CPA. Independence shall be considered to be impaired if a member engages in any type of transaction, interest, or relationship that, for example, had a direct or material financial interest; was a trustee or executor of an estate; had any closely held or joint interest in an enterprise; had a loan to or from an enterprise or its officers or stockholders; or was connected with the enterprise as a promoter, underwriter, or trustee for a pension or profit-sharing trust of the enterprise.

5. **C** CS 100 provides the standards that apply to consulting services. As to communication with the client, CS 100 provides that the client should be informed of any significant reservations concerning the scope or benefits of the engagement.

6. **C** CPA's preparing tax returns are not required to examine or verify supporting materials or data. In preparing the tax return, the CPA may generally rely on information provided by the client unless such information appears to be incorrect, incomplete, or inconsistent (TX 132). The CPA should consider any relevant information or data actually known by that CPA from the return of another client.

7. **A** When a CPA discovers an error, he or she must inform the client and recommend appropriate measures to be taken. It is the responsibility of the client to correct such errors. If the IRS is considering bringing criminal charges, the client should be advised to obtain counsel. In the event the error is not corrected, the CPA should consider whether or not to continue the professional relationship with the client (TX 162).

8. **B** An accountant will be liable for negligence, under the Ultramares ruling, only when the plaintiff is in privity of contract with the accountant or is a primary beneficiary of the engagement. Privity of contract was required to pursue a cause of action based on negligence. However, in recent years a majority of states and the Restatement of Torts adopts a foreseen users test which expands the class of protected to those the accountant knew would use the work product.

9. **C** According to AU 325, an auditor is required to report to the client's audit committee any deficiencies in the design or operation of the internal control structure. Failure to comply with professional standards will result in evidence of malpractice.

10. **D** The required elements of fraud include a false representation; of fact; that is material; that is made with knowledge (scienter) of its falsity and intention to deceive; justifiably relied upon and; causes damages to the plaintiff. The CPA firm's best defense is that the injured party (the plaintiff) failed to prove knowledge—scienter.

11. **D** A key element of fraud is knowledge, scienter, which constitutes an intent to defraud. When a CPA acts in good faith, he or she can assert "good faith" as a proper defense because it lacks the element of scienter.

12. **B** Generally, a CPA will be strictly liable to investors under Section 11 of the 1933 Securities Act; however he or she will not be liable upon proper proof of due diligence. Adhering to GAAP and GAAS will generally be a basis for a due diligence defense. In essence, if part of a registration statement prepared by the accountant was not prepared fraudulently or negligently, the accountant will be free of liability upon demonstrating proper due diligence.

13. **C** Under Section 11, an investor need prove only that he or she sustained losses as a result of the transaction covered by the registration statement, and the registration statement contained a false or untrue statement or a material omission for which the CPA was responsible. The investor is not required to prove reliance or negligence. The investor merely has to establish the existence of the untrue statement or omission and will prevail barring a showing of "due diligence" on the part of the CPA. Sharp will not prevail under the Securities Exchange Act of 1934 because of the failure to prove scienter.

14. **D** Rule 301 (Confidential Client Information) provides a CPA may voluntarily disclose in court information:

a) Needed to defend himself or herself against a negligence suit

b) About a client's secret formulas

c) To justify claims when suing a client for fees

This does not affect the CPA's duty to comply with a validly issued subpoena. There is no accountant-client privilege at the federal level.

Therefore a federal court can subpoena a CPA's working papers.

15. A Although there exists an attorney-client privilege, there is no communication privilege at common law as between CPA and client. However, there are some states that have enacted such confidential privileges.

16. D A partnership is an association between two or more parties engaged in a business enterprise as co-owners for profit. It is not the partnership entity that pays federal income taxes. It is rather an entity in which income or losses are reported on the individual returns of the owners. Further, a partnership does not have ongoing, indefinite continuity.

17. A Partners are jointly and severally liable for a tort or breach of trust committed by any partners in the course of the partnership business. Joint and several liability occurs where, for example, a creditor may sue the partners jointly as a group or separately as individuals.

Because a partner is a general agent of the partnership, the act of every partner binds the partnership on transactions within the scope of the partnership business unless the partner lacks actual or apparent authority to act. A partner may bind the partnership by his or her act if there exists actual authority, express or implied to perform the act. Because he or she has apparent authority, the partner may bind the partnership to contracts with third parties in the course of carrying out partnership business.

18. C The partnership agreement always governs, particularly as it provides for partnership profits and losses. Absent any agreement or provision to the contrary, partners share in the profits and losses equally, regardless of the pro-rata contribution of their financial investment.

19. D A partner may sell or assign his or her interest in the partnership without dissolving the partnership. The assignee does not become a partner, does not have the right to participate in management, and does not have the right to inspect partnership books or records.

20. A The U.P.A. provides that dissolution is a change in the relations between partners caused by a partner's ceasing to be associated in the carrying out of the partnership business. A partner always has the power to dissolve a partnership. Whether the partner has the right to do so is determined by the partnership agreement. A partner who wrongfully dissolves the partnership may be liable to the other partner(s) for breach of the partnership agreement. Where there is no specific provision as to the duration of the partnership, it is a partnership at will, and as such, may be dissolved at any time.

21. A The Articles of Incorporation should include a) the name of the corporation, b) the number of authorized shares, and c) the address of the registered office and the name of registered agent, and the names of the incorporators. Matters and procedures affecting internal grievance should be contained in the corporate by laws.

22. C Unless otherwise provided in the articles of incorporation, the corporate entity has a perpetual existence and does not terminate upon death, withdrawal, or addition of shareholders, directors, or officers.

23. **C** Any shareholder has the right to inspect corporate books and records provided the inspection is for proper purpose related to corporate business or interests. Inspection for personal use or business is not a proper purpose.

24. **C** The board of directors has the authority to declare dividends and other distributions. A stock dividend is a distribution of additional shares of the corporation in proportion to current holdings. The value is transferred from earned or capital surplus. The earnings and profits are a tax account, which does not change by a declaration of a stock dividend. It does not affect the corporation's ability to pay a cash or property dividend.

25. **D** A merger is the combination of the assets of two or more corporations into one corporation. The surviving corporation receives title to all of the assets. The target or merged corporation ceases to exist as a separate entity. The law generally requires approval by a majority vote of the board and majority vote of the shares of each corporation. A special shareholders' meeting, giving proper notice and purpose of such a meeting, must be given to the shareholders of each corporation.

26. **B** Federal Law, not State statutes, exempt a debtor's assets from federal tax liens. Social Security is exempt from garnishment.

27. **A** A lien creditor is a creditor who has acquired a lien in the property by judicial decree and includes an assignee for the benefit of creditors. A lien securing claims arising from services, repairs, or materials furnished with respect to goods (i.e., mechanics lien or artisan's

lien) "takes priority over a perfected security interest unless the lien is statutory and specifically provides otherwise." (See UCC 9-310)

28. **D** Contribution is where there is more than one surety. The co-sureties are jointly and severally liable for the principle—debtor's default up to the amount of each surety's undertaking. When a surety pays the oligation of the principal-debtor, the surety is entitled to have any co-sureties pay their proportionate share of the obligation. Payment from the cosureties of their pro-portionate share is referred to as *contribution*.

29. **D** A surety will be released to the extent that the principal-debtor's obligation under the contract between the debtor-creditor has been performed. It is immaterial as to who tenders performance.

30. **C** Once a surety has paid the principal-debtor's entire obligation, he "steps into the shoes" of the creditor and thereafter seeks recovery from the debtor.

31. **A** Employees subject to FICA taxes are required to file quarterly returns and to deposit the proper amounts on a monthly or semi-weekly basis to an appropriate banking institution. Failure to do so will result in penalties. Penalties may also be imposed on parties who file returns or other documents without indicating tax identification numbers.

32. **B** Federal unemployment tax must be paid by an employer employing one or more employees covered under the Social Security Act or who pays more than $1,500 in wages in a calendar quarter. Such payments are a business expenses and are deductible for tax purposes.

33. **A** Workers' compensation insurance provides benefits to an employee injured during the course of employment and within the scope of employment. Workers' compensation is a form of strict liability whereby the employer is liable to the employee for such injuries or disease sustained by the employee that occur in the course of employment.

34. **B** Workers' compensation is a form of strict liability whereby the employer will be liable to an employee for injuries sustained in the course of employment. The employee will be entitled to recover regardless of

a) Absence of fault on the part of the employer

b) Assumption of the risk by the employee taking a hazardous job

c) Negligence by a co-worker or employee

d) Contributory negligence where the injury was caused by the employee's negligence.

35. **C** Age Discrimination in Employment Act (ADEA) remedies include back pay as well as other benefits denied as a result of the discriminatory act. Remedies also include attorney's fees and reinstatement.

36. **A** Equal Pay Act of 1963 amends the Fair Labor Standards Act. It prohibits an employer from discriminating in paying different wages based on gender when the same or equal work is being performed. Title VII of the 1964 Civil Rights Act prohibits discrimination on the basis of race, color, religion, national origin, or sex.

37. **A** The FLSA requires nonexempt employers to pay an established minimum-hour pay base for a covered employee provided the minimum-hour pay rate and overtime standards are satisfied.

38. **B** As indicated in the answer to Question 37, the FLSA provides for a minimum hourly rate of pay and further provides for payment of time and one-half (150%) of a covered nonexempt employee's hourly rate of compensation for every hour in excess of 40 hours. Therefore, the employee will be paid for 5 hours overtime in the first week and 2 hours for the second week.

39. **A** Under ERISA, private pension and retirement plans are protected, as are the rights to retirement benefits. ERISA imposes a fiduciary duty on the managers-trustees, which duties include record keeping, reporting, and disclosure. Vesting rules generally require that employee contributions vest immediately and employer contributions may vest after specified annual intervals, e.g., after 5 years.

40. **D** Under the National Labor Relations Act of 1935 employees have the right to formally organize the workplace and engage in the collective bargaining process. The NLRA also defines "unfair labor practices" by employers. For example, employers are required to bargain (negotiate) in good faith issues affecting conditions of employment, e.g. wages and hours. The NLRA does not exempt sick pay or vacation pay, both of which are considered compulsory bargaining issues.

41. **B** Under Article 2 of the UCC a firm offer is an assurance in a writing and signed by the merchant-offeror that the offer will remain open. A firm offer will remain open for the stated time period. No consideration is necessary. If no time period is specified, then it is for a reasonable time. The firm offer can remain open for 90 days (3 months).

42. C Under Article 2 of the UCC an offer to make a contract invites an acceptance in any manner and by any medium reasonable under the circumstances unless indicated otherwise. A mailed or faxed acceptance is deemed acceptable under given circumstances and is effective upon dispatch. Consequently both methods resulted in a valid acceptance because they were dispatched prior to the ten-day exemption period.

43. B The warranty of title provides that there is an obligation on the part of the seller to convey the right of ownership—title free of any liens. The Code provides that the seller warrants that the title being conveyed is good, and the transfer of the goods is proper.

44. D Section 402A Restatement, Second, Torts imposes strict liability in tort on merchants for personal injuries and property damage resulting from the selling of a product in a defective condition, unreasonably dangerous to the user or consumer.

45. B Under Article 2 an agreement as to the risk of loss is either express or implied by virtue of custom or trade usage. If the contract does not require the seller to deliver the goods at a specified destination but only to the common carrier, risk of loss passes to the buyer when the goods are delivered to the carrier. If the seller is required to deliver to a specified destination, risk of loss passes to the buyer at the destination point where the goods are tendered to the buyer.

46. C F.O.B. (Free on Board) indicates that the seller bears the risk of loss and expense of shipping the goods to the point of destination. If it is F.O.B. place of shipment, seller will bear the risk and expense of delivering goods to the common carrier. Thereafter, risk and expenses are borne by the buyer.

47. B When either party has reasonable grounds for insecurity as to performance of the other, the insecure party may suspend performance and demand reasonable assurances from the other party. Under Article 2, if the seller defaults, it usually involves a repudiation of the contract or failure to deliver conforming goods. Remedies include recovery of any payments made, cover damages, recovery for breach of warranty, recovery for consequential and incidental damages. Generally, barring a showing of bad faith or vindictive conduct, punitive damages are not recoverable for breach of contract actions.

48. B Where the parties have contracted, the seller is obligated to transfer and deliver goods, and the buyer is obligated to accept and pay the contract price. If the goods are nonconforming in any respect, the buyer may reject the goods or revoke acceptance if goods are not cured as promised by the seller. The seller must put and hold goods for the buyer and must give the buyer reasonable notice to take possession.

49. B A liquidated damages clause is a provision in a contract that specifies a dollar amount for damages to be paid in the event of a breach. The amount agreed upon by the parties must be reasonable in consideration of the anticipated losses. If the amount is excessive, or too low, it will be deemed a penalty and will be unenforceable. If there is no liquidated damages clause, Article 2 provides that the seller may keep 20% of the contract price or $500, whichever amount is less.

50. A When a buyer wrongfully rejects goods, fails to pay for goods, or in any way repudiates the contract, the seller has the following remedies: withhold and suspend delivery of goods, stop shipment of goods in transit, resell the goods and recover damages, recover the price, recover incidental damages, cancel the contract, and reclaim the goods from a buyer who is insolvent (see UCC.)

51. B Joint tenancy with the right of ownership provides that the interest of a decedent tenant will revert to the first tenants. However, the conveyance in this case by deed during the lifetime of one of the joint tenants severed joint tenancy. It results in a tenancy in common of one-third (1/3) ownership to Green and the remaining 2/3 ownership interest held jointly with rights of survivorship. Consequently, Fall's and Dear's deaths resulted in their interests' passing to the heirs of the later to die receiving the 2/3 interest.

52. D The sale of real property must be entered into in good faith and at arms length distance. Each party must be independent and have his or her own interest properly and effectively represented.

53. B In most states leases for a period of longer than one year must be in a writing to satisfy the Statute of Frauds. Generally a valid, enforceable lease must demonstrate an interest in property that conveys certain possessory rights without conveying ownership, specifying the lease term and reversion to the landlord, the rent to be paid, and description of the premises to be occupied.

54. C The deed is an instrument demonstrating the seller's intent to convey or pass title of real property to a grantee (buyer). Deed contains the names of the grantor, grantee, words of conveyance, proper and adequate description of the real property, and the signature of the grantor. The deed must be delivered to the grantee.

55. B If the interest of the mortgagee is recorded, a subsequent purchaser of the property will have notice of the recorded mortgage and takes the property subject to that. Recording also gives Marsh priority over a subsequent mortgagee.

56. C A fixture is an item of personal property that is so firmly attached to real property that an interest in the fixture arises under real property law. In determining whether personal property becomes a fixture, the intention of the parties with conflicting claims to it as expressed in their agreement will be the controlling factor. Absent any agreement, the following factors will be relevant in determining whether the item is a fixture: 1) the physical relationship of the item to the property, 2) the intent of the party who attached the item to the property or building, 3) the purpose served by the item in relation to the land, 4) the intent of the person in that land or building at the time of the attachment of the item.

57. A Under the Federal Water Pollution Control Act (Clean Water Act), standards have been established regulating the discharge of pollutants into waterways. It specifically prohibits thermal pollution since the discharge of heated waters or materials may upset the ecological balance. This also covers wetlands which include swamps, marshes, and other similar areas that support birds, animals, and other vegetative life. It forbids the dredging of wetlands, unless a permit has been secured from the Army Corps of Engineers.

58. C In certain cases a party may acquire title to abandoned personal property by taking possession of it. Abandoned property is property intentionally disposed of by the owner. If the property has been intentionally abandoned, the finder is entitled to the property. A lease, however, gives possession but not ownership.

59. D A common carrier is anyone who transports goods from one place to another for a fee. The common carrier is strictly liable for damage to or loss of goods being transported. However, loss will be borne by the bailor if it is caused by force majeur, action by an enemy, order of public authority, or the shippers negligence in packaging.

60. A In order to collect a property insurance policy claim, a party must have an insurable interest in the property at the time of loss. An insurable interest is a financial interest or close personal interest or relationship in someone's life or property that justifies insuring the particular life or property.

61. B *Agency* is a consensual relationship between a principal and agent through which the agent is authorized to act for and on behalf of the principal in entering legal relationships with third parties.

This particular agreement calls for Banks to represent Lace on customer-service calls, in effect, forming an agency relationship. Unless the agency relationship falls within the Statute of Frauds, requiring a specific writing (such as to sell the land), the oral agreement is sufficient to create the agency agreement.

62. A Express authority is that which expressly conferred to the agent by actual instructions of the principal. Banks, as Laces agent, was expressly authorized to provide computer services that included customizing software for Lace's customers. Agency Law provides a principal is bound on contracts with third parties if the agent has actual and apparent authority. Actual authority includes both express and implied. Clear Company relied on Banks's implied authority to customize software. Clear Company should not have relied on Banks's express authority when purchasing a computer. The express authority did not exist.

63. B An agency may be terminated at will by either party or by operation of law: death or insanity of either party, bankruptcy, or destruction of the subject matter of the agency. An agent's breach or disregard for the express limitation of his or her authority is cause for termination. A terminated agent continues to have apparent authority until actual notice is given to Clear Co. and those that have had business dealings with the agent. Others who have not had any business dealings must be given constructive notice, e.g., trade publication.

64. D Banks lacked the actual authority to sell Clear Co. However, based on previous purchases made from other agents and not objected to by Lace, Banks did have apparent authority to engage in computer sales and receive deposits. Lace is bound by the agreement between Banks and Clear Company and may not make any changes in the contract without consent of Clear Company.

65. **A** A disclosed principal exists if a third party entering the contract knows that the agent is acting for a principal and knows the actual identity of the principal. A disclosed principal is liable on contracts with third parties by an agent with actual or apparent authority. The agent, however, who breaches his or her instructions, as in Banks's case, will be liable to the principal for actual damages. (2.703)

66. **C** The Rule Against Perpetuities requires that an interest in property must vest, if at all, within a period that is measured by the life of a person in being plus twenty-one years. Glenn's trust provides for the income to be paid out to Glenn's children for life. The principal of the trust then vests in Glenn's grandchildren. The trust does not violate the rule.

The powers and authority conferred to a trustee are derived from the trust instrument. The trust was properly formed, and the discretion granted to the trustee does not affect the validity of the trust, permitting the trust to make payments of principal to the income beneficiaries.

67. **A** A trust generally can be terminated upon completion of its purpose or by order of the court. The terms of the trust specifically provide that the trust will continue until the death of the last income beneficiaries (the children of Glenn). Thereafter, the assets are to be distributed to the remaining beneficiaries.

A trust is not terminated because of the unauthorized activity or conduct engaged in by the trustees. Trustees have a fiduciary duty to the beneficiaries and the trust itself. They will be liable for any damages resulting from a breach of that duty.

68. **B** A trustee has a legal duty to carry out the terms of the trust document and likewise owes a fiduciary trust to the beneficiaries. A fiduciary has a duty to act in good faith, with the highest degree of loyalty exercising the utmost care for the parties to whom they owe that duty. Failure to distribute the annual income, as provided for in the trust, was a breach of the fiduciary duty. However, exercising prudent discretion as to the distribution of the principal to income beneficiaries was exercised in good faith. The trust provided the principal and income was to be distributed in accordance with the trust investment.

69. **B** A stock dividend is payable in the stock of the dividend paying corporation. It does not increase the equity of the shareholder because stock dividends are issued in proportion to the number of shares owned by the shareholder. Generally, dividends are not income and should be allocated as principal remaining as trust assets unless the trustees have been granted such discretion to distribute from the principal.

70. **D** The powers of a trustee are determined by the authority granted by the settlor in the trust instrument. Here the provisions of the trust allow the trustee to make discretionary distributions from the principal when such distribution is serving the best interest of the beneficiary. The interest of the settlor was to restrict and limit distribution from principal to the income beneficiaries. The $5,000 payment to the grandchild was not authorized. The $10,000 to Glenn's child was provided for and the trustee did not act in excess of or without discretionary authority.

71. **A** The priority among creditors in a bankruptcy action is 1) secured creditors 2) priority creditors and 3) general creditors. A secured creditor has a secured claim only to the extent of the collateral. The balance of the claim is unsecured. A secured creditor has the right to take possession of the asset securing the claim if the secured interest was perfected. If the collateral is insufficient, they are treated as general creditors. The Bank, a secured creditor, will be entitled to the funds from the sale of the warehouse to pay the balance of the mortgage.

72. B   There is a priority of claims to creditors under the Bankruptcy Act. These priorities are before any assets can be paid to general creditors. The priority is as follows: 1) administrative costs, 2) post-petition creditors, for debts arising between the filing of bankruptcy and the granting of relief, 3) employee wages and benefit plans, 4) farmers and fishermen, 5) advance from customers, 6) alimony and child support, 7) taxes.

Here, the employee wage claims are limited by the priority rule to $4,000. Any unpaid balances will be treated as general claims.

73. B   Federal income taxes are a priority claim under the Bankruptcy Code. They are not a secured creditor claim. Priority claims are paid after secured claims and prior to general creditor claims.

74. C   The trustee may recover certain property transferred by the debtor to others under the following circumstances: 1) to or for the benefit of a creditor, 2) for or on account of an antecedent debt owed by the debtor before the transfer was made, 3) while the debtor was insolvent 4) made on or within 90 days before the date of the filing of the petition or if the creditor was an "insider" within one year of the date of filing. To void the "insider" transaction taking

place more than 90 days prior to the filing, the trustee must establish insolvency at the time of the transfer. Rusk had paid off the loans while insolvent and the directors should return their payments to the trustee.

75. A   A nonpreferential transfer, payment of a debt in the ordinary course of business, made in accordance with normal business terms within 45 days of when the debt was incurred, will not result in a voidable transfer. Likewise, payments of alimony, support, and consumer debts less than $600 are not considered preferential.

76. A   Coffee Corporation is permitted to make a private offering under Regulation D if the offering is in fact private—it may not be announced or advertised except in limited circumstances under Rule 504. The security may not be immediately reoffered by purchasers to the general public. The S.E.C. must be notified within 15 days. The Securities Exchange Act (SEA) of 1934 provides that publicly held corporations with more than 500 shareholders and assets exceeding $5 million must register with the S.E.C. and file periodic reports. Being covered under the SEA of 1934 does not affect eligibility for an offering under regulation D.

77. B   Under Regulation D, Rule 506, shares may be purchased by any number of accredited investors, and up to 35 unaccredited investors. Nonaccredited investors must be provided with material information about the issuer. The nonaccredited purchaser must show sufficient knowledge and experience in financial matters to be in a position to prudently evaluate the risk of the investment.

78. **B** An offering under Rule 506 has no dollar amount limitation. Under Rule 504 dollar limit is $1 million; under Rule 505 the dollar amount is $5 million.

79. **B** Under Regulation D issues are required to exercise reasonable care to assure that purchases of the exempt offering are purchasing for their own investment and are not underwriters. The issuer requires the purchaser to sign a statement indicating the purchase is for investment purposes and not for resale. Securities sold under Rule 506 are restricted securities that have limited transferability. In essence, the security may not be resold without full registration under the 1933 Act unless there exists some other exemption. The resale restriction is to prevent an issuing company from selling securities in an exempt transaction to an underwriter who in turn would resell them to the public. After a two-year period, limited sales by noninsiders are permitted without restriction. Unlimited sales by noninsiders are permitted after three years. A restriction of sale for nine months is imposed on securities purchased in an intrastate offering exemption.

80. **D** Private placements under Regulation D are exempt from registration. The issuing company must notify the S.E.C. of the offering within 15 days after the first sale of the security. Notification is given on Form D.

Notification

4. **a.** Korn would argue the following points demonstrating there was not a valid contract.

As to Korn's offer dated July 15, 19X5, the offer lacked definitiveness and specificity as to length and time and consideration (compensation), which are essential to a valid and proper offer.

Wilson's response on September 28 proposed different terms. As such it constituted a counteroffer and did not to the mirror image requirement. Korn did not accept the counter-offer made by Wilson.

Korn specifically requested acceptance on or before October 1 and not October 3. Korn's offer in effect terminated October 1.

Because the degree of snowfall could very well vary, heavier snowfalls would require increased costs and expenses. This in itself would be cause for termination of the agreement without performance.

b. Arguments supporting a valid contract.

Korn's writing of July 5 showed a manifestation of intent to make a serious offer providing snow-removal service for a specified period for a specified amount of compensation.

Wilson responded to the offer September 28. He agreed to all the terms. He proposed that the agreement be in effect from January 1 through March 31. It can be argued that Wilson did not condition his acceptance to the extension and complied with the mirror image rule.

Inasmuch as no specific instructions were given as to mode of acceptance, using the mail was a reasonable means of acceptance. The acceptance became effective upon mailing and thus a contract became effective September 28.

Heavier snowfalls were reasonably foreseeable and should have been anticipated, and therefore Korn's call to Wilson asking for additional consideration (compensation) is not a justifiable claim of hardship. Wilson did not agree to the changes. Contracts can be modified only as a result of mutual agreement between the contracting parties.

Further, the revocation of the September 30 offer is not valid because there was a valid and effective acceptance made on September 28.

c. Korn effectively breached the contract on September 30 by repudiating the contract. It was an anticipatory breach on his part indicating his unwillingness or inability to perform the contract before actual performance time.

The appropriate remedies for breach of contract include compensatory damages, which are intended to put the nonbreaching party in a position that is economically equivalent to that which he or she expected to be in had the contract been fully performed. Wilson is under a legal duty to mitigate his damages by securing some other snow-removal service and may thereafter recover from Korn any additional costs and expenses over the original contract that are incidental to the breach.

5.

Memo To: Audit Partner

From: Staff Accountant

Our client, Crane Corp. received a promissory note from one of its customers, Jones Corp., in payment for a tractor. Crane accepted a security interest from customer Harper for the purpose of securing the balance of the price of the tractor. Harper has granted to Acorn Trust a security interest covering all of Harper's equipment, including the tractor sold to Harper. Copies of the security agreement, financing statement, and copies of proof of filings are secured. Acorn Trust has also filed a financing statement.

Issues and principles of law that are applicable are as follows:

a. Is Crane Corp. a holder in due course of the promissory note? Is the instrument negotiable?

In order for an instrument to be negotiable and valid, the following elements must be satisfied:

1) it must be in writing

2) signed by the maker

3) as an unconditional promise to pay a sum certain in money

4) on demand or at a time certain

5) payable to bearer or to the order of someone.

These elements according to the facts have been satisfied. Therefore, the note is negotiable.

b. Is Crane a holder in due course?

Crane Corp. is a holder. It is in possession of the paper issued, and it has been properly endorsed. Jones endorsed the note in blank and delivered it to Crane Corp. Crane is therefore a holder. A holder in due course is a party who takes the instrument a) for value, b) in good faith, and c) without any notice that the note is without any defenses, is not overdue, and has not been dishonored. Since the facts only indicate that there was a contract dispute between Oval and Jones, the payee prior to the execution of the note, Crane, did not have knowledge of such claims and therefore was a holder in due course.

c. Is Oval Corp. liable on the note?

Crane is a holder in due course. As such, Crane Corp. takes the instrument free of personal defenses. In this case, Oval's defense is fraud in the inducement. Oval is liable to Crane. Oval will have to seek recovery from Jones Corp.

d. Is Jones liable to Crane on the note?

Jones avoided contractual liability by the qualified endorsement. However, Jones is still obligated under warrant liability. Jones warranted that there were no defenses that were good against Jones. Jones had knowledge of Oval's claim prior to the endorsement. This constitutes a breach of warranty and thus Jones is liable on the note for its face amount.

e. Did Crane Corp. have a valid security interest? Was it perfected? Did it have priority over Acorn's interest?

Crane's security interest was perfected by its filing on October 10. Acorn's security interest was filed on October 9. Generally this would have had priority over Crane's. In this case, however, a Purchase Money Security Interest (PSMI) as collateral is given priority over a conflicting security interest (noninventory), even if filed first, provided the PSMI is perfected at the time the debtor takes possession or within 10 days. Since Crane Corp. filed timely within a 10-day period, the PSMI has priority over the security interest held by Acorn.

TEST 2: SOLUTIONS
AUDIT

1. **D** In considering the objectivity of the internal audit staff, the independent auditor should consider the organizational level to which it reports the results of its work. The other choices relate to determining the competence of the internal audit staff.

2. **A** Obtaining knowledge about the design of internal control policies and procedures in order to identify the potential types of misstatements that might occur is a typical part of the planning process. Documenting the assessed level of control risk occurs after performing tests of controls. Evaluating operational efficiency or determining that collusion exists is not part of the auditor's planning process.

3. **B** Edit tests are used to check input data for validity. A file of rejected sales transactions would likely identify the reason for rejection and thus allow for correction and re-entry. The circumstances identified in the other responses do not relate to input validity and would not be detected by edit checks.

4. **B** If the integrity of an entity's management is suspect, representations, assertions, and records provided by management would be of questionable value. While the other choices indicate inappropriate practices, those practices are not so significant as to preclude the ability to conduct an audit.

5. **B** Management is responsible for the establishment and ongoing supervision of the internal control. When management is dominated by one individual, the credibility of the internal control is impaired. The other choices do not relate directly to management philosophy and operating style.

6. **C** Establishing budgets and forecasts and investigating identified variances for correction of potential problems is an effective supervisory tool. The other choices identify methods that might be desirable business practices, but do not directly relate to improving management's ability to supervise activities.

7. **C** A credit sale or a collection on account would require the updating of the accounts receivable master file. Receiving reports and cash disbursement transactions are associated with the expenditures cycle. Unless an entity is utilizing electronic data interchange, remittance advices are not likely maintained in a computerized format.

8. **D** A sales invoice would be generated as part of the revenue cycle. Customer orders and customer checks would be incoming items, while receiving reports are associated with the expenditures cycle.

9. A Auditors are required to document the understanding of the internal control to plan an audit. The form and extent of the documentation is influenced by the size, complexity, and nature of the internal control of the entity.

10. C A validity check compares the bit structure of a data item with a list of all possible valid bit structures. If no match is found, there is an indication the data item that was input was not properly coded. Response A is an example of a limit test, response B is an error listing of errors detected and corrected, and response D is and example of an echo check.

11. C An examination of client records of the use of EDP programs is appropriate for determining whether internal control is operating as designed. The types of evidence presented in the other choices are the types obtained in the performance of substantive tests.

12. A The use of a lockbox prevents employees from having access to cash receipts and, therefore, is superior to the other choices.

13. A Auditors are required to obtain a sufficient understanding of the internal control to enable them to plan an audit. In obtaining an understanding for planning purposes, auditors are not required to obtain knowledge about the effectiveness or the consistent application of policies and procedures, nor are auditors required to obtain knowledge of control procedures related to each principal transaction class and account balance.

14. B The segregation of programming and operations is the most effective control to prevent EDP personnel from modifying programs. None of the other choices prevent EDP personnel from gaining access to programs for purposes of alteration.

15. A The notification of the payroll supervisor by the personnel department of terminated employees allows the payroll supervisor to remove the terminated employee from the payroll to prevent a check from being issued.

16. B Dual custody is a desirable control over marketable securities when an independent trust agent is not employed. Neither the review of the investment decisions nor the tracking of sales and purchases safeguard securities already acquired. The annual verification of securities by the chairman of the board is too infrequent to be an adequate control.

17. C If the auditor assesses control risk too low, the auditor's sample results indicate the maximum deviation rate in the population is less than the tolerable rate. In fact, the deviation rate exceeds the tolerable rate. Thus, the auditor has overrelied on the control. This condition is represented by situation III.

18. B Reperformance and observation are audit procedures commonly used in tests of controls. The other choices represent audit procedures more commonly associated with substantive tests.

19. D The risk of incorrect acceptance implies that the auditor accepts an account balance as being fairly stated when it is materially misstated. The risk of assessing control risk too low implies that the auditor has relied on a control as functioning acceptably when the actual state is that the control is not functioning acceptably. The auditor then incorrectly relies on a poorly functioning control. Relying on ineffective controls and accepting material misstated accounts as fairly stated relates to the effectiveness of the audit.

20. A For reasons of efficiency, assessing control risk may be done in conjunction with obtaining an understanding of the entity's internal control. Auditors may consider knowledge obtained in prior audits is assessing the current year's control risk. If auditors assess control risk at less than the maximum, they must document the basis of their conclusions. The lower the level of assessed control risk, the more assurance the evidence must provide.

21. D An auditor assesses control risk in conjunction with inherent risk in order to determine the level of detection risk, given a desired level of audit risk (the audit risk model). The auditor's understanding of the control environment is the basis of the assessment of control risk. The assessment of control risk is not a factor in determining materiality levels. Inherent risk is evaluated assuming no related internal control policies or procedures.

22. D In order to assess control risk at less than the maximum, the auditor must both identify internal control policies and procedures that are relevant to specific assertions and test the effectiveness of those policies and procedures. Assessing control risk at less than the maximum normally allows less substantive testing with smaller sample sizes. Inherent risk is evaluated assuming no related internal control policies or procedures. Assessing control risk at less than the maximum normally allows more testing at interim, not less.

23. D After assessing control risk at less than the maximum and desiring to seek a further reduction for some assertions, auditors should consider gathering additional evidence to support a further reduction. The other choices all deal with procedures performed prior to the decision to assess control risk at less than the maximum.

24. C The understanding of the entity's control environment should always be documented. Only when auditors assess control risk below the maximum are they required to document the basis for that conclusion.

25. D When an auditor reduces the planned reliance on a prescribed control, the auditor has concluded from the tests of controls that the control is not functioning sufficiently to enable the auditor to rely on the control. This condition occurs when the achieved upper precision limit is greater than the tolerable rate. The achieved upper precision limit is the sum of the sample rate of deviation and the allowance for sampling risk.

26. D In considering the qualitative aspects of deviation, the auditor should attempt to distinguish between errors and irregularities. A deviation concealed by a forged document is an irregularity. Because irregularities are intentional and relate to employee dishonesty, they may have implications beyond the control being tested.

27. C When there are numerous property transactions during the year, an auditor may wish to assess control risk at less than the maximum in order to reduce the amount of substantive tests. In order to assess control risk at a low level, the auditor must test controls. If they are found to be reliable, then only limited tests of current year property transactions need be performed.

28. A Lapping is a technique designed to conceal the theft of customer receipts on account by applying subsequent customer receipts on account to those accounts from which the receipts were previously stolen. Thus, the date the check is deposited will be prior to the date the remittance was credited to the account.

29. D The normal procedure is for the check signer, or someone in the same department, to mail the checks after signing. Supporting documentation should be available to the signer and be canceled by the signer or someone acting under the signer's supervision. To promote adequate segregation of duties, the check signer should not review the bank reconciliation or return checks to accounts payable.

30. D Agreeing the vendor's invoice with the receiving report ensures that the company is billed only for what it receives. Agreeing the vendor's invoice with the purchase order ensures that the company was bill for what it ordered. After establishing agreement, a voucher is prepared and submitted for payment.

31. A Observation of the distribution of the payroll checks to valid employees by someone other than the personnel department is an important test of the existence assertion. Inspecting evidence of prenumbering relates to completeness. Recomputation relates to valuation. Verification of the monthly payroll bank reconciliation may provide information about the total checks distributed, but not about whether they were distributed to valid employees.

32. C Reviewing an entity's description of inventory policies and procedures in a standard procedure in obtaining an understanding of an entity's internal control related to inventory. The

procedures identified in the other choices are substantive tests.

33. A Attribute sampling is normally employed in tests of controls. To determine sample size in attribute sampling, the auditor must specify: the expected deviation rate, the tolerable deviation rate, and the allowable risk of assessing control risk too low.

34. D By vouching assets recorded in the accounting records to the actual assets, the auditor would gather evidence concerning failure to record retirements (a weakness in internal control over retirements). Inspecting equipment and tracing it to plant asset records will not detect failures to record retirement, because the population being sampled does not include any retired assets. If an asset is in the subsidiary ledger, even though it may have actually been retired, depreciation is normally taken on the asset. The most likely scenario for equipment that is unused, but still on hand, is to leave it in the plant asset records. It is not likely that unused assets would be transferred to other assets.

35. D According to SAS No. 60, a communication of reportable conditions should be made to the audit committee, or its equivalent. The report should indicate that the purpose of the audit is to report on the financial statements and not to provide assurance on the internal control, define reportable conditions, and restrict distribution of the report to the management, the audit committee, and others within the entity.

36. C Management may present its written assertion about the effectiveness of internal control in a separate report accompanying the CPA's report, or a representation letter to the CPA. If the written assertion is presented in a representation letter, there is a limitation on the distribution of the report of the CPA. Otherwise, there is no limit on the distribution of the report.

37. A The report for a service center on policies and procedures placed in operations includes a description of the scope and nature of the procedures. The report should not state that management has disclosed all design weaknesses, contain an opinion on the operating effectiveness, or make any reference to the assessment of control risk.

38. A Auditors develop particular audit objectives to test specific management assertions. The goal of the auditor is to satisfy these audit objectives by the completion of evidence gathering procedures. The evidence gathering procedures are substantive tests. Analytical procedures are the only substantive tests identified among the available responses.

39. C Customers have more incentive to report an overstatement error in their account than an understatement. Therefore, if an understatement error is present in a confirmation, the customers may be inclined not to return the confirmation.

40. B The standard form to confirm account balance information with financial institutions requests information on deposit account balances as well as information on loans, including balance, interest rate, and collateral.

41. B Analytical procedures are substantive tests that involve an evaluation of relationships between data to determine the reasonableness of the data. A standard cost system produces reports showing the difference between standard and actual costs. This would be a possible source of

data used by auditors for analytical tests. All other responses do not relate to comparisons of data and an evaluation of their relationship.

42. B The formula for calculating inventory turnover is: Cost of Goods Sold / Average Inventory.

43. C An increase in tolerable misstatement will decrease sample size. An increase in the assessed level of control risk will increase sample size.

44. C An advantage of statistical sampling is that it allows auditors to select a sample size and evaluate the sample results based on the laws of probability, including measuring sampling risk. Determining sample size while measuring sampling risk is directly related to measuring the sufficiency of evidential matter. Neither statistical nor nonstatistical sampling can eliminate nonsampling error (human error). Auditors determine audit risk and materiality independent of the type of sampling method employed. Auditors may fail to detect errors and irregularities under either statistical or nonstatistical sampling.

45. D Employees who complete the bank confirmation form may not have access to information regarding loan balances, interest rates, or collateral. The standard bank confirmation form is widely used and contains a place for the customer's signature authorizing the release of the requested information. Normally the bank reconciliation is prepared by the client, and it is unlikely that the bank employee responding to the confirmation request has access to the bank reconciliation. The bank employee may have access to the cutoff bank statement, but that should have no effect on the usefulness of the bank confirmation.

46. B When auditing balance sheet accounts, auditors frequently gather evidence regarding related income statement accounts. When auditors gather evidence regarding accounts receivable, evidence related to credit sales is obtained. Additionally, when auditors gather evidence regarding cash receipts, evidence related to cash sales is obtained.

47. C When searching for liabilities unrecorded at the balance sheet date, auditors commonly examine documentation supporting cash disbursements made after year's end. The examination of receiving reports provides evidence as to when goods were received and the period in which the liability should have been recorded. The examination of vendors' invoices provides evidence of the amount of the liability.

48. C Tracing a sample of purchase orders and related to receiving reports to the purchases journal and the cash disbursements journal provides evidence concerning the completeness and propriety of the recording of purchase transactions.

49. B When plant assets are retired, the asset account will be credited and the accumulated depreciation account will be debited. The upward revision of the useful lives of plant assets would be treated as a change in estimate and would result in smaller credits to the accumulated depreciation account as less depreciation is taken in years following the upward revision. If the prior year's depreciation was understated, then accumulated depreciation would be credited when the error was corrected. Revision of overhead allocations are also changes in estimates and would not result in debits to accumulated depreciation.

50. A Analytical procedures revealing a large difference between actual labor costs and standard labor costs would alert the auditor to possible employee payroll fraud. All other choices consist of standard payroll procedures.

51. C Substantive tests consist of tests of details of balances and transactions and analytical procedures. The objective of substantive tests is to detect material misstatements in the financial statements. Auditors may comply with GAAS without performing tests of details of transactions. Test of controls would be used to attain assurance about the reliability of the accounting system and to evaluate whether management's policies and procedures operate effectively.

52. A One of the big advantages of generalized audit software packages is their applicability to many different computer systems. Instead of detailed knowledge of many different computer systems, the auditor needs only detailed knowledge of the generalized audit software and limited knowledge of the client's computer system.

53. D The work of internal auditors may affect the independent auditor's procedures performed in many areas of audit. Before relying on internal auditors the independent auditor must assess the competence and objectivity of the internal auditors. However, with proper supervision and review, the independent auditor may use the internal auditors to assist in the performance of substantive tests or tests of controls.

54. D The work of a specialist who has a relationship with a client may be acceptable if the auditor performs additional procedures to determine the reasonableness of the specialist's findings.

55. C In investigating litigation, claims, and assessments, the auditor should initially obtain information from discussions with management. The auditor then seeks corroboration of management's disclosures and assessments from the client's attorney. Evaluation of a going concern is the auditor's responsibility. Auditor's have no responsibility to examine legal documents in the possession of the client's attorney. Attorneys are not in a position to know if all litigation, claims, and assessments have been recorded or disclosed in the financial statements.

56. D Procedures performed at or near the completion of fieldwork to identify any subsequent events include inquiring and discussing with management whether any unusual adjustments were made during the period from the balance sheet date to the date of the inquiry.

57. B The management representation letter confirms the oral responses of management to the inquiries of auditors during the course of the audit. It is addressed to the auditors and usually is signed by the chief executive officer and the chief financial officer. A request for all available minutes of stockholders' and directors' meetings is a normal audit procedure, and one significant enough that auditors would seek management acknowledgment of compliance.

58. C Related parties are entities that have a relationship such that one of the transacting parties may be prevented from fully pursuing its own separate interests. SAS No. 45 specifically identifies the review of confirmations of loans receivable and payable for indications of guarantees as a procedure to identify related party transactions.

59. D If an auditor believes that substantial doubt exists about the ability of an entity to continue as a going concern, the auditor should consider management's plans for dealing with the adverse effect of the conditions and events that are causing the doubt. Management's plans may include disposing of assets, borrowing money or restructuring debt, reducing or delaying expenditures, or increasing ownership equity.

60. D The permanent file contains items of continuing audit significance. Because debt agreements are likely to affect the audited financial statements of several years, they would likely be included in the permanent workpaper file. All other choices are items that would likely be contained in current-year workpapers.

61. C An engagement to report on one basic financial statement is a limited reporting engagement, not a scope limitation. An auditor may accept this type of engagement as long as there is no limitation on the audit procedures the auditor seeks to perform.

62. C The auditor's standard report includes the statement, "[a]n audit also includes assessing the accounting principles used and the significant estimates made by management . . . ."

63. B Auditors may not issue a qualified opinion when they lack independence. Auditors must disclaim an opinion when they lack independence. Qualified opinions may be expressed in all the situations described by the other responses.

64. D If the auditor believes that the likelihood of a material loss from an uncertainty is only remote, an unqualified opinion without an explanatory paragraph is appropriate. Emphasis of a matter, lack of consistency, and the omission of supplementary information required by the FASB are all conditions requiring the addition of an explanatory paragraph to the audit report.

65. D An unjustified accounting change is a departure from GAAP, which requires an a qualified or adverse opinion. A material weakness in internal control does not affect the auditor's opinion on the financial statements, only the way in which that opinion is formulated. In other words, a material weakness in internal control may affect the nature, extent, and timing of substantive tests, but the auditor may still be able to express an unqualified opinion based on those tests.

66. B A departure from GAAP results when management does not provide reasonable justification for a change in accounting principle.

67. A The use of FIFO for a subsidiary and LIFO for the parent is not a departure from GAAP and would not preclude an unqualified opinion. Qualifications due to a lack of consistency are no longer appropriate. Additionally, this question does not deal with a lack of consistency, because there has not been a change in accounting principle from one period to the next.

68. C The fourth standard of reporting states "the report should contain a clear-cut indication of the character of the auditor's work, if any, and the degree of responsibility the auditor is taking."

69. D If an auditor is unable to obtain sufficient competent evidential matter, a scope limitation is present. A qualified opinion or disclaimer of opinion is appropriate when a scope limitation is present. An unqualified opinion would be appropriate in the circumstances presented in the other responses.

70. D When the audit report is modified to reflect an uncertainty, an unqualified opinion is appropriate in most circumstances. In cases of extreme uncertainty, auditing standards permit a disclaimer of opinion.

71. C When expressing a qualified opinion because of inadequate disclosure, the auditor should include the phrase *except for the omission of the information discussed in the preceding paragraph*. Subject to opinions are no longer appropriate. Audit reports should not include the phrase, with the foregoing explanation. An adverse opinion includes the phrase does not present fairly.

72. D While the auditor is required to add an additional paragraph to the end of the audit report when substantial doubt exists about the entity's ability to continue as a going concern, neither of the presented phrases are used in the paragraph.

73. A When doubt about the ability of an entity to continue as a going concern has been resolved in the year subsequent to issuing a going concern opinion, the auditor should not repeat the going concern explanatory paragraph in the updated audit opinion.

74. B In a first year audit of a new client, if the auditor is able to perform auditing procedures sufficient to establish the consistent application of GAAP, the audit report should make no reference to consistency. Because the auditor has been able to obtain satisfaction concerning consistency, a report may be issued on the income statement. The consistency standard does apply to new clients. The standard audit report does not make reference to consistency.

75. **A** If the prior year's financial statements are restated to conform with GAAP, the implication is that the prior year's financial statements received a report containing a qualified or adverse opinion due to a GAAP departure. When the financial statements are restated to conform to GAAP, an unqualified opinion is appropriate in the updated report.

76. **D** If the financial statements of a prior period were audited by a predecessor auditor whose report is not presented, the successor auditors must modify their report to indicate that the financial statements of the prior period were audited by another auditor, the date of the predecessor's report, the type of report issued, and, if the report was other than a standard report, the reasons therefore. The predecessor auditor should not be mentioned by name.

77. **A** The language used is appropriate to indicate a division of responsibility between the principal auditor and the other auditor. If the principal auditor had assumed responsibility for the other auditor, there would have been no division-of-responsibility language. Dividing responsibility does not result in a departure from an unqualified opinion.

78. **A** The audit report is normally addressed to whoever hired the auditor. In this instance, a company other than the one being audited engaged the auditor. Therefore, it is appropriate to address the report to the client who engaged the auditor, rather than the company being audited.

79. **C** The review report states that "[a] review consists principally of inquiries of company personnel and analytical procedures applied to financial data." No reference is made to providing limited assurance. A review does not examine information. While the review report does indicate that a review is substantially less in scope than an audit, how they differ is not extensively addressed.

80. **C** The standard language included in an accountant's compilation report on financial statements compiled without review or audit states that "[w]e . . . do not express an opinion or any other form of assurance on them." Compilations do not involve testing financial information, so there can be no scope limitation. An audit involves the assessment of the accounting principles used and significant estimates made by management. A review consists principally of inquiries and analytical procedures.

81. **A** Reports on agreed-upon procedures should restrict the distribution of the report to the board of directors and management of the entity and the parties to the contract containing the specified requirements.

82. **A** The accountant's report on an examination of projected financial statements should describe the limitations on the usefulness of the presentation. There is no practical difference between an examination and an audit. No statement is included in the accountant's report, which expands the accountant's responsibility for events after the date of the report. Examination reports express an opinion, not a disclaimer on whether the assumptions provide a reasonable basis for the projection.

83. A SAS No. 35 states, "[i]f a specified element, account, or item is, or is based upon, an entity's net income or stockholders' equity or the equivalent thereof, the auditor should have audited the complete financial statements to express an opinion on the specified element, account, or item."

84. B GAAS require auditors to communicate certain matters to the audit committee or comparable group having oversight of the financial reporting process. The communication may be written or oral, although the auditor should document any oral communications. Matters to be communicated include the following: the auditor's responsibility under GAAS, selection and changes in significant accounting policies, management judgments and accounting estimates, significant audit adjustments, auditor's responsibility for other information in documents containing audited financial statements, disagreements with management, consultations between management and other accountants concerning accounting and auditing matters, significant issues discussed with management related to the retention of the auditor, and difficulties encountered in performing the audit. None of these matters must also be communicated to the entity's management.

85. C Once an auditor has issued the report on the audited financial statements, the auditor has no further obligation to perform procedures with respect to those financial statements unless new information that may affect the report comes to the auditor's attention. Undisclosed lease transactions of the audited period might affect the report on that period. Uninsured natural disasters and the sale of a subsidiary occurring after the issuance of the audit report would not affect the report on the audit financial statements.

Resolution of properly disclosed contingencies would not require further inquiries.

86. A The predecessor auditor of financial statements filed in a registration statement should normally only obtain a letter of representation from the successor auditor. The representation letter should address whether the successor auditor's examination revealed any matters that would have a material effect on the financial statements reported on by the predecessor auditor.

87. A An auditor may report on information included in a client-prepared document containing audited financial statements. The report should be limited to data derived from the audited financial statements. There is no limitation on the distribution of the report. The information should be derived from audited financial statements prepared in conformity with GAAP. The report should state that the information is fairly stated in all material respects in relation to the basic financial statements taken as a whole. If the auditor is unwilling to accept responsibility for the other information, a disclaimer of opinion should be issued.

88. B It is the auditor's responsibility to assess whether management has identified laws and regulations that have a direct and material effect on the entity's financial statements. The auditor should issue a separate report on internal control. The audit should be designed to provide reasonable assurance of detecting material errors and irregularities. The auditor should not express an opinion on continued eligibility for assistance.

89. **B** Under the Single Audit Act, materiality is determined separately for each major program. Materiality is calculated in relation to the financial statements taken as a whole for GAAS audits of financial statements. Materiality would be determined prior to risk assessment, but should be considered in deciding which account balances to test.

90. **B** *The Yellow Book* requires that CPAs seeking to enter into a contract of perform an audit to provide their most recent external quality control review report to the contracting party. CPAs who conduct government audits should have an appropriate internal quality control system in place, and should have an external quality control review every three years. An external quality control review should involve selecting, on a test basis, audits performed since the last review. It is recommended that the external quality review report be made available to the public.

91. **D** Management acknowledges primary responsibility for the financial statements in the management representation letter. One of the key responsibilities acknowledged is the recording of all material transactions in the financial statements.

92. **I** Auditors seek corroboration of management assertions regarding contingencies from the client's attorney's through an audit inquiry letter to legal counsel.

93. **D** This statement is related to management's acknowledgment of their primary responsibility for the assertions contained in the financial statements and is contained in the primary source of management's written representations, the management representation letter.

94. **C** The auditor's engagement letter is the contractual basis for the audit. Appropriately included in the engagement letter is information about audit fees.

95. **C** The auditor's engagement letter is the contractual basis for the audit. Indicating the objective of the engagement is appropriate for inclusion in the engagement letter.

96. **D** Management acknowledges primary responsibility for the financial statements in the management representation letter. Denying the existence of irregularities that could have a material effect on the financial statements provides written corroboration of verbal representations made to the auditors during the audit.

97. **B** The successor auditor is required to make inquires of the predecessor auditor concerning, among other things, the integrity of management. The purpose of this inquiry is to assist the successor in making the decision whether or not to accept the client.

98. **A** Documenting resolution of differences of opinion in the partner's engagement review program is designed to demonstrate that the audit was conducted in accordance with GAAS.

99. **E** The standard financial institution confirmation request includes this statement with a place for an authorized representative of the institution to sign.

100. C The auditor's engagement letter is the contractual basis for the audit. As such, it details not only what can be expected of the auditor, but also what the auditor expects from the client.

101. D Management acknowledges primary responsibility for the financial statements in the management representation letter. Appropriately, management should indicate that there are no plans which would materially affect the presentation of those statements.

102. G Emphasis of a matter reporting allows the addition of a paragraph to the standard audit report without negating the unqualified nature of the report.

103. F Unreasonable delays and failure to provide needed information are appropriately reported to the audit committee.

104. J This statement is excerpted from a negative accounts receivable confirmation.

105. G This statement indicates doubt in the auditor's mind about the entity's ability to continue as a going concern. The statement is appropriately placed in an explanatory paragraph following the opinion paragraph.

106. A, A Establishing an understanding with an entity regarding the nature and limitations of services to be performed is required for both types of engagements.

107. A, B Inquiry is required only for review engagements.

108. B, B Communication with a predecessor accountant is not required for compilations or reviews.

109. A, A Obtaining knowledge of accounting principles and practices is required for both compilations and reviews.

110. B, B Obtaining an understanding of the entity's internal control is not required for compilations or reviews.

111. A, B Analytical procedures are required only for review engagements.

112. B, B An assessment of control risk is not required for compilations or reviews.

113. B, B A letter of inquiry to the entity's attorney is not required for compilations or reviews.

114. A, B Management representation letters are not required for compilations.

115. A, B Analytical procedures are required only for review engagements.

116. B, B Communicating inconsequential illegal acts by employees is not required for compilations or reviews.

117. A, B Inquires about subsequent events are required only for review engagements.

118. B, B Modifying the accountant's report for an adequately disclosed change in accounting principles is not required for compilations or reviews.

119. B, B Financial statements with an accompanying accountant's report may be submitted either on a computer disk or as hard copy.

120. B, B Procedures to evaluate the entity's ability to continue as a going concern are not required for compilations or reviews.

4. a. Irregularities may be classified as intentional distortions of financial statements, such as deliberate misrepresentations by management, sometimes referred to as management fraud; or misappropriations of assets, sometimes called defalcations.

b. The auditor should assess the risk that irregularities (management fraud) may cause the financial statements to be materially misstated. Based on that assessment, the auditor should design the audit to provide reasonable assurance of detecting management fraud that is material to the financial statements.

c. The characteristics of management fraud that are relevant because of their potential to influence the auditor's ability to detect such matters are: the materiality of the effect on the financial statements, the level of management involved, the extent and skillfulness of any concealment, the relationship to established control procedures, and the specific financial statements affected.

d. The factors that should heighten an auditor's concern about the existence of management fraud include: operating and financing decisions are dominated by a single person, management's attitude toward financial reporting is unduly aggressive, management turnover is high, management places undue emphasis on meeting earnings projections, management's reputation in the business community is poor, and known circumstances indicate a management predisposition to distort financial statements.

5. a. SAS No. 31 notes that assertions are representations of management that are embodied in financial statement components.

b. In obtaining evidential matter in support of financial statement assertions, SAS No. 31 requires the auditor to develop specific audit objectives in light of those assertions.

c. In developing the audit objectives of a particular engagement, SAS No. 31 states the auditor should consider the specific circumstances of the entity, including the nature of its economic activity and the accounting practices unique to the industry.

d. SAS No. 31 notes that there is not necessarily a one-to-one relationship between audit objectives and procedures. Some procedures may relate to more than one objective, while a combination of procedures may be needed to achieve a single objective.

e. In selecting particular substantive tests to achieve audit objectives, an auditor considers, among other things, the risk of material misstatement of the financial statements, including the assessed level of control risk, and the expected effectiveness and efficiency of such tests. Other considerations include the nature and materiality of the items being tested, the kinds and competence of the evidence, and the nature of the audit objective to be achieved.

TEST 2: SOLUTIONS

ACCOUNTING & REPORTING—
Taxation, Managerial, and Governmental and
Not-for-Profit Organizations

1 **C** Schedule M-1 of Form 1120 is a book income to taxable income reconciliation.
Taxable income would be determined as follows:

Book income (after tax)	$380,000
Tax-exempt municipal bond interest income	(50,000)
Federal income tax expense (nondeductible)	170,000
Interest expense to carry municipal bonds (nondeductible)	2,000
Taxable income	$502,000

2. **D** Accrual-basis taxpayers report prepaid rental income when received (unless the lease ends by the end of the year following the year of receipt—not the case here). The lease cancellation payment is also reported as income when received. $125,000 + $50,000 = $175,000.

3. **B** A regular or C corporation nets capital gains against capital loses first. Any net capital loss is then carried back 3 years and forward 5 years, applied against capital gains in those prior or future years. Individuals may deduct net capital losses against ordinary income to the extent of $3,000, but corporations may not.

4. **D** Taxable income, not dividends received, is multiplied by the applicable percentage when the corporation has a positive taxable income and its taxable income before the dividends received deduction (DRD) is less than the dividends received. That is the case in this problem ($90,000 is less than $100,000). The applicable percentage is 70% since the corporations are unrelated. 70% × $90,000 = $63,000.

5. **C** When a taxpayer places into service during the year more than 40% of his personal property in the last quarter of the year, it must use the mid-quarter convention for all personal property placed into service that year. Data Corp. placed all of its personal property (office equipment) into service in the last quarter of the year (November, and it's a calendar-year corporation). Therefore, it must use the mid-quarter convention instead of the half-year convention. The full-year convention does not exist in taxation. The mid-month convention applies to real property only.

6. **C** Capital assets include primarily investment property (e.g., stocks and bonds and other investments) and personal use property (personal residence, personal automobile . . .). A corporation's accounts receivable from sale of inventory as well as unimproved land to build homes for sale (effectively inventory) are ordinary income assets. Property used in a trade or business like equipment is Sec. 1231 property.

7. **D** Baker Corp. would first net its short-term capital gains (losses): $8,500 + ($4,000) = $4,500 net short-term capital gain. It would then do the same with its long-term capital gains (losses): $1,500 + ($3,500) = ($2,000) net long-term capital loss. The two net numbers are further netted: $4,500 + ($2,000) = $2,500 capital gain net income. Since all capital gains are taxed as ordinary income to corporations, taxable income = $36,000 + $2,500 = $38,500.

8. **B** A corporation is limited in its charitable contribution deduction to 10% of its taxable income before the charitable contribution deduction, the dividends-received deduction, and NOL and capital loss carrybacks 10% × ($820,000 + $40,000) = $86,000. Cable can deduct the $80,000 current year contribution plus $6,000 of the $10,000 prior-year carryover, for a total of $86,000.

9. **C** If a corporation's charitable contributions exceed the 10% of taxable income limitation, the excess is carried forward to a maximum of 5 succeeding years, but cannot be carried back.

10. **B** If a corporation accrues an income estimate in Year 1, and in Year 2 determined the amount to be different from the accrual, the corporation would simply include the difference in Year 2. No IRS notification or amended return is required.

11. **A** The uniform capitalization (unicap) rules are the tax rules for determining the costs that must be capitalized as part of inventory. The unicap rules apply to all manufacturers. They also apply to retailers and wholesalers if their average annual gross receipts for the past 3 years exceed $10 million (not $2 million).

12. **A** Undistributed personal holding company income (prior to the dividend-paid deduction) is taxable income adjusted for certain items. Those items include deductions for federal income taxes and for net long-term capital gains less related taxes.

13. **D** In a consolidated tax return, intercompany dividend revenue is $0 since it is eliminated completely in the consolidation process.

14. **C** To eliminate or reduce any accumulated earnings tax, a corporation can demonstrate that the "reasonable needs" of its business required its retention of all or part of its accumulated taxable income. It can also pay dividends during the year, within 2 1/2 months of year-end (throwback dividends), or consent dividends.

15. **A** Alternative minimum taxable income is taxable income adjusted for certain items. In this case, the adjustment for accelerated depreciation is added back to taxable income. Tax-exempt interest from specified private activity bonds (PABs) is taxable for AMT purposes, so it too is added back. $300,000 + $1,000 + $5,000 = $306,000.

16. **D** Civil fraud is a willful and deliberate attempt to evade taxes. It is more than simply negligent acts, errors, or omissions by the taxpayer. Maintaining false records and reporting fictitious transactions to minimize corporate tax liability would most likely subject the corporation to the civil fraud penalty.

17. **B** A corporation may reduce its regular income tax by taking a tax credit for foreign income taxes. The dividends-received deduction, state income taxes, and accelerated depreciation are all deductions and reduce taxable income, not the tax.

18. **D** The accumulated earnings tax can be imposed regardless of the number of stockholders in the corporation. It cannot be imposed on partnerships or personal holding companies. It is a tax that can be avoided by making distributions of earnings. Therefore, companies that make distributions in excess of accumulated earnings would not be subject to the tax.

19. **C**   Dividend income are distributions out of the current and accumulated earnings and profits (E&P) of the corporation. Total E&P, current and accumulated, is $280,000 ($160,000 + $120,000 = $280,000). Distributions equal $360,000. Therefore, dividend income equals $280,000; the remaining $80,000 is a liquidating distribution that is nontaxable to the extent of the shareholders' bases and capital gain beyond bases.

20. **C**   Nonliquidating corporate distributions are taxable to the shareholders as ordinary dividend income to the extent of the corporation's current and accumulated earnings and profits ($750,000 in this case). The rest is nontaxable to the extent that it reduces the shareholders' bases to zero; beyond that it is treated as a capital gain. In this case, the $250,000 remainder would reduce the shareholders' bases by $250,000 (assuming shareholders have at least that much bases).

21. **C**   When shareholders contribute property solely in exchange for stock in a corporation and the shareholders own at least 80% of the stock after the exchange, no gain or loss is recognized by the shareholders. In addition, their basis in the stock is the adjusted basis they had in the property contributed. In this case, Clark contributed $60,000 cash plus other property in which he had a $50,000 basis. Therefore, his basis in the stock is $110,000.

22. **A**   When A Corp. and B Corp. combine in a qualifying reorganization to form C Corp., the reorganization is tax free to both the shareholders and the corporation.

23. **A**   Bass Corp. must pay interest on the $400 tax payment made after the original due date, even if it filed an automatic extension request. The automatic extension is an extension on filing, not on paying. Bass Corp. is not subject to a tax delinquency penalty since it filed a timely extension and the amount paid by the original due date is at least 90% (here it's 95%) of the corporation's total tax.

24. **B**   The total of the quarterly payments that corporations make must equal the lesser of 100% of the current year tax liability or 100% of the preceding tax year liability, except that the latter is not available to corporations that had a net operating loss in the preceding tax year. The quarterly payments may always be computed using the annualized income method.

25. **B**   If the tax return has a nonfraudulent omission of income, the statute of limitations **cannot** be reopened after it has expired. If the corporation prevails in a determination allowing a deduction in an open tax year that was taken by the corporation erroneously in a closed tax year, the corporation's closed year can be reopened by the IRS in order to disallow the deduction in the previous year. This is equitable because otherwise the same deduction would be taken twice by the corporation.

26. **D**   A penalty for understated corporate tax liability can be imposed on a tax preparer for failing to make reasonable inquiries when taxpayer information appears incorrect. A tax preparer need not audit the records or examine business operations or copy all underlying documents.

27. B Barker's interest in the partnership is determined as follows:

Cash contributed	$20,000
Adjusted basis of building contributed	26,000
Liability assumed by partnership	(10,000)
Barker's share of liability (50% × 10,000)	5,000
	$41,000

28. D Black does **not** recognize gain if the fair market value of the contributed property is more than his adjusted basis in the property. Black also does **not** recognize gain as long as the mortgage encumbering the property does not cause a negative basis. If the mortgage is $100,000 and he has a 50% interest in the partnership, his basis in the partnership is the $250,000 adjusted basis less the $100,000 liability plus his 50% share of the $100,000, which equals $200,000. Since this is not a negative basis, no gain is recognized. If it had been a negative, gain would be recognized to the extent needed to bring the basis to zero.

29. A Evan should report the following income on her tax return:

25% of the $60,000 net business income **after** guaranteed payments ($80,000 – $20,000)	$15,000
25% of the $10,000 net long-term capital gain	2,500
Guaranteed payment received by Evan	20,000
	$37,500

30. A A partner increases his basis in the partnership by his share of the increase in partnership liabilities. Smith would increase his basis by 40% of the $40,000 mortgage note, or $16,000.

31. B Hart's basis in the land would be determined as follows:

Hart's adjusted basis in partnership	$9,000
Cash distributed to Hart	(5,000)
Remaining basis	4,000
Hart's basis in the land	(4,000)
Hart's adjusted basis in partnership	0

Even though the land's basis is $7,000, it will flow through to Hart at only $4,000 since that is his remaining basis in the partnership.

32. D Nonliquidating distributions of assets reduce the partner's basis by the assets' adjusted basis. No gain or loss is recognized by either the partner or the partnership. In this case, Stone recognizes no gain or loss. His basis in the partnership is reduced to $5,000 ($70,000 – $65,000 = $5,000). His basis in the capital assets is $65,000.

33. B A partnership terminates on the day that 50% or more of the total interests in capital and profits are sold within a 12-month period. In this case, 30% is sold on February 4, 19X4 and 25% is sold on December 20, 19X4. Therefore, 55% is sold within a 12-month period. The partnership is technically terminated on December 20, 19X4.

34. C In a technical termination, the old partnership is deemed to make a distribution of all assets to its partners. The partners are deemed to immediately recontribute the assets back to a new partnership.

35. C The amount of the distribution taxable to the beneficiary is the lesser of the amount required to be distributed ($15,000) or the fiduciary's distributable net income ($40,000 – $34,000 = $6,000). The estate's taxable income after the distribution's deduction would be $0 ($6,000 – $6,000). The $9,000 excess distributed over the $6,000 taxable amount is considered a distribution out of principal.

36. C When a married couple elects gift splitting, half the gift is deemed to come from one spouse, the other half is deemed to come from the other spouse. Gift splitting is elected to maximize the benefit of the $10,000 gift exclusion for each spouse. Each spouse would have taxable gifts of $15,000 less the $10,000 exclusion, or $5,000. Their total taxable gifts equal $10,000 ($5,000 + $5,000).

37. A The organizational test to qualify a public service charitable entity as tax exempt requires the articles of organization to limit the purpose of the entity to a charitable purpose. However, it does not have to state that an information return should be filed annually with the IRS. Although most tax-exempt organizations must file an annual return, some (e.g., churches) are exempt from the requirements.

38. D Selling articles made by disabled persons as part of their rehabilitation, when the organization is involved exclusively in their rehabilitation, is **not** unrelated business income (UBI). The income in such case would be from the sale of products, the production of which contributes importantly to the accomplishment of the organization's purpose, namely, rehabilitation of the disabled.

Operating a grocery store almost fully staffed by emotionally disabled persons as part of a therapeutic program would also not be UBI as the conduct of the business is substantially related to the purposes for which exemption was granted, namely, the therapy of emotionally disabled persons.

39. C The estimated cost for mailing 12,000 parcels consists of a fixed cost and a variable cost. The fixed cost is $15,000 since that is the cost to mail 0 parcels. The variable cost per unit is calculated as follows:

$$\frac{\text{high cost} - \text{low cost}}{\text{high units} - \text{low units}} = \frac{\$75,000 - \$15,000}{20,000 - 0}$$
$$= \$60,000 \div \$20,000$$
$$= \$3$$

The total variable cost to mail 12,000 parcels is $3 × 12,000 = $36,000. The total cost is $15,000 + $36,000 = **$51,000.**

40. C The budgeted purchases of Loire is calculated as follows:

Budgeted sales of Nous	$53,000
Desired increase in Nous inventory	6,000
Budged production of Nous	59,000
× 4 kilos of Loire per Nous	× 4
Kilos of Loire needed for production	236,000
Desired reduction in Loire inventory	(50,000)
Budgeted purchases of Loire	$186,000

41. C The basis difference between a master budget and a flexible budget is that a master budget is based on one specific level of production and a flexible budget can be prepared for any production level within a relevant range. A master or comprehensive budget is an overall budget consisting of many smaller budgets. It is based on one specific level of production. A flexible budget is a series of several budgets prepared for many levels of sales or production.

42 D The lease's after-tax present value is calculated as follows:

Operating net cash inflow per year	$7,500
Tax expense (7,500 × 40%)	(3,000)
After-tax annual operating net cash inflow	4,500
Amortization expense tax shield/ savings (5,000 × 40%)	2,000
After-tax annual net cash inflow	6,500
Times PV of ordinary annuity at 10% for 2 years	× 1.74
PV after-tax annual net cash inflow	$11,300

43. B Cott's fixed cost would be calculated as follows:

Sales

Break-Even Sales	=	Margin of Safety
Break-Even Sales	=	Sales – Margin of Safety
	=	$200,000 – $80,000
	=	$120,000
Break-Even Sales	=	Fixed Cost
		Contribution Margin %
Fixed Cost	=	Break-Even Sales × CM%
	=	120,000 × 20%
	=	**$24,000**

44. B Break-even analysis assumes, among other things, that over the relevant range unit variable costs are unchanged or constant. Unit revenues and total fixed costs are also linear. Total costs do change with the level of production because of the variable costs.

45. A Payments to employees who develop computer programs to meet customers' special requirements are direct costs that are traceable to the specific job or customer. They are essentially part of direct labor. They are also value-adding costs in that they are necessary costs which add value or worth to the product.

46. C Using the weighted-average method, Forming's conversion cost transferred to the second production department would be calculated as follows:

Equivalent Units of Production (EUP)

Units completed and transferred (100%)	7,000
* Spoiled units (100%)	500
Ending WIP (80% × 2,500)	2,000
Total EUP (weighted average)	9,500

* Spoilage is identified when the units have completed the Forming process; therefore, they are 100% complete in this department.

Conversion Costs Per EUP

Total conversion costs	$85,500
Divided by EUP	÷ 9,500
Equals Cost Per EUP	$9

Conversion Cost Transferred

Units completed and transferred	7,000
*Spoiled units	500
7,500	
Times cost per EUP	× $9
	$67,500

*Cost of spoiled units are assigned to units completed and transferred to the second department in the period spoilage is identified.

47. B Material price variance (MPV) is calculated as follows:

$$
\begin{aligned}
\text{MPV} &= (\text{Actual Price} - \text{Standard Price}) \times \\
&\quad (\text{Actual Quantity Purchased}) \\
&= (\$2.40^* - \$2.50)\,(4{,}200) \\
&= \$420 \text{ favorable}
\end{aligned}
$$

*$\$10{,}080 \div 4{,}200 = \$2.40$

The variance is favorable because the actual cost is less than the standard cost.

48. C For purposes of allocating joint costs to joint products, the sales price at point of sale, reduced by the cost to complete after split-off, is assumed to be equal to the net sales value at split-off (also known as the relative sales value at split-off). Joint costs and total costs are not necessarily equal to net sales price at split-off. Normal profit margin does not necessarily equal the cost to complete after split-off.

49. C The step method allocates costs sequentially, with the costs of the service department rendering the greatest service/cost allocated first, then the second greatest is similarly allocated, and so on. Once a service department's costs are allocated, it never receives a subsequent allocation from another service department.

50. D Residual income equals operating income less investment capital multiplied by an inputted interest rate.

Capital turnover = Sales ÷ Investment capital
Investment capital = Sales ÷ Capital turnover
= $400,000 ÷ 4
= $100,000
Residual income = $40,000 − ($100,000) (10%)
= $40,000 − $10,000
= $30,000

51. A A just-in-time (JIT) operation will decrease inspection costs due to the total quality control that occurs before and during production in a JIT operation. A backflush costing system is a simplified approach to product costing that does not distinguish between raw materials and work-in-process inventories since in a JIT environment they are kept very low. However, this system provides much less detailed costs tracked to jobs than a job-order costing system provides.

52 A The economic order quantity (EOQ) formula assumes that demand is known and both order costs and unit carrying costs are constant. Purchase costs are not relevant to the EOQ formula.

53. B With an unprotected crop and frost, Cal loses $20,000 in market value ($60,000 − $40,000). With a protected crop and frost, Cal gains $30,000 ($90,000 − $60,000), but the cost for protection is $10,000. At what probability is Cal indifferent to spending the $10,000? Let x = probability %.

$$
\begin{aligned}
(20{,}000)x &= 30{,}000x - 10{,}000 \\
10{,}000 &= 50{,}000x \\
x &= 20\% \\
&= \underline{.200}
\end{aligned}
$$

54. C The estimated savings would be calculated as follows:

Cost savings:	
1 outage × 2 months × $400	$ 800
2 outages × 4 months × $400	3,200
3 outages × 3 months × $400	3,600
Total cost savings	$7,600
Cost of leasing: $500 × 12	(6,000)
Estimated savings, net	$1,600

55. A The target price to obtain a 15% profit margin on sales is calculated as follows: x = target sales price.

Sales	=	Traceable Costs + Profit
$500x$	=	$990,000 + 15\% (500x)$
x	=	$990,000 \div 425$
x	=	**$2,329** (rounded to nearest dollar)

56. C Absorption costing inventories fixed overhead whereas variable costing expenses it currently. The current ratio (current assets over current liabilities) would be greater under absorption costing because of the higher inventory value. Return on stockholders' equity (net income over stockholders' equity) would be higher under absorption costing. Stockholders' equity would be higher under absorption costing since stockholders' equity equals assets minus liabilities and inventory, an asset, is greater under absorption costing. Net income would be the same under both methods since there was no change in inventory.

57. C The general funds and expendable trust funds, both of which use modified accrual accounting, do not have income determination as a measurement focus. Their measurement focus is on the determination of financial position and flow of financial resources. The proprietary funds (enterprise fund and internal services fund), which use full accrual accounting, have income determination as a measurement focus.

58. B Fixed assets donated to a governmental unit should be recorded at estimated fair value when received.

59. A Interperiod equity is the extent to which revenues generated during a given period are sufficient to cover expenditures made during the period. The issue of interperiod equity is addressed by adopting a balanced budget. The equality of residual equity transfers in and out has no relationship to the interperiod equity concept.

60. C Fund accounting is used for resources that must be segregated for the purpose of carrying on specific activities or attaining certain objectives in accordance with special regulations, restrictions, or limitations. This is part of the GASB definition of funds.

61. A In this combined statement of revenues, expenditures, and changes in fund balances—budget and actual—the amounts in the actual column are to be reported on the same basis as required for budget preparation, even if that basis differs from the GAAP basis. Therefore, the cash basis should be used for this statement since the city uses a cash-basis budget, even though the modified accrual basis is the GAAP basis for governmental funds.

62. D The basic criterion used to determine the reporting entity is the concept of financial accountability. A primary government is financially accountable for the organizations that make up its legal entity. It is also financially accountable for legally separate organizations if the primary government appoints a voting majority of the organization's governing body and it is able to impose its will on the organization.

63. B The statement of cash flows (SCF) is required of the proprietary fund types only (enterprise fund, internal service fund, and non-expendable trust fund). The cash inflow from issuing bonds to finance city hall construction would be recorded in a capital projects fund, which does **not** issue a SCF. The cash outflow from a city utility representing payments in lieu of property taxes would be recorded in an enterprise fund, which does issue a SCF.

64. **A** An agency fund should be used where a government has no obligation to assume debt service on special assessment debt in the event of the property owners' default, but does perform the functions of billing property owners for the assessments, collecting payments, and from the collections paying principal and interest on the debt. The government is, in effect, acting as a collection and paying agent for the property owners and the debt holders.

65. **C** The revenue control account is increased when property taxes are recorded. Property taxes receivable is debited and revenue is credited. Estimated revenues, not revenues, would be increased when the budget is recorded.

66. **D** Both of these bonds will be recorded in an enterprise fund that records its own long-term debt and does **not** use the general long-term debt account group.

67. **A** Capital leases are recorded as assets in the GFAAG and also as capital lease obligations payable in the GLTDAG. Therefore, they increase both the asset amount and the liability amount. If the possibility of lease cancellation is considered remote, the lease should be disclosed in the financial statements and accounted for in the manner specified for capital leases.

68. **C** According to GASB Statement 18, equipment included in the estimated total current cost of closure and postclosure care should be reported as a reduction of the reported liability when they are acquired, and not as capital assets. Therefore, there is no effect to the asset amount in the GFAAG and a decrease in the liability amount in the GLTDAG.

69. **B** Proprietary funds such as the enterprise fund report retained earnings. Capital projects funds, special revenue funds, and expendable trust funds report fund balances.

70. **C** The salary rate used to calculate the compensated absence liability should normally be the rate in effect at the balance sheet date.

71. **D** When the township issues a purchase order for supplies, it should debit Encumbrances and credit Reserve for encumbrances.

72. **C** Estimated revenues is debited when the budget is recorded. Appropriations is credited, and the difference is debited/credited to Budgetary fund balance. When actual revenues are recorded, revenues control is credited. When the budget is closed at year-end, estimated revenues is credited.

73. **B** Billings to other governmental units is recorded by the internal service fund as operating revenues. The journal entry would be a debit to Due from other funds and a credit to Billings to departments.

74. **A** A not-for-profit organization's statement of activities should report the net change in net assets that are unrestricted, permanently restricted, and temporarily restricted.

75. **B** Both room-and-board fees from patients and recovery-room fees are considered ongoing or central transactions for a not-for-profit hospital. They are part of patient service revenue.

76. **$6,140** Net business or ordinary income includes the gross receipts less the supplies. $7,260 − $1,120 = $6,140. Interest income and charitable contributions are separately stated items on Schedule K.

77. $2,700 (rounded to the nearest hundred)
Pike's share of the net business income is calculated as follows:

S Corporation's net business income	$14,520
× Percentage stock ownership (40/200)	× 20%
	2,904
× Number of days	
Pike owned stock*/363	× 333/363
	$2,664

*363 – 30 = 333; stock was sold to Pike January 31, and the calendar year had 363 days.

78. $3,150. Pike's basis in the stock is reduced by his share of S corporation loss and increased by his share of interest income, even if nontaxable as in this case. His share is reported to him on a Schedule K-1.

Pike's stock basis January 31	$4,000
His share of ordinary business loss	(1,000)
His share of municipal bond interest	150
	$3,150

79. $9,000 Taylor's basis in Lan shares for determining gain or loss from the sale to Pike is calculated as follows:

Taylor's stock basis on January 3	$10,000
Taylor's share of ordinary income to the date of sale	2,000
Cash distribution to Taylor	(3,000)
	$9,000

80. B S corporations may only have one class of stock outstanding. This is one of the eligibility requirements to be an S corporation.

81. B This would be true only if the S corporation had accumulated earnings and profits (from a previous existence as a C corporation) at the end of each of the 3 consecutive years. Since Lan has been an S corporation since inception, it could not possibly have any accumulated earnings and profits.

82. $3,000 The $10,000 ($15,000 – $25,000) long-term capital loss from Revco is netted against the $4,000 ($8,000 – $4,000) short-term capital gain from Abbco, to yield a net long-term capital loss of $6,000. An individual can deduct up to $3,000 of capital losses against ordinary income. The remaining $3,000 excess net long-term capital loss would be carried over to next year.

83. 0 When a gift is received whose fair market value at the date of gift is less than the donor's adjusted basis ($50,000 < $60,000) and the property is subsequently sold at a price in between fair market value and donor's basis (e.g., $56,000), no gain or loss is recognized by the seller.

84. 0 No income is reported on a refundable security deposit since there is an obligation to return it to the tenant in the future.

85. $55,000 Wages of $53,000 are included in income. In addition, the value of employer-paid group-term life insurance coverage in excess of $50,000 is included in income. $53,000 + $2,000 = $55,000.

86. $1,250 Under the tax benefit rule, the Moores would include in income the $1,250 state tax refund. They deducted the amount last year and received a $1,250 benefit from the deduction as their itemized deductions were $1,450 in excess of the standard deduction.

87. $1,300 Unemployment compensation benefits ($1,300) are fully taxable. The $100 unemployment insurance fund contribution made by the employer on her behalf is not taxable to her, but it is deductible by the employer.

88. $2,500 Net rental income equals gross receipts less rental deductions. All of the expenses listed are deductible, for a total of $5,900.

Net rental income = $8,400 − $5,900 = $2,500.

89. $900 If the taxpayer has the option of receiving a cash dividend or a stock dividend, the dividend is fully taxable at fair market value even if the taxpayer opts for the stock. The fair market value of the stock is $900, the amount includable as dividend income.

90. $0 Death benefits are excludable up to $5,000, allocated pro rata to all beneficiaries. Here the death benefit is $3,500, and we assume Joan is the only beneficiary.

91. $5,000 Since Laura is **not** their dependent, the interest income does not qualify for exclusion as education savings bonds used for college education expenses. Therefore, the $5,000 interest is taxable when the bonds are redeemed since the taxpayer elected not to report the yearly increases in income.

92. $8,000 The $8,000 alimony paid is deductible to arrive at adjusted gross income (AGI). On the other hand, child support payments are not deductible.

93. A Under the wash-sale rules, if the taxpayer sells stock at a loss and then buys it back within 30 days before or after the sale, the loss is disallowed and added to the basis of the shares bought.

94. B Personal property tax based on value ("ad valorem") are fully deductible on Schedule A.

95. D Used clothes donated to the church are deductible as charitable contributions on Schedule A, subject to an overall ceiling of 50% of AGI.

96. A Income protection insurance premiums are not deductible.

97. F Unreimbursed employee business expenses are deductible on Schedule A as miscellaneous itemized deductions subject to a 2% of AGI floor.

98. B Home-equity loan interest is deductible on Schedule A up to a $100,000 loan. The interest on a $10,000 loan would be fully deductible. There is no restriction on the use of the loan proceeds.

99. C Unreimbursed medical expenses and prescription drugs are deductible on Schedule A subject to a 7.5% of AGI floor.

100. A Funeral expenses are not deductible on Form 1040.

101. E Unreimbursed theft and casualty losses are deductible on Schedule A, after subtracting $100 and 10% of AGI.

102. A Loss on the sale of a personal use asset is not deductible.

103. B Home mortgage interest is fully deductible on Schedule A up to $1,000,000 of acquisition debt.

104. A Only out-of-pocket expenses to do charity work are deductible. The value of the taxpayer's services performed for a charity is not deductible.

105. B For married couples filing jointly, the phaseout of personal and dependency exemptions begins at an AGI of $167,700 in 19X4. There would be no phaseout at an AGI of $75,000.

106. A For alternative minimum tax (AMT) purposes, unreimbursed medical expenses are deductible to the extent they exceed 10% (not 7.5%) of AGI.

107. A Personal and dependency exemptions are **not** permitted for AMT purposes.

108. A A taxpayer avoids the underpayment penalty if his tax withholdings for the current year equal at least 100% of last year's tax liability or 90% of this year's tax liability. It is 110% of last year's tax liability (not 100%) if the taxpayer's AGI last year was over $150,000 (not the case here).

109. A Amounts withdrawn from an IRA before the age of 59 1/2 are subject to a 10% withdrawal penalty unless they are withdrawn after the taxpayer dies or becomes disabled. A withdrawal used for medical expenses is not one of the exceptions.

110. B The Moores are not allowed an earned income credit because their AGI of $75,000 is too high (needs to be under $9,000 with no dependent children in 19X4).

111. E Guard-designated funds are still classified as unrestricted. Only outside-donor restrictions make an asset temporarily restricted or permanently restricted. Since the $1,000,000 is currently unrestricted, the board designation is not a required reportable event.

112. A Income from unrestricted board-designated funds are increases in unrestricted revenues.

113. C An outside-donor gift for building expansion is an increase in **temporarily** restricted net assets since the funds will be released from restriction when the building is expanded.

114. A When the temporarily restricted funds are used for the intended purpose (purchase a building), there is a decrease in temporarily restricted net assets and an increase in **unrestricted** net assets.

115. A When services are contributed to a not-for-profit organization, the fair value of the services is recognized as an increase in unrestricted expense and unrestricted revenue if the services require specialized skills and would normally be purchased if not donated.

116. D These investments result in an increase in **permanently** restricted net assets because the outside-donor restriction states that the investment cannot be spent, only the income can be used for a specified purpose.

117. $104,500 The 19X4 general fund (GF) operating transfers out consists only of the transfer from the GF to a debt service fund to be used to repay the bond principal and interest.

118. $17,000 The 19X4 GF liabilities from entitlements for compensated absences consists of the $17,000 available at December 31, 19X4 in the GF to be used for compensated absences entitlements. This amount would be reported as an expenditure and a liability in the GF. The remaining $69,000 would be reported in the general long-term debt account group.

119. $125,000 The 19X4 reserved amount of the GF balance consists of $83,000 Reserve for Encumbrances (the outstanding GF encumbrances) and $42,000 Reserve for Supplies (the 12/31/X4 supplies inventory balance) under the purchases method.

120. $236,000 The 19X4 capital projects fund balance equals the $600,000 other financing source from the bond issuance less the $364,000 of construction expenditures, or $236,000.

121. $6,000 The 19X4 fund balance on the special revenue fund for tourist promotion equals the $109,000 revenues from taxes less the expenditures for promotions, $81,000, and for the motor vehicle, $22,000, for a net of $6,000.

122. $104,500 The amount of 19X4 debt service fund expenditures equals the expenditures for principal payment, $100,000, plus the expenditures for interest payment, $4,500, for a total of $104,500.

123. $386,000 The amount that should be included in the general fixed assets account group (GFAAG) for the cost of assets acquired in 19X4 is $22,000 for the motor vehicle plus the construction in progress of $364,000 for a total of $386,000. The citizens center was not acquired in 19X4, but earlier, when the 15-year-old bonds were issued.

124. $100,000 The amount stemming from 19X4 transactions that **decreased** the liabilities reported in the general long-term debt account group (GLTDAG) would be the maturity of the $100,000 15-year term bonds.

125. $181,000 Under the purchases method, the 19X4 supplies expenditures equals the amount purchased (e.g., credited to vouchers payable) of $181,000.

126. $190,000 The total amount of 19X4 supplies encumbrances equals the amount of purchase orders during 19X4, $190,000.

1. D One of the objectives of financial reporting identified by SFAC No. 1 is to provide information that is useful to users in their decision making. Response A is incorrect because GAAP is derived from the objectives. Response B is incorrect because financial statements report on the business entity, not the management. Management's stewardship may only be indirectly inferred from the financial statements. Response C is incorrect because conservatism is a fundamental concept of SFAC No.1.

2. B SFAC No. 1 states that the cost of providing information should be considered in relation to benefits provided. Responses A, B, and C are incorrect because consistency, reliability, and representational faithfulness are qualities of accounting information.

3. A According to SFAS No. 5, gain contingencies should not be recognized until realized in accordance with conservatism. Relevance is concerned with the usefulness of information for decision making. Consistency relates to the application of the same accounting principles from period to period. Reliability is a qualitative characteristic concerned with representational faithfulness, verifiability, and neutrality.

4. A SFAS No. 7 states that development stage enterprises should follow the same GAAP that apply to established enterprises.

5. D The present value of future cash flows is used to measure long-term receivables and payables. All other responses are appropriate to measure inventory.

6. A Because interim financial statements are prepared for periods of less than one year, they may be considered as providing timely information. However, reliability may be reduced by the use of estimates in the preparation of interim financial statements.

7. D SFAS No. 57 specifically limits nondisclosure of material related party transactions to ". . . compensation arrangements, expense allowances, and other similar items in the ordinary course of business . . . ." All other material related party transactions require disclosure.

8. D SFAS No. 14 defines a reportable segment as one that has 10% of all revenue, including sales to unaffiliated customers and intersegment sales. Terra Co.'s combined revenues total $150,000. Each segment has greater than 10% of the combined total revenue and each would be a reportable segment.

9. C In a period of rising prices, the use of LIFO will result in a lower value for ending inventory than under FIFO because older and lower costs are assigned to the ending inventory. Cost of goods sold will be higher under LIFO than FIFO in periods of rising prices because newer and higher costs will be assigned to the cost of goods sold.

10. **C** The gross profit rate for 19X3 is equal to 50% (19X3 sales of $80,000 less 19X3 cost of goods sold of $40,000/19X3 sales of $80,000). The gross profit rate for 19X4 is equal to 33.3% (19X4 sales of $90,000 less 19X4 cost of goods sold of $60,000/19X4 sales of $90,000). The deferred gross profit associated with 19X3 sales is $15,000 (19X3 gross profit rate of 50% × 19X4 installment receivables on 19X3 sales of $30,000). The deferred gross profit associated with 19X4 sales is $23,000 (19X4 gross profit rate of 33.3% × 19X4 installment receivables on 19X4 sales of $69,000). The deferred gross profit at December 31, 19X4 is $38,000 ($15,000 + $23,000).

11. **B** In a sale-leaseback transaction when the seller-lessee retains the right to substantially all of the remaining use of the property, SFAS No. 28 requires the gain that results from a sale to be deferred and amortized in proportion to the amortization of the leased asset.

12. **C** Interest is recognized based on the passage of time from the creation of a liability. Because the first payment is made at the inception of the lease, the full payment would be applied to the lease liability and no interest would be recognized.

13. **D** The payroll tax expense is comprised of the employer's share of FICA ($10,000 × 7% = 700). The payroll tax liability is comprised of the federal income tax withheld + the employees' share of FICA + the employer's share of FICA ($1,200 + $700 + $700 = $2,600).

14. **C** SFAS No. 87 requires employers to report a minimum pension liability that is at least equal to the unfunded accumulated benefit obligation ($25,000 in this problem). If the accrued pension costs are less than the minimum liability, an additional liability must be recognized for the difference. The accrued pension cost is $8,000 since Hall made no contributions in 19X4. Therefore, the additional pension liability is equal to $17,000 ($25,000 – $8,000).

15. **A** The excess of additional pension liability over unrecognized prior service cost is $5,000 and is determined as the difference between the additional pension liability of $17,000 (calculated in the previous problem) and the unrecognized prior service cost of $12,000.

16. **D** Accrued interest at December 31, 19X4 would be $2,320, calculated as (12% × $10,000 × 10/12) + (12% × $11,000 × 12/12). Interest is compounded annually in this problem so interest for 19X4 would be based on the total liability of $11,000, which includes $10,000 principal and $1,000 accrued interest from 19X3.

17. **A** SFAS No. 5 specifically requires that debt guarantees be disclosed even if the possibility of loss is considered remote.

18. **A** The statement in this problem that "[l]aws in Nest's state of incorporation protect treasury stock from dilution" means that stock splits will apply to treasury stock. Therefore, the shares issued are 220,000 [(100,000 + 10,000) × 2]. The shares outstanding are 212,000 [(95,000 + 1,000 + 10,000) × 2)].

19. **A** Under the cost method of accounting for treasury stock, when treasury stock is reissued at a price higher than its cost, an additional paid-in capital account is credited. The only item affecting retained earnings in 19X4 would be net income of $60,000. Retained earnings would be reported as $360,000.

20. B Under the par value method of accounting for treasury stock, when treasury stock is acquired, additional paid-in capital is debited for the excess of the issue price over the par value. The transaction on July 14 would result in a debit to additional paid-in capital of $25,000 [($15-original issue price) – ($10-par) × 5,000 shares)]. When treasury stock is reissued, additional paid-in capital is credited for the excess of the reissue price over par. The transaction on December 27 would result in a credit to additional paid-in capital of $50,000 [$20 (reissue price) – $10(par) × 5,000 shares]. Therefore, additional paid-in capital in excess of par is $125,000 ($100,000 – $25,000 + $50,000).

21. C No entry is made when rights are issued without consideration. Common stock and additional paid-in capital would be affected if the rights are exercised.

22 C Stockholder's equity should be reduced by the $12,000 cost of the rights (120,000 × $0.10). No value was assigned to the rights at issuance, because no consideration was received.

23. A

	Young	Zinc	Profit
Capital balances	$160,000	$100,000	$ 4,000
Interest	16,000	10,000	(26,000)
			(22,000)
Loss allocation	(11,000)	(11,000)	22,000
	$165,000	$99,000	$ 0

The partners receive 10% interest on their average capital balances and divide residual profit and loss equally. The interest allowance creates a residual loss, which must be divided equally.

24. C Capital reported on March 31, 19X5 under the cash-basis method of accounting is $6000 ($2000 beginning balance + $5,000 cash receipts – $1,000 cash disbursements). No expenses are recognized under the cash-basis method because they were not paid until April. Cash receipts for services were received and recognized in March.

25. C Additional paid-in capital is credited for $250,000 upon the reduction of the par value of the common stock to $5 ($25 × 10,000 shares), bringing the balance to $400,000. Retained earnings would be credited for $210,000 to bring the balance to zero and additional paid-in capital would be debited for $210,000. The result of the two transactions is to arrive at a balance in additional paid-in capital of $190,000.

26. B Because Grant, Inc. owns 30% of the voting stock of South Co. and has the ability to exercise significant influence over South's operating and financial policies, Grant should employ the equity method in accounting for its investment in South Co. Under the equity method, income from the investee is recognized based on the percentage of ownership of the investor. Thus, Grant would recognize $24,000 in investee income for 19X3 ($80,000 × 30%).

27. B Under the equity method of accounting, the investment account is debited for the cost of the investment. Subsequently, the recognition of income results in a debit to the investment account and the receipt of dividends results in a credit to the investment account. Therefore, the carrying amount of the investment in South Co. should be $209,000 ($200,000 + $24,000 – $15,000). The $24,000 was calculated in the previous problem and the $15,000 is the ownership percentage times the dividends received (30% × $50,000).

28. B The carrying value of the investment is $239,000 based on adding 30% of South's $100,000 income at June 30, 19X5 to the carrying value of the investment at December 31, 19X3 ($209,000, calculated in the previous problem). The gain is equal to the proceeds less the carrying value, or $150,000 – $119,500 (only 1/2 of the investment was sold) = $30,500.

29. A The total of the annual lease payments less the fair value of the asset will equal the interest earned over the life of a direct-financing lease ($375,000 – $323,400 = $51,600). The annual lease payment is $75,000, which is calculated by dividing the fair value of the leased asset by the annuity factor (323,400/4.312). The total of the lease payments is obtained by multiplying the annual lease payment by the lease term ($75,000 × 5 = 375,000).

30. C Royalty revenue reported for 19X4 equals $149,000 [20%($400,000 – $50,000 + $325,000 + $70,000)]. Note that the $50,000 for December 19X3 is included in the $400,000 for the period December 1, 19X3 – May 31, 19X4. In order to avoid double-counting the $50,000 must be subtracted from the $400,000.

31. D Revenue is not recognized prior to the sale of merchandise under either the installment sales or cost recovery methods. A portion of the deferred gross profit is recognized as cash is received under the installment sales method and deferred gross profit is recognized after all costs have been recovered under the cost recovery method.

32. A Changes in the exchange rates between the functional currency and the currency in that the transaction is denominated result in gains or losses which are reported as a component of income form continuing operations.

33. B The gain of $24,000 from the sale of the patent is the proceeds less the carrying value ($75,000 – $51,000). The $51,000 carrying value is the cost of $45,000 less accumulated amortization [3($45,000/15 years)] plus the $15,000 in legal costs for the successful defense.

34. D A nonrefundable lease bonus should be recognized as revenue over the lease term. The receipt of the lease bonus creates deferred revenue.

35. B The revenue recognized is the proceeds less the cash surrender value. As the cash surrender value of the policy increased in previous years, revenue was recognized in the amount of the increase in the previous years.

36. C The income tax expense for the year consists of the current portion of income taxes payable and the deferred portion, which is the sum of the net changes in the deferred tax asset and deferred tax liability accounts. In this problem, the current portion equals $13,000. The deferred portion is calculated by netting the change in the deferred asset account $5,000 ($20,000 less $15,000) and the increase in the valuation account of $2,000, and subtracting the net amount from the current portion [$10,000 = $13,000 – ($5,000 – $2,000)].

37. B The current portion of income tax expense is income tax payable, which is calculated as the current rate × taxable income. Thus, income tax expense – current will equal $56,000 ($140,000 × 40%).

38. C In order to calculate the deferred tax liability, all noncurrent deferred tax assets and liabilities should be netted. Therefore, the deferred tax asset of $10,000 (associated with the long-term loss accrual) is netted with the deferred tax liability of $25,000 (arising from excess depreciation). Multiplying the net by the current tax rate of 40% yields the deferred tax liability of $6,000 (40% × $15,000).

39. B The gain or loss from discontinued operations is the net of the income or loss from the measurement date to the disposal date and the gain or loss on disposal. When the measurement date and disposal date occur in different periods, an estimated net gain or loss must be calculated. If an expected loss is indicated, conservatism requires recognition in the current period. If an expected gain is indicated, the gain should not be recognized until realized. Hart's net gain from the disposal of the discontinued operation is $250,000 [($900,000 – $50,000) – $600,000]. Because the gain is not realized until 19X4, no gain or loss should be recognized in 19X3.

40. D Results of operations of discontinued segments prior to the measurement date are reported as a gain or loss from operations of a discontinued segment. Deer Corp. has a $300,000 loss ($500,000 revenue – $800,000 of expenses) on operations that should be reported as a loss from operations of a discontinued segment.

41. D Gains or losses from early extinguishment of debt are required to be reported as extraordinary items by SFAS No. 4. Losses on sales of investments are not extraordinary items. For accounting purposes, no netting of the transactions should occur.

42. A In order to be classified as an extraordinary item, an event must be unusual and infrequent. Cane has never before had flood losses and is located fifty miles from the river. Because the flood is unusual (flooded by a river fifty miles away) and infrequent (had not occurred in the previous twenty years), Cane should classify the event as an extraordinary item. Based on history and location, Raim should report the loss as a component of income from continuing operations.

43. A Changing from an accounting principle that is not GAAP to one that is GAAP is a correction of an error and should be treated as a prior period adjustment.

44. A APB No. 20 requires that changes in estimates be accounted for prospectively. A change in the estimated rate for warranty costs would be treated as a change in estimate.

45. B Net income less current dividends (the annual dividend that accumulates or is declared) on cumulative preferred stock equals the earnings available to common shareholders. To calculate EPS, net income less current dividends on cumulative preferred stock is divided by the weighted average number of shares of common stock outstanding. Therefore, EPS = $2.45[($500,000 – $10,000)/200,000 shares].

46. C APB No. 15 classifies all stock options as common stock equivalents. However, if the options are antidilutive they are not included in calculations for primary earnings per share. The options in this problem increase EPS, making them antidilutive. It is given that the convertible bonds are not common stock equivalents. Accordingly, there is no adjustment of the $15.00 EPS.

47. D Cash equivalents are liquid investments that are readily convertible to cash and so near maturity (three months or less) that changes in interest rates are not likely to affect their value. A three-month U.S. Treasury bill meets the definition of cash equivalents as defined by SFAS No. 95. Therefore, purchasing a Treasury bill would not affect the statement of cash flows.

48. D The statement of cash flows does not reconcile ending retained earnings to net cash flow from operations. A statement of cash flows prepared under the direct method does present the major classes of cash receipts and cash payments (choice A), and statements of cash flows prepared under the direct or indirect method present the amount of income tax paid (choice B). A reconciliation of net income to net cash from operations is presented in a separate schedule.

49. B The consolidated statement of retained earnings should only report the dividends paid by Pare. Dividends paid by Kidd are eliminated.

50. B The minority interest in net assets should be reported as $30,000 [25%($180,000 – $60,000)].

51. B The consolidated balance sheet should report only common stock of $100,000. The common stock of Kidd is eliminated.

52. C The pooling of interest method requires that liabilities be reported at their carrying values. The purchase method requires liabilities to be reported at their fair value.

53. C The purchase method requires the excess of the appraised values of identifiable assets over the acquisition price to be allocated to reduce the values of the noncurrent assets. The allocation is done on a relative value basis and no allocation is made to noncurrent investments in marketable securities. Any remaining amount is recorded as a deferred credit and amortized.

54. D A personal statement of financial position presents a business interest constituting a large part of an individual's total assets as a single amount valued at its estimated current value, not at the proprietorship equity. Separate listings of assets and liabilities, either individually or net, is not appropriate.

55. D A personal statement of financial position presents assets at their estimated current value. The buyout value is a better measure than the tax basis of the current fair value of the stock of Ink Corp. The appraisal value is a better estimate of current fair value than the tax basis for the jewelry. Accordingly, the total amount that should be presented is $745,000($675,000 + $70,000).

56. A Nondeductible expenses should be fully reported in financial statements prepared on the income tax basis. It is appropriate to make footnote disclosure of any differences between the amounts reported for tax purposes and the amounts reported for financial statement purposes.

57. C Current cost accounting reflects specific price changes because it attempts to present financial statement items at their current value. Constant dollar accounting reflects changes in the general price level.

58. A Trading securities are current assets and quick assets, as is cash. If they are sold for their carrying value, one quick current asset (cash) is merely substituted for another quick current asset (trading securities). Therefore, the sale would have no effect on either the current or the quick ratios.

59. B After issuing an additional $300,000 in common stock, stockholder's equity will total $1,000,000. The debt-to-equity ratio allowed by the bank is .75, allowing $750,000 (.75 × $1,000,000 of stockholder's equity) of debt after the issuance of the common stock. Barr currently has total debt of $420,000, thus allowing for maximum additional borrowing of $330,000 ($750,000 - $420,000).

60. B Rate of return is net income divided by average total assets. Thus, rate of return equals 6% [$150,000/(($2,000,000 + $3,000,000)/2)].

This question is in the form of a set of objective questions related to financial statement ratios. The candidate was required to determine the impact that each of several transactions would have on the current ratio, the inventory turnover, and the total debt/total assets ratio. The candidate was given the following:

I. Current ratio 3 to 1
Current assets = 3 × current liabilities

II. Inventory turnover 4 times
Cost of sales = 4 × average inventories

III. Total debt/total assets ratio 0.5 to 1
Total liabilities = 1/2 × total assets

The candidate would indicate that each of the above would increase (I), decrease (D), or would not change (N) as a result of each transaction.

61. B Trading securities include both debt and equity securities that are held with the intent to sell them in the near term.

62. A Held-to-maturity securities are debt securities that the investor has the intent and ability to hold to maturity.

63. C Available-for-sale securities include both debt and equity securities that management has the intent to sell in other than the near term, rather than hold indefinitely or to maturity. This security should not be classified as a trading security because management does not intend to sell it in the near term.

64. C Available-for-sale securities include equity securities that management has the intent to sell in other than the near term.

65. G Held-to-maturity securities are reported at their carrying value. Thus, ABC should be reported at $100,000.

66. I Trading securities are reported at their fair value at the balance sheet date. DEF's fair value is $155,000.

67. J Available-for-sale securities are reported at their fair value at the balance sheet date. JKL's fair value is $160,000.

68. D, B The realized loss is $15,000 ($190,000 cost – $175,000 cash proceeds). Adjustments in the carrying value of available-for-sale securities do not affect the realized gain or loss on the sale of the security. The $25,000 unrealized loss from 19X3 will result in an adjustment to the 19X4 balance sheet.

69. B, B Only changes in the fair value of trading securities are reflected in the income statement. Therefore, the reported unrealized loss is $5,000 ($155,000 fair value – $160,000 carrying value).

70. C, B Only changes in the fair value of available-for-sale securities are reported as a component of stockholder's equity. Security GHI was sold in 19X4, leaving only Security JKL in the available-for-sale securities. The unrealized gain or loss to be reported at December 31, 19X4 is $10,000 ($170,000 cost of JKL – $160,000 fair value of JKL). The balance in the unrealized gain and loss account at December 31, 19X4 was a $20,000 debit. The adjustment to bring the unrealized gain or loss account to the required $10,000 debit balance would involve a debit to a valuation account and a credit to the unrealized gain and loss account.

71. G Face – Discount = Carrying value, substituting and rearranging terms, we get: Face – Carrying Value = Discount, and $480,000 – $363,600 = $116,400.

72. C The semiannual cash payments do not change over the life of the bond. The cash payment at 12/31/X4 is $14,400, thus the cash payment at 6/30/94 is $14,400.

73. H The original discount would be the discount at 6/30/X4 plus the amortization recognized at 6/30/X4 or: $116,400 + $3,600 = $120,000. Face – Original Discount = Original Carrying Value or: $480,000 – $120,000 = $360,000.

74. D The stated annual interest rate is equal to the annual cash payments divided by the face value [(2 × $14,400) / $480,000 = 6%].

75. F The effective annual interest rate is equal to the interest expense divided by the carrying value [($18,000/$360,00 = 5%). Because the calculation is based on a semiannual period, the rate must be multiplied by two in order to annualize it (2 × 5% = 10%).

76. E Interest expense is equal to the carrying value times the effective interest rate (10% × 6/12 × $363,600 = $18,180).

77. A Amortization is equal to the difference in the cash payment for interest and the interest expense recognized ($18,180 – $14,400 = $3,780).

78. C Normally a gain contingency is neither accrued nor disclosed. However, the verdict was not appealed, the event giving rise to the contingency occurred in 19X4, and the amount was actually received prior to the issuance of the 19X4 financial statements. Thus, the judgment should be accrued and the circumstances disclosed.

79. D Normally no disclosure is required for contingencies that are remote.

80. N Losses on purchase commitments are accrued; gains are not accrued. When the market price is higher than the contracted price, a gain results. Accordingly, neither accrual nor disclosure are required.

81. A A loss contingency that is reasonably possible should be disclosed, but not accrued.

82. C A loss contingency that is probable and subject to reasonable estimation should be accrued. Based on the unusual nature and the large cost, disclosure is warranted.

83. D Early extinguishment of debt would be reported as an extraordinary item in the 19X5 financial statements because the event of refinancing arose subsequent to the balance sheet date. However, because of the significance of the refinancing, disclosure should be made in order to prevent the financial statements from being misleading.

4.

Baron Flowers
Worksheet to Convert Trial Balance to Accrual Basis
December 31, 1994

Account Title	Cash Basis Dr.	Cash Basis Cr.	Adjustments Dr.	Adjustments Cr.	Accrual Basis Dr.	Accrual Basis Cr.
Cash	$ 25,600				$ 25,600	
Accounts Receivable	16,200		(1) $ 15,800		32,000	
Inventory	62,000		(4) 10,800		72,800	
Furniture & Fixtures	118,200				118,200	
Land Improvements	45,000				45,000	
Accumulated deprec. & Amortization		32,400		(6) 14,250		$ 46,650
Accounts payable		17,000		(3) 13,500		30,500
Baron, Drawings			(9) 61,000		61,000	
Baron, Capital		124,600	(7) 2,000	(5) 2,600		125,200
Allowance for doubtful accounts				(2) 3,800		3,800
Prepaid Insurance			(5) 2,900		2,900	
Utilities payable				(7) 1,500		1,500
Payroll taxes payable				(7) 1,600		1,600
Contingent loss liability				(8) 50,000		50,000
Sales		653,000		(1) 15,800		668,800
Purchases	305,100		(3) 13,500	(4) 10,800	307,800	
Salaries	174,000			(9) 48,000	126,000	
Payroll Taxes	12,400		(7) 500		12,900	
Insurance	8,700		(5) 2,600	(5) 2,900	8,400	
Rent	34,200				34,200	
Utilities	12,600		(7) 600		13,200	
Living expenses	13,000			(9) 13,000	0	
Bad debt expense			(2) 3,800		3,800	
Amortization expense			(6) 2,250		2,250	
Depreciation expense			(6) 12,000		12,000	
Contingent loss			(8) 50,000		50,000	
	827,000	827,000	177,750	177,750	928,050	928,050

a. Adjustments to Convert to the Accrual Basis

1.
Accounts Receivable	15,800	
Sales		15,800

To adjust accounts receivable to 32,000 per Baron

2.
Uncollectible Accounts Expense	3,800	
Allowance for Uncollectible Accounts		3,800

To recognize appropriate expense and establish allowance

3.
Purchases	13,500	
Accounts Payable		13,500

To adjust accounts payable to 30,500 from examination of unpaid invoices

4.
Inventory	10,800	
Purchases		10,800

To adjust inventory to physical count

5.
Prepaid Insurance	2,900	
Insurance Expense		2,900

To establish a prepaid asset for the 4 months coverage remaining in 19X5 ($8,700 \times 4/12 = 2,900$)

Insurance Expense	2,600	
Baron, Capital		2,600

To recognize in 19X4 the portion of the previous year's policy which was expensed under the cash basis method ($7,800 \times 4/12 = 2,600$)

6.
Depreciation Expense	12,000	
Amortization Expense	2,250	
Accumulated Depreciation and Amortization		14,250

To recognized amortization of land improvements ($45,000/15 = 2,250$) and depreciation

7.
Payroll Taxes	500	
Utilities	600	
Baron, Capital	2,000	
Utilities Payable		1,500
Payroll Taxes Payable		1,600

To recognize the accrued liabilities and adjust the expense accounts at 12/31/X4, and to adjust the capital account for expenses not accrued in the prior year

8.
Estimated Loss from Litigation	50,000	
Contingent Litigation Liability		50,000

To accrue an estimated loss and related liability for the portion of the probable litigation loss not covered by insurance

9.
Baron, Drawings	61,000	
Salaries		48,000
Living Expenses		13,000

To reclassify personal expenditures

b. Memo

TO: Baron Flowers
FROM: Muir, CPA
SUBJECT: Accrual versus Cash Basis Accounting

Accrual accounting is generally considered preferable to cash basis accounting in that it achieves a better matching of expenses and revenues. In other words, revenues are recognized when actually earned, rather than when collected. Expenses are recognized when incurred, rather than when paid. Recognition of revenues and expenses is not dependent upon the receipt or payment of cash. Therefore, accrual accounting provides a better measure of a company's performance. Users of financial statements generally find accrual based statements to be more informative in evaluating company performance and financial position as it relates to a company's ability to meet forthcoming obligations.

5. a

1. Intangible assets are noncurrent operating assets. They represent probable, future economic benefits. Intangible assets lack physical substance and frequently prove difficult to value and/or determine the appropriate useful life. Intangible assets which are purchased should be capitalized. Intangible assets that are developed internally are not capitalized. Rather, the costs of internally developed intangible assets are expensed as incurred, (e.g., research and development costs). Intangible assets that are capitalized, yet have an indeterminate life should be amortized over a period not to exceed forty years.

2. Intangible assets should be amortized over their period of utility to the economic entity. That period should be the shorter of the useful life, the legal life, or forty years. The useful life of an intangible asset is affected by factors like obsolescence and competition. The legal life of an intangible is determined by statute, contract, or regulation. APB Opinion No. 17 established the maximum amortization period as forty years. Amortization is traditionally calculated on a straight-line basis. The justification to amortize an intangible asset with an indeterminate life is based on matching. Failure to recognize a portion of the cost of the intangible asset as an expense would result in the overstatement of income.

3. Broca's Balance Sheet should report the intangible assets at cost, of net accumulated amortization. The Income Statement should report the amortization expense associated with the intangibles. Footnotes should disclose the method of amortization and the useful life of the intangible assets.

b.

Broca Co.
Intangible Assets
December 31, 19X4

Goodwill: Cost	$188,000	
Less: Accumulated Amortization	4,700	$183,300
Franchise: Cost	60,000	
Less: Accumulated Amortization	12,000	48,000
Patent: Cost	136,000	
Less: Accumulated Amortization	13,600	122,400
Total Intangibles		$353,700

Calculations:

Goodwill = purchase price less fair value of net assets ($360,000 – $172,000 = $188,000)
Franchise = purchase price of $60,000 (annual fees should be expensed)
Patent = registration costs plus costs of successful defense ($51,000 + $85,000 = $136,000)

Broca Co.
Schedule of Intangible Related Expenses
For the Year Ended December 31, 19X4

Goodwill Amortization	$ 4,700
Franchise Fee Amortization	12,000
Patent Amortization	13,600
Annual Franchise Fee	200
	$30,500

Calculations:

Goodwill Amortization: $188,000/40 years = $4,700
Franchise Fee Amortization: $60,000/5 years = $12,000
Patent Amortization: $136,000/10 years = $13,600
Annual Franchise Fee: $20,000 × 1% = $200

APPENDICES

APPENDIX I:
STATE BOARDS OF ACCOUNTANCY

Alabama
ph: (334) 242-5700
fax: (334) 242-2711
Alabama State Board of Public Accountancy
RSA Plz, 770 Washington Ave
Montgomery, AL 36130

Alaska
ph: (907) 465-2580
fax: (907) 465-2974
Alaska State Board of Public Accountancy
Commerce Dept Occ Lic, Box 110806
Juneau, AK 99811-0806

Arizona
ph: (602) 255-3648
fax: (602) 255-1283
Arizona State Board of Accountancy
3110 N 19th Ave. Suite 140
Phoenix, AZ 85015-6038

Arkansas
ph: (501) 682-1520
fax: (501) 682-5538
Arkansas State Board of Accountancy
101 East Capitol, Suite 430
Little Rock, AR 72201

California
ph: (916) 263-3680
fax: (916) 263-3675
California State Board of Accountancy
2000 Evergreen Street, Suite 250
Sacramento, CA 95815-3832

Colorado
ph: (303) 894-7800
fax: (303) 894-7790
Colorado State Board of Accountancy
1560 Broadway, Suite 1370
Denver, CO 80202

Connecticut
ph: (860) 566-7835
fax: (860) 566-5757
Connecticut State Board of Accountancy
30 Trinity Street, P.O. Box 150470
Hartford, CT 06115-0470

Delaware
ph: (302) 739-4522
fax: (302)739-2711
Delaware State Board of Accountancy
Cannon Building, Suite 203, P.O. Box 1401
Dover, DE 19903

District of Columbia
ph: (202) 727-7468
fax: (202) 727-8030
District of Columbia Board of Accountancy
614 H Street NW, c/o P.O. Box 37200
Washington, DC 20013-7200

Florida   ph: (352) 955-2165   Florida Board of Accountancy
             fax: (352) 955-2164   2610 NW 43rd Street, Suite 1A
                                      Gainsville, FL 32606-4599

Georgia   ph: (404) 656-2281   Georgia State Board of Accountancy
             fax: (404) 651-9532   166 Pryor Street SW
                                      Atlanta, GA 30303

Guam   ph: (671) 646-3884   Guam Territorial Board of Accountancy
             fax: (671) 649-4932   Deloitte & Touche, LLP
                                      361 South Marine Drive
                                      Tamuning, GU 96911

Hawaii   ph: (808) 586-2694   Hawaii Board of Accountancy
             fax: (808) 586-2689   Dept Com & Cons. Aff., P.O. Box 3469
                                      Honolulu, HI 96801-3469

Idaho   ph: (208) 334-2490   Idaho State Board of Accountancy
             fax: (208) 334-2615   P.O. Box 83720
                                      Boise, ID 83720-0002

Illinois   ph: (217) 785-0800   Illinois Department of Professional Regulation
             fax: (217) 782-7645   Public Accty Section, 320 W
                                      Washington Street, 3rd Fl
                                      Springfield, IL 62786-0001

Indiana   ph: (317) 232-5987   Indiana Board of Accountancy
             fax: (317) 232-2312   IN Prof. Lic. Agc., IN Gov. Ctr.
                                      302 W Washington, Room E034
                                      Indianapolis, IN 46204-2246

Iowa   ph: (515) 281-4126   Iowa Accountancy Examining Board
             fax: (515) 281-7411   1918 SE Hulsizer Ave.
                                      Ankeny, IA 50021-3941

Kansas   ph: (913) 296-2162   Kansas Board of Accountancy
             fax: (913) 296-6296   Landon State Office Building
                                      900 SW Jackson Suite 556
                                      Topeka, KS 66612-1239

Kentucky   ph: (502) 595-3037   Kentucky State Board of Accountancy
             fax: (502) 595-4281   332 Broadway, Suite 310
                                      Louisville, KY 40202-2115

Louisiana   ph: (504) 566-1244   State Board of CPAs of Louisiana
                fax: (504) 566-1252   Pan-American Life Ctr, 601 Poydras Street
                                      Suite 1770
                                      New Orleans, LA 70139

Maine   ph: (207) 624-8603   Maine Board of Accountancy
            fax: (207) 624-8637   Dept. of Prof. & Fin. Reg., Div. of Lic. & Enf.
                                  State House Station 35
                                  Augusta, ME 04333

Maryland   ph: (410) 333-6322   Maryland State Board of Public Accountancy
               fax: (410) 333-6314   501 St. Paul Place, 9th Floor
                                     Baltimore, MD 21202-2272
                                     Sue Mays, Executive Director

Massachusetts   ph: (617) 727-1806   Massachusetts Board of Public Accountancy
                    fax: (617) 727-0139   Saltonstall Bldg., Gov't. Center
                                          100 Cambridge Street, Room 1315
                                          Boston, MA 02202-0001

Michigan   ph: (517) 373-0682   Michigan Board of Accountancy
               fax: (517) 373-2795   Dept. of Commerce—BOPR, P.O. Box 30018
                                     Lansing, MI 48909-7518

Minnesota   ph: (612) 296-7937   Minnesota State Board of Accountancy
                fax: (612) 282-2644   85 East 7th Place, Suite 125
                                      St. Paul, MN 55101

Mississippi   ph: (601) 354-7320   Mississippi State Board of Public Accountancy
                  fax: (601) 354-7290   653 North State Street
                                        Jackson, MS 39202

Missouri   ph: (573) 751-0012   Missouri State Board of Public Accountancy
               fax: (573) 751-0890   P.O. Box 613
                                     Jefferson City, MO 65102-0613

Montana   ph: (406) 444-3739   Montana State Board of Public Accountants
              fax: (406) 444-1667   Arcade Bldg, Lower Level
                                    111 North Jackson, P.O. Box 200513
                                    Helena, MT 59620-0513

Nebraska   ph: (402) 4710-3595   Nebraska State Board of Public Accountancy
               fax: (402) 471-4484   P.O. Box 94725
                                      Lincoln, NE 68509-4725

Nevada	ph: (702) 786-0231 fax: (702) 786-0234	Nevada State Board of Accountancy 200 South Virginia Street, Suite 670 Reno, NV 89501-2408
New Hampshire	ph: (603) 271-3286 fax: (603) 271-2856	New Hampshire Board of Accountancy 57 Regional Drive Concord, NH 03301
New Jersey	ph: (201) 504-6380 fax: (201) 648-3355	New Jersey Board of Accountancy P.O. Box 45000 Newark, NJ 07101
New Mexico	ph: (505) 841-9108 fax: (505) 841-9113	New Mexico State Board of Public Accountancy 1650 University NE, Suite 400 A Albuquerque, NM 87102
New York	ph: (518) 474-3836 fax: (518) 473-6995	New York State Board for Public Accountancy State Education Dept. Cultural Education Ctr. Room 3013 Albany, NY 12230-0001
North Carolina	ph: (919) 733-4222 fax: (919) 733-4209	North Carolina State Board of CPA Examiners 1101 Oberlin Road, Suite 104 P.O. Box 12827 Raleigh, NC 27605-2827
North Dakota	ph: (701) 775-7100 fax: (701) 775-7430	North Dakota State Board of Accountancy 2701 S Columbia Road Grand Forks, ND 58201
Ohio	ph: (614) 466-4135 fax: (614) 466-2628	Accountancy Board of Ohio 77 South High Street, 18th Floor Columbus, OH 43266-0301
Oklahoma	ph: (405) 521-2397 fax: (405) 521-3118	Oklahoma Accountancy Board 4545 N. Lincoln Blvd, Suite 165 Oklahoma City, OK 73105
Oregon	ph: (503) 378-4181 fax: (503) 378-3575	Oregon State Board of Accountancy 3218 Pringle Road, SE #110 Salem, OR 97302

Pennsylvania	ph: (717) 783-1404 fax: (717) 787-7769	Pennsylvania State Board of Accountancy 613 Transportation & Safety Bldg. P.O. Box 2649 Harrisburg, PA 17105-2649
Puerto Rico	ph: (787) 722-2122 fax: (787) 721-8399	Puerto Rico Board of Accountancy Box 3271, Old San Juan Station San Juan, PR 00902-3271
Rhode Island	ph: (401) 277-3185 fax: (401) 277-6654	Rhode Island Board of Accountancy Dept. of Bus. Reg., 233 Richmond Street Suite 236 Providence, RI 02903-4236
South Carolina	ph: (803) 734-4228 fax: (803) 734-9571	South Carolina Board of Accountancy Bd. of Accty., Suite 101, P.O. Box 11329 Columbia, SC 29211-1329
South Dakota	ph: (605) 367-5770 fax: (605) 367-5773	South Dakota Board of Accountancy 301 E. 14th Street, Suite 200 Sioux Falls, SD 57104
Tennessee	ph: (615) 741-2550 fax: (615) 532-8800	Tennessee State Board of Accountancy 500 James Robertson Parkway, 2nd Floor Nashville, TN 37243-1141
Texas	ph: (512) 505-5500 fax: (512) 505-5575	Texas State Board of Public Accountancy 333 Guadalupe Tower III, Suite 900 Austin, TX 78701-3900
Utah	ph: (801) 530-6730 fax: (801) 530-6511	Utah Board of Accountancy 160 East 300 South, P.O. Box 45805 Salt Lake City, UT 84145-0802
Vermont	ph: (802) 828-2837 fax: (802) 828-2496	Vermont Board of Public Accountancy Pavilion Office Building, Montpelier, VT 05609-1106
Virginia	ph: (804) 367-590 fax: (804) 367-2474	Virginia Board of Accountancy 3600 West Broad Street Richmond, VA 23230-4917

Virgin Islands ph: (809) 773-4305   Virgin Islands Board of Public Accountancy
fax: (809) 773-9850   P.O. Box 3016, No. 1A Gallows
Bay Market Place

Washington   ph: (360) 753-2585   Washington State Board of Accountancy
fax: (360) 664-9190   210 E. Union, Suite H, P.O. Box 9131
Olympia, WA 98507-9131

West Virginia   ph: (304) 558-3557   West Virginia Board of
fax: (304) 558-1325   201 L & S Bldg., 812 Quarrler Street
Charleston, WV 25301-2695

Wisconsin   ph: (608) 266-1397   Wisconsin Accounting Examining Board
fax: (608) 267-0644   1400 E. Washington Ave., P.O. Box 8935
Madison, WI 53708-8935

Wyoming   ph: (307) 777-7551   Wyoming Board of Certified Public Accountants
fax: (307) 777-3796   First Bank Building, 2020 Carey Avenue
Cheyenne, WY 82002-0610

APPENDIX II:
KAPLAN CPA
REVIEW PRODUCTS

Kaplan's CPA review products give students the skills and confidence they need to get a passing score on exam day. We've designed them to help you focus on what you need to know to pass the exam.

CPA VIDEO REVIEW COURSE

The backbone of Kaplan's CPA test prep is the video review course, consisting of an introductory class (including a diagnostic exam), twenty-eight comprehensive video lessons, and a final exam. By offering a video review course, Kaplan ensures that all students, no matter at which Kaplan Center they take the course, get the same superior quality of instruction.

The course features Dauberman-Chaykin course content and is taught by top-of-the-line accounting professors and practitioners. You get clear, concise, easy-to-read boardwork, graphics, and animation that bring concepts to life and make them more memorable.

Kaplan believes the key to successful studying rests in diagnosis. During the first class, every student has the option of taking a Diagnostic Skills Test, a compilation of various released CPA exams. The exam analysis helps determine your testing strengths and weaknesses. Through Kaplan's Computerized Assisted Feedback System (CAF), you will receive computerized feedback highlighting your individual strengths and weaknesses. CAF ensures that each student can focus on their individual needs, allowing students to spend their time wisely.

After each class, there will be assigned homework problems to answer. Kaplan invites students to complete their homework on scannable grids and bring the completed grids to the next class. All homework will be graded and answers, as well as computer-assisted feedback, will be provided to each student.

And, if you can't attend a particular class, you can still make it up, either by sitting in on the same class at another location, or by working through the video of that particular lesson at a Kaplan Training Library.

The video review course ends with a Final Exam. By this time, you will have learned a great deal of Kaplan's CPA wisdom, and the CPA Final Exam will help you get ready for exam day. If you have gone to class, done your homework problems, and read over the solutions, you should see a noticeable improvement from the Diagnostic Exam to the Final Exam and on exam day itself. However, your score on the Final Exam—good or bad—is simply an indicator of what you might receive on the CPA exam. There are several factors that influence performance on Exam Day, the most common of which is exam anxiety. Of course, the best way to beat exam anxiety is to **STUDY!** Learning the material, applying what you've learned to the problems, and familiarizing yourself with the format of the exam is critical to ensure your success on exam day.

CPA BOOKS

Kaplan offers eight books—one lesson book and one homework book for each section of the exam. The set of books includes detailed instruction in over one hundred heavily tested topics, and the material provides coverage of the American Institute of Certified Public Accountants (AICPA) Content Specification Outline. Each book is clearly referenced, easy to read, and revised regularly to ensure you have the most updated material available.

Kaplan's review material provides you with the technical knowledge you need to pass the Uniform CPA Examination. However, knowledge is not enough. You need to apply that knowledge over and over to actual examination questions. That's why Kaplan's CPA books include questions from the ten most recently released examinations. How much you practice on these questions will have a significant impact on your overall success.

CPA SOFTWARE

Kaplan's *CPA RoadTrip Software* is a fun and engaging software package. It includes extensive tutorials on CPA content, advice on writing skill, test-taking strategies, and careers in accounting. *CPA RoadTrip Software* also provides users with one hundred "hot topic" flashcards, and the ten most recently released examinations.

In order to help students focus in on specific areas of study, *CPA RoadTrip Software* provides dozens of topical tests comprising both multiple-choice and other objective format (OOF) questions. These topical tests, in conjunction with Kaplan's detailed explanations and feedback on questions provide a thorough preparation for the Uniform CPA Examination.

CPA FLASHCARDS

Kaplan offers 500 well-indexed flashcards that thoroughly cover the topics on the CPA exam. CPA flashcards eliminate the countless hours usually spent by candidates in creating their own notecards, making studying-on-the-go that much easier.

KAPLAN'S 24-HOUR TUTORING HOTLINE

For enrolled students who have questions involving their CPA preparation, Kaplan provides a free 24-hour tutoring hotline. When you call our hotline accounting professionals and professors familiar with the examination will answer your questions. Please call us at 1-800-KAP-TEST for more information.

Want more information about our services, products, or the nearest Kaplan educational center?

HERE

Call our nationwide toll-free numbers:

1–800–KAP–TEST
(for information on our live courses, private tutoring and admissions consulting)

1–800–KAP–ITEM
(for information on our products)

1–888–KAP–LOAN*
(for information on student loans)

Connect with us in cyberspace:
On **AOL**, keyword **"Kaplan"**
On the Internet's World Wide Web, open **"http://www.kaplan.com"**
Via E-mail, **"info@kaplan.com"**

Write to:
Kaplan Educational Centers
888 Seventh Avenue
New York, NY 10106

Test (circle one):   One   Two

Section (circle one):   LAW   AUDIT   ARE   FARE

Question number _____   ☐ begins on this page.

☐ continues from page _____.

_____

_____

_____

_____

_____

_____

_____

_____

_____

_____

_____

_____

_____

_____

_____

_____

_____

_____

_____

_____

_____

_____

_____

Name _____

Address _____

_____

Phone _____

Question number _____   ☐ continues on page _____.

☐ ends on this page.

page 2 Essay and Problem Response Sheet

Test (circle one):   One   Two
Section (circle one):   LAW   AUDIT   ARE   FARE

Question number _____   ☐ begins on this page.
                        ☐ continues from page _____.

_____

_____

_____

_____

_____

_____

_____

_____

_____

_____

_____

_____

_____

_____

_____

_____

_____

_____

_____

_____

_____

_____

_____

_____

_____

Question number _____   ☐ continues on page _____.
                            ☐ ends on this page.

Test (circle one):   One   Two
Section (circle one):   LAW   AUDIT   ARE   FARE

Question number _____   ☐ begins on this page.
                         ☐ continues from page _____.

_____

_____

_____

_____

_____

_____

_____

_____

_____

_____

_____

_____

_____

_____

_____

_____

_____

_____

_____

_____

_____

_____

_____

Name _____

Address _____   Question number _____   ☐ continues on page _____.

_____   ☐ ends on this page.

Phone _____

Test (circle one):   One   Two
Section (circle one):   LAW   AUDIT   ARE   FARE

Question number _____   ☐ begins on this page.
                          ☐ continues from page _____.

_____

_____

_____

_____

_____

_____

_____

_____

_____

_____

_____

_____

_____

_____

_____

_____

_____

_____

_____

_____

_____

_____

_____

_____

_____

_____

Test (circle one):   One   Two
Section (circle one):   LAW   AUDIT   ARE   FARE

Question number _____   ☐ begins on this page.
                          ☐ continues from page _____.

_____

_____

_____

_____

_____

_____

_____

_____

_____

_____

_____

_____

_____

_____

_____

_____

_____

_____

_____

_____

_____

_____

_____

_____

_____

_____

Name _____

Address _____   Question number _____   ☐ continues on page _____.
        _____   ☐ ends on this page.

Phone _____

Test (circle one):   One   Two
Section (circle one):   LAW   AUDIT   ARE   FARE

Question number _____   ☐ begins on this page.
                           ☐ continues from page _____.

_____

_____

_____

_____

_____

_____

_____

_____

_____

_____

_____

_____

_____

_____

_____

_____

_____

_____

_____

_____

_____

_____

_____

Question number _____   ☐ continues on page _____.
                             ☐ ends on this page.

Test (circle one):   One   Two
Section (circle one):   LAW   AUDIT   ARE   FARE

Question number _____   ☐ begins on this page.
                        ☐ continues from page _____.

_____

_____

_____

_____

_____

_____

_____

_____

_____

_____

_____

_____

_____

_____

_____

_____

_____

_____

_____

_____

_____

_____

Name _____

Address _____   Question number _____   ☐ continues on page _____.

_____   ☐ ends on this page.

Phone _____

Test (circle one):   One   Two

Section (circle one):   LAW   AUDIT   ARE   FARE

Question number _____   ☐ begins on this page.

☐ continues from page _____.

_____

_____

_____

_____

_____

_____

_____

_____

_____

_____

_____

_____

_____

_____

_____

_____

_____

_____

_____

_____

_____

_____

_____

Question number _____   ☐ continues on page _____.

☐ ends on this page.

Test (circle one):   One   Two
Section (circle one):   LAW   AUDIT   ARE   FARE

Question number _____   ☐ begins on this page.
                          ☐ continues from page _____.

_____

_____

_____

_____

_____

_____

_____

_____

_____

_____

_____

_____

_____

_____

_____

_____

_____

_____

_____

_____

_____

_____

_____

Name _____
Address _____   Question number _____   ☐ continues on page _____.
                                                                            ☐ ends on this page.
_____

Phone _____

Test (circle one):   One   Two

Section (circle one):   LAW   AUDIT   ARE   FARE

Question number _____   ☐ begins on this page.
                         ☐ continues from page _____.

_____

_____

_____

_____

_____

_____

_____

_____

_____

_____

_____

_____

_____

_____

_____

_____

_____

_____

_____

_____

_____

_____

_____

_____

Question number _____   ☐ continues on page _____.
                            ☐ ends on this page.

Test (circle one):   One   Two

Section (circle one):   LAW   AUDIT   ARE   FARE

Question number _____   ☐ begins on this page.

☐ continues from page _____.

_____

_____

_____

_____

_____

_____

_____

_____

_____

_____

_____

_____

_____

_____

_____

_____

_____

_____

_____

_____

_____

_____

Name _____

Address _____

_____

Phone _____

Question number _____   ☐ continues on page _____.

☐ ends on this page.

page 12   Essay and Problem Response Sheet

Test (circle one):   One   Two

Section (circle one):   LAW   AUDIT   ARE   FARE

Question number _____   ☐ begins on this page.

☐ continues from page _____.

_____

_____

_____

_____

_____

_____

_____

_____

_____

_____

_____

_____

_____

_____

_____

_____

_____

_____

_____

_____

_____

_____

_____

_____

Question number _____   ☐ continues on page _____.

☐ ends on this page.

Test (circle one):   One   Two

Section (circle one):   LAW   AUDIT   ARE   FARE

Question number _____   ☐ begins on this page.

☐ continues from page _____.

_____

_____

_____

_____

_____

_____

_____

_____

_____

_____

_____

_____

_____

_____

_____

_____

_____

_____

_____

_____

_____

_____

_____

_____

_____

_____

Name _____

Address _____

_____

Phone _____

Question number _____   ☐ continues on page _____.

☐ ends on this page.

Test (circle one):   One   Two
Section (circle one):   LAW   AUDIT   ARE   FARE

Question number _____   ☐ begins on this page.
                        ☐ continues from page _____.

_____

_____

_____

_____

_____

_____

_____

_____

_____

_____

_____

_____

_____

_____

_____

_____

_____

_____

_____

_____

_____

_____

_____

Question number _____   ☐ continues on page _____.
                          ☐ ends on this page.

Test (circle one):   One   Two
Section (circle one):   LAW   AUDIT   ARE   FARE

Question number _____   ☐ begins on this page.
                         ☐ continues from page _____.

_____

_____

_____

_____

_____

_____

_____

_____

_____

_____

_____

_____

_____

_____

_____

_____

_____

_____

_____

_____

_____

_____

_____

_____

_____

Name _____

Address _____   Question number _____   ☐ continues on page _____.
_____   ☐ ends on this page.

Phone _____

Test (circle one):   One   Two
Section (circle one):   LAW   AUDIT   ARE   FARE

Question number _____   ☐ begins on this page.
                          ☐ continues from page _____.

_____

_____

_____

_____

_____

_____

_____

_____

_____

_____

_____

_____

_____

_____

_____

_____

_____

_____

_____

_____

_____

_____

Question number _____   ☐ continues on page _____.
                            ☐ ends on this page.

Test (circle one):   One   Two
Section (circle one):   LAW   AUDIT   ARE   FARE

Question number _____   ☐ begins on this page.
                        ☐ continues from page _____.

_____

_____

_____

_____

_____

_____

_____

_____

_____

_____

_____

_____

_____

_____

_____

_____

_____

_____

_____

_____

_____

Name _____

Address _____   Question number _____   ☐ continues on page _____.

_____   ☐ ends on this page.

Phone _____

page 18 Essay and Problem Response Sheet

Test (circle one):   One   Two
Section (circle one):   LAW   AUDIT   ARE   FARE

Question number _____   ☐ begins on this page.
                        ☐ continues from page _____.

_____

_____

_____

_____

_____

_____

_____

_____

_____

_____

_____

_____

_____

_____

_____

_____

_____

_____

_____

_____

_____

_____

_____

_____

                    Question number _____   ☐ continues on page _____.
                                              ☐ ends on this page.

Test (circle one):   One   Two
Section (circle one):   LAW   AUDIT   ARE   FARE

Question number _____   ☐ begins on this page.
                        ☐ continues from page _____.

_____

_____

_____

_____

_____

_____

_____

_____

_____

_____

_____

_____

_____

_____

_____

_____

_____

_____

_____

_____

_____

_____

_____

Name _____

Address _____   Question number _____   ☐ continues on page _____.
        _____   ☐ ends on this page.
Phone _____

page 20 Essay and Problem Response Sheet

Test (circle one):   One   Two
Section (circle one):   LAW   AUDIT   ARE   FARE

Question number _____   ☐ begins on this page.
                          ☐ continues from page _____.

_____

_____

_____

_____

_____

_____

_____

_____

_____

_____

_____

_____

_____

_____

_____

_____

_____

_____

_____

_____

_____

_____

_____

Question number _____   ☐ continues on page _____.
                            ☐ ends on this page.

Test (circle one):   One   Two
Section (circle one):   LAW   AUDIT   ARE   FARE

Question number _____   ☐ begins on this page.
                        ☐ continues from page _____.

_____
_____
_____
_____
_____
_____
_____
_____
_____
_____
_____
_____
_____
_____
_____
_____
_____
_____
_____
_____
_____
_____

Name _____
Address _____
        _____   Question number _____   ☐ continues on page _____.
Phone _____   ☐ ends on this page.

Test (circle one):   One   Two
Section (circle one):   LAW   AUDIT   ARE   FARE

Question number _____   ☐ begins on this page.
☐ continues from page _____.

_____
_____
_____
_____
_____
_____
_____
_____
_____
_____
_____
_____
_____
_____
_____
_____
_____
_____
_____
_____
_____
_____
_____
_____
_____
_____

Question number _____   ☐ continues on page _____.
☐ ends on this page.

Test (circle one):   One   Two
Section (circle one):   LAW   AUDIT   ARE   FARE

Question number _____   ☐ begins on this page.
                          ☐ continues from page _____.

_____

_____

_____

_____

_____

_____

_____

_____

_____

_____

_____

_____

_____

_____

_____

_____

_____

_____

_____

_____

_____

_____

_____

_____

Name _____

Address _____   Question number _____   ☐ continues on page _____.
                                                                          ☐ ends on this page.
_____

Phone _____

Test (circle one):   One   Two
Section (circle one):   LAW   AUDIT   ARE   FARE

Question number _____   ☐ begins on this page.
                        ☐ continues from page _____.

_____

_____

_____

_____

_____

_____

_____

_____

_____

_____

_____

_____

_____

_____

_____

_____

_____

_____

_____

_____

_____

_____

Question number _____   ☐ continues on page _____.
                            ☐ ends on this page.

Test (circle one):   One   Two
Section (circle one):   LAW   AUDIT   ARE   FARE

Question number _____   ☐ begins on this page.
                        ☐ continues from page _____.

_____

_____

_____

_____

_____

_____

_____

_____

_____

_____

_____

_____

_____

_____

_____

_____

_____

_____

_____

_____

_____

_____

_____

_____

_____

Name _____

Address _____   Question number _____   ☐ continues on page _____.
        _____   ☐ ends on this page.

Phone _____

Test (circle one):   One   Two
Section (circle one):   LAW   AUDIT   ARE   FARE

Question number _____   ☐ begins on this page.
                          ☐ continues from page _____.

_____

_____

_____

_____

_____

_____

_____

_____

_____

_____

_____

_____

_____

_____

_____

_____

_____

_____

_____

_____

_____

_____

_____

_____

Question number _____   ☐ continues on page _____.
                            ☐ ends on this page.